How to Open a Financially Successful

Coffee, Espresso & Tea Shop

With Companion CD-ROM

Elizabeth Godsmark, Lora Arduser
and Douglas R. Brown

How to Open a Financially Successful Coffee, Espresso & Tea Shop

Copyright © 2014 Atlantic Publishing Group, Inc.
1405 SW 6th Avenue • Ocala, Florida 34471 • Phone 800-814-1132 • Fax 352-622-1875
Website: www.atlantic-pub.com • E-mail: sales@atlantic-pub.com
SAN Number: 268-1250

No part of this publication may be reproduced, stored in a retrieval system, or transmitted in any form or by any means, electronic, mechanical, photocopying, recording, scanning, or otherwise, except as permitted under Section 107 or 108 of the 1976 United States Copyright Act, without the prior written permission of the Publisher. Requests to the Publisher for permission should be sent to Atlantic Publishing Group, Inc., 1405 SW 6th Avenue, Ocala, Florida 34471.

Library of Congress Cataloging-in-Publication Data

Brown, Douglas R.
How to open and operate a financially successful coffee, espresso and tea shop : with companion CD-ROM / by Douglas R. Brown. -- Revised 2nd edition.
pages cm
Includes bibliographical references and index.
ISBN-13: 978-1-60138-905-3 (alk. paper)
ISBN-10: 1-60138-905-1 (alk. paper)
1. Coffeehouses--Management. 2. Coffeehouses--Finance. I. Godsmark, Elizabeth. How to open a financially successful coffee, espresso & tea shop. II. Title. III. Title: How to open and operate a financially successful coffee, espresso & tea shop.
TX911.3.M3G63 2014
647.95068--dc23
                2013045801

LIMIT OF LIABILITY/DISCLAIMER OF WARRANTY: The publisher and the author make no representations or warranties with respect to the accuracy or completeness of the contents of this work and specifically disclaim all warranties, including without limitation warranties of fitness for a particular purpose. No warranty may be created or extended by sales or promotional materials. The advice and strategies contained herein may not be suitable for every situation. This work is sold with the understanding that the publisher is not engaged in rendering legal, accounting, or other professional services. If professional assistance is required, the services of a competent professional should be sought. Neither the publisher nor the author shall be liable for damages arising herefrom. The fact that an organization or website is referred to in this work as a citation and/or a potential source of further information does not mean that the author or the publisher endorses the information the organization or website may provide or recommendations it may make. Further, readers should be aware that Internet websites listed in this work may have changed or disappeared between when this work was written and when it is read.

TRADEMARK DISCLAIMER: All trademarks, trade names, or logos mentioned or used are the property of their respective owners and are used only to directly describe the products being provided. Every effort has been made to properly capitalize, punctuate, identify, and attribute trademarks and trade names to their respective owners, including the use of ® and ™ wherever possible and practical. Atlantic Publishing Group, Inc. is not a partner, affiliate, or licensee with the holders of said trademarks.

COVER & INTERIOR DESIGN: Meg Buchner • megadesn@mchsi.com

Printed in the United States

Table of Contents

Chapter 1 Successful Pre-Opening Activities

Business Plan Outline 14
What to Include in Your Business Plan... 15
Business Plan: Section 1 Description of Your Coffee, Espresso & Tea Shop 15
Business Plan: Section 2 The Marketing Plan 17
Business Plan: Section 3 The Management Plan... 19
Business Plan: Section 4 The Financial Management Plan 20
Legal Forms of Business 22
Choosing a Name... 23
Marketing Research: Identifying Your Target Market.................................. 23
Selecting a Site for Your Coffee, Espresso & Tea Shop 27
Competition 27
Laws, Regulations, and Licenses 29
Opening a Bank Account 34
Insurance 35

Chapter 2 Organizing Pre-Opening Activities

First Priorities.. 37
Additional Pre-Opening Activities — Payroll 38
Pre-Opening Promotion... 39
Selecting Coffee and Tea Suppliers 40
Installation of Coffee- and Tea-Making and Related Equipment 41
Organizing Public Utilities... 42
Securing Other Essential Services 43
Ordering China, Glassware, Flatware,
Utensils, and Miscellaneous Items 47
Worksheets... 48
Business Logo and Business Cards.. 51

Chapter 3   The Basics of Buying a Coffee, Espresso & Tea Shop

Choosing the Best Location 55
Real Estate and Its Value 63
The Value of Other Assets 63
Goodwill 64
Terms, Conditions and Price 65
Determining Price from a Buyer's Perspective 65
Initial Investment 67
Strategies for Buying 68
Financing 69
How to Write a Loan Proposal 71
How Your Loan Request Will Be Reviewed 71
Closing the Sale 72

Chapter 4   How to Invest in a Franchise

Definition of Franchising 76
Advantages of Franchising 76
Disadvantages of Franchising 77
Minority Participation in Franchising 78
Franchise Financing 78
Evaluating a Franchising Opportunity 79
Conclusion 83

Chapter 5   Basic Cost Control for Beverage and Food Service Operations — An Overview

Cost Controls Are Crucial 85
The Bottom Line 86
Cost-Control Program 86
Cost Ratios 88
Controlling Beverage and Food Costs 88
Inventory and Product Management 88
Menu Sales Mix 89
The Menu Itself 89
Pricing 90
Financial Analysis 91

Internal Controls 91
Guest Tickets and the Cashier 92
Purchasing and Ordering 94
Production Controls 96
Ordering Coffee and Tea Supplies 96
Inventory, Storage and Accounts Payable 96
Labor Productivity 97
Alcoholic Beverages Control 97

Chapter 6 Choosing the Best Equipment, Coffees, Teas and Food Products

Choosing the Right Equipment 99
Coffee- and Tea-Making Equipment 100
The Espresso Machine 101
Grinders 102
Milk Steamers 103
Equipment Maintenance and Repair 103
Choosing Gourmet Coffee and Tea Supplies 104
Understanding Coffee Beans and Blends 104
Coffee Beans with "Customer Appeal" 105
Tasting 107
Coffee Suppliers/Roasters 109
Tips for Brewing Coffee 110
Espresso 110
Standard Espresso Recipes 110
Tips for Making Great Espresso 112
Specialty Teas 113
Types of Tea 113
Tips for Preparing/"Steeping" Tea 115
Popularity of Iced Tea 116
Herbal Teas 116
Other Beverages 117
Food Products 117

Chapter 7 Profitable Menu Planning — For Maximum Results

Menu Style 121
Developing the Menu Selections 123

Portion Control 123
Truth and Accuracy in the Menu 123
Nutritional Claims on Menus 124
Menu Size and Cover 124
Menu-Design Software 125
Copyrighting the Menu 125
Printing the Menu 126
Projecting Menu Costs 126
Menu Prices 127

Chapter 8   Inventory Control — For Maximum Profits

Establishing an Inventory-Control System 131
Choosing an Inventory-Control System for Your Establishment 132
Purchasing 133
Inventory Levels 133
Beginning Inventory — The Math 134
Determining Reorder Levels 134
Receiving and Storing Inventory 135
Rotation Procedures 136
Issuing 136

Chapter 9   Successful Management of Operational Costs and Supplies

Operational Categories 138
Ordering Operational Supplies 139
Beginning Inventory 139

Chapter 10   The Essentials of Beverage and Food Safety, HACCP, and Sanitation Practices

What Is HACCP? 142
Why Use HACCP in Your Facility? 142
HACCP's Eight Key Steps for the Beverage and Food Service Process 143
Sanitary Self-Service 145
A First-Rate Facility 145
Dangerous Forms of Bacteria 147

Controlling Bacteria 148
Bugs, Insects, and Animal Pests 150
Safety in the Beverage and Food Preparation Areas 151
Sanitation Information Resources 154

Chapter 11   Computers and Your Beverage and Food Service Operation

Computer Systems for the Beverage and Food Service Industry 157
Front-of-the-House Computer Systems 158
Stand-Alone Software Applications 159
Desktop Publishing Applications and Ideas 161
What Is the Future of Computers in Beverage and Food Service? 162
Effective Use of Email 162
Why Use Email? 163
Do I Need a Website? 163
What to Put on Your Website 164
How Do You Get an Effective Website? 165

Chapter 12   Successful Employee Recruitment

The Labor Problem in the Beverage and Food Service Industry 167
The Beverage and Food Service Labor Shortage 168
Recruiting Sources 168
Hiring Employees for Your Coffee, Espresso & Tea Shop 169
Hiring the Best Barista 171
Specifics of What to Look for When Hiring a Barista 171
Specifics to Look for in Servers and Food Preparation Staff 172
Hiring a Dishwasher 173
Key Points for Conducting Employment Interviews 173
Unlawful Pre-Employment Questions 174
Screening Potential Employees 176
The Final Selection and Decision 177
Rejecting Applicants 178
Employee Handbook/Personnel Policy Manual 178
Personnel File 180
Job Descriptions 180

Chapter 13 Successful Employee Motivation and Training

Employee Motivational Factors 183
How to Motivate Employees 184
How to Create a Contented Workforce and Retain Employees 184
Training 185
Training Objectives: An Overview 186
Tailoring Training to Meet Individual Requirements 187
Orientation and Instruction for New Employees 188
Training for Food Preparation and Waitstaff 189
Special Training for the Barista 190
Outside Help in Training 190
Training Management 190
Role of Communication 191
Evaluating Performance 194
Ongoing Training 195

Chapter 14 Successful Labor Cost Control

Scheduling 197
Computer Software for Improved Labor Scheduling 198
Prepared Beverages and Foods 199
Work Area Layout and Equipment Design 199
The Decision to Terminate an Employee 200

Chapter 15 Successful Public Relations: How to Get Customers in the Door

What is Public Relations? 204
What PR Does (and Doesn't Do) for You 204
The Marriage of PR and Marketing 205
How to Apply Your PR Plan 205
Building and Supporting Strong Media Relations 207
Marketing Your Coffee, Espresso & Tea Shop 207
What's News? 209
PR is Different from Advertising 210
Launching a Campaign 211
Special Events 212

Communicating to Your Guests — The Value of Loyalty 215
Customer Loyalty Schemes 215
Employee Relations Is Also Public Relations 217
Talking to Your Community 218
Planning for the Unforeseen 219

Chapter 16   Internal Marketing: How to Keep Customers Coming Back to Your Establishment

Customers for Life 221
Focus Your Attention on Delighting Your Guests 222
Ways to Delight 223
Word-of-Mouth 223
Educating Guests on the Differences 224
Incentives 224
Creative Ways to Win Repeat Customers 226
People, People, People 229
Staff 231
A Truly Effective Staff Meeting 237
Conclusion: Focus on Making Your Guests Happy 239

Chapter 17   Internal Bookkeeping: Accounting for Sales and Costs

The Role of the Bookkeeper 241
Accounting Software 242
Section 1: Accounts Payable 242
Invoices 243
Coding Invoices 243
Total Monthly Purchases 245
Managing the Shop's Cash Flow 246
Section 2: Revenue Accounts and Reconciliation 246
Preparing and Auditing Sales Reports 246
Tipped Employees 249
Tip Rate Determination and Education Program 249
Tip Credits for Employers Are Possible 250
Additional Information on Tip Reporting 250
Employee Tip Reporting "Frequently Asked Questions" 250

What an Employer Must Record for Tip Records 253
Section 3: Payroll 255
Payroll Accounting 255
Employer Tax Calendar 256
Forms You May Need 256
General Tax Calendar 263

Chapter 18   Successful Budgeting and Profit Planning — For Maximum Results

Projecting the Operational Budget 274
Sales 274
Material Costs 276
Labor 277
Controllable Operational Costs 278
Services 279
Utilities 279
Fixed Operating Costs 280
General Operating Costs 281
Conclusion 283

Index 285

Introduction

The market for specialty, gourmet coffees and teas is an exciting growth area of the beverage service industry. Sales of specialty coffees alone increased from approximately $45 million in the early 1960s to more than $10 billion in the United States by 2014, and steady growth is forecasted in this buoyant sector of the beverage market.

Today, the United States consumes more coffee per capita than any other country in the world and consumption is likely to increase at a rate of 2.7 percent per year through 2015 according to the SBA National Information Clearinghouse. According to market analysts, the increase in coffee consumption is entirely attributable to the rapid growth of the specialty coffee segment of the beverage industry. About 37 percent of the U.S. population are regular consumers of gourmet coffee; a remarkable achievement considering that, just over a decade ago, only 3 percent of the population indulged in such delights on a regular basis. The percentage reached a pre-recession peak of 40 percent between 2004 through 2006. In 1991, there were as few as 500 coffee bars throughout the United States, today there are in excess of 20,000!

To succeed, new coffee shops have to offer more than a decent cup of coffee or tea and acceptable service, they need to serve up more than the sum of their individual parts; they need to serve up a gourmet beverage experience. Consumer expectations have never been higher. The demand for quality products, in general, and a willingness to spend more disposable income on small, daily indulgences, such as the perfect cup of coffee or tea, has never been greater.

In response to this growing demand for the espresso experience, a café culture is emerging that offers ambience, buzz, and relaxed social interaction reminiscent of the vibrant European-style coffee houses. Indeed, the desire to linger at leisure over an up-market coffee or tea, in a relaxed and welcoming environment, is hugely appealing to a broad section of the population, not only in the United States but also throughout the Western world. The café culture scene has truly taken hold in the United States, with 27 percent of all coffee now consumed outside the home according to 2011 statistics from the National Coffee Association of U.S.A. More important, this burgeoning trend presents an area of potential opportunity for the prospective coffee, espresso, and tea shop entrepreneur.

How to Open a Financially Successful Coffee, Espresso & Tea Shop offers a wealth of information and practical advice for the prospective specialty beverage operator. From inception all the way to fruition, this comprehensive manual directs you through the various stages of setting up a successful coffee, espresso, and tea shop.

What sets this guide apart is its "no-holds-barred" approach to steering the reader through the many pitfalls that the potential coffee and tea shop owner is likely to encounter, en route to success! Its honesty is refreshing — as refreshing, possibly, as the specialty coffees and teas you intend to serve in your unique beverage establishment!

Sincerely,

Douglas R. Brown

1

Successful Pre-Opening Activities

This chapter lists and describes the essential pre-opening activities and procedures which must be completed by any prospective coffee, espresso, and tea shop owner. There are bucks to be made in quality beans and loose tea leaves, but only if you get it right from the start.

Before engaging in any business activity, seek the guidance of a lawyer who can guide you through the many legal issues that are specific to your requirements. You can save yourself a lot of hassle if you seek legal counseling during the early stages of the opening period. The services of a local accountant or CPA also should be retained. The accountant will be instrumental in helping you set up the business, and can provide you with a great deal of financial advice to inform your decision-making.

A carefully structured, formal business plan is fundamental to the setup of any successful venture is; your future success depends upon it. Your formal business plan will be your road map for success.

Business Plan Outline

Elements of a Business Plan

    I. Cover sheet
    II. Statement of purpose
    III. Table of contents

    A. The Business
        1. Description of business
        2. Marketing
        3. Competition
        4. Operating procedures
        5. Personnel
        6. Business insurance
        7. Financial data

    B. Financial Data
        1. Loan applications
        2. Capital equipment and supply list
        3. Balance sheet
        4. Break-even analysis
        5. Pro forma income projections (profit and loss statements)
            a. Three-year summary
            b. Detail by month, first year
            c. Detail by quarters, second and third years
            d. Assumptions upon which projections were based
        6. Pro forma cash flow
            a. Follow guidelines for number 5

    C. Supporting Documents
        1. Tax returns of principals for last three years
        2. Personal financial statement (all banks have these forms)
        3. Copy of proposed lease or purchase agreement for building space
        4. Copy of licenses and other legal documents
        5. Copy of resumes of all principals
        6. Copies of letters of intent from suppliers, etc.

What to Include in Your Business Plan

It is vital that your business plan shows clearly where you want to go with your coffee, espresso, and tea shop business; the plan must include immediate and short- and long-term goals. You also must indicate that you are prepared to cope with the challenges and setbacks that will inevitably occur at various stages along the route to success. Questions need to be asked, and answers provided to cover all likely eventualities.

The body of the business plan can be divided into four distinct sections: 1) the description of the business, 2) the marketing plan, 3) the management plan, and 4) the financial management plan. Addenda to the business plan should include the executive summary, supporting documents and financial projections.

Business Plan: Section 1
Description of Your Coffee, Espresso & Tea Shop

In this section of the business plan, provide a detailed description of your shop. Ask yourself, "What business am I in?" and "What makes my coffee and tea shop special?" In answering these questions, include your products, market and services, as well as a thorough description of what makes your coffee, espresso, and tea shop unique. As you develop your business plan, be prepared to modify or revise your initial questions.

The business description section is divided into three primary sections: Section 1 actually describes your business; Section 2, the product or service you will be offering; and Section 3, the location of your business and why this location is desirable (if you have a franchise, some franchisers assist in site selection). When describing your coffee, espresso, and tea shop, you should explain:

- **Legalities.** Business form: proprietorship, partnership, or corporation. What licenses or permits you will need?
- **Business type**
- **What your product or service is.** Perhaps sample beverages and food menus could be included.
- **Type of business.** Is it a new independent business, a takeover, an expansion, a franchise?
- **Why your business will be profitable.** What are the growth opportunities? Will franchising impact growth opportunities?
- **When your business will be open.** What days? Hours?

- **What you have learned about your kind of business from outside sources** (trade suppliers, bankers, other franchise owners, franchiser, publications)?

Cover Sheet

Place a cover before the description. Include the name, address, and telephone number of your shop and the names of all principals.

Description

In the explanation of your business, describe the unique aspects of your shop and how or why they will appeal to consumers. Emphasize any special features that you feel will particularly appeal to customers and explain how and why these features are appealing. The description of your business should clearly identify goals and objectives. It should also clarify why you are, or why you want to be, in business.

Products and Services

Try to describe the benefits of your products and services from your customers' perspective. Successful coffee, espresso, and tea shop owners will have carefully researched what their prospective customers want or expect from them. This anticipation can be helpful in building customer satisfaction and loyalty. And, it is certainly a good strategy for beating the competition or retaining a competitive edge. You will need to describe:

- What you are selling — include your beverage and food menus here.
- How your product or service will benefit the customer
- Which specific products/services are in demand and whether these products or services can maintain a steady cash flow
- What is different about the product or service your shop is offering.

Location

The location of your coffee, espresso, and tea shop can play a decisive role in its success or failure. Your chosen location should be customer-centered; the location should be accessible and provide a sense of security. Consider these questions when addressing this section of your business plan:

- What are your location needs?
- What kind of space will you need?
- Why is the building or area desirable?
- Is it easily accessible? Is public transportation available? Is street lighting adequate?
- Are market shifts or demographic shifts occurring?

Finally, make a checklist of questions you identify when developing your business plan. Categorize your questions and, as you answer each question, remove it from your list.

Business Plan: Section 2 The Marketing Plan

How well you market your coffee, espresso, and tea shop, along with a few other considerations, will ultimately determine degree of success or failure for your business. The key element of a successful marketing plan is to know your customers — their likes, dislikes, and expectations. By identifying these factors, you can develop a marketing strategy that will allow you to arouse and fulfill their needs.

Identify your customers by their age, gender, income/educational level, and residence. At first, target only those customers who are most likely to visit your shop. As your customer base expands, you may need to consider modifying the marketing plan to include other customers.

Develop a marketing plan for your business by answering these questions (potential franchise owners will have to use the marketing strategy the franchiser has developed). Your marketing plan should answer the questions outlined below:

- Who are your customers? Define your target market(s).
- Are your markets growing? Steady? Declining?
- Is your market share growing? Steady? Declining?
- If a franchise, how is your market segmented?
- Are your markets large enough to expand?
- What pricing strategy have you devised?
- How will you attract, hold, and increase your market share? If a franchise, will the franchiser provide assistance in this area? Based on the franchiser's strategy, how will you promote your sales?

The Competition

Competition in the specialty coffee and tea segment of the beverage service industry is fierce. Because of the volatility and competitiveness in this area of the beverage market, it is vital that you know and understand your competitors. Questions like these can help you stay ahead of the competition:

- Who are your five nearest direct competitors?
- Who are your five nearest indirect competitors; for example, gourmet coffee, and tea retail stores?
- Are their businesses steady? Increasing? Decreasing?
- What have you learned from their operations? From their advertising?

- What are their strengths and weaknesses?
- How does their menu or service differ from yours?

Create a file on each of your competitors containing examples of their advertising, promotional materials, and pricing strategy techniques. Review these files periodically, determining when and how often they advertise, sponsor promotions, and offer sales. Study, for example. Is their copy is short, descriptive or catchy? Do they reduce prices for certain promotions?

Pricing and Sales

You can use your pricing strategy to improve your overall competitiveness. Get a feel for the pricing strategy your competitors are using. That way you can determine if your prices are in line with your competitors and if they are in line with specialty coffee and tea service industry averages. Pricing considerations should include:

- Beverage and food menu cost and pricing
- Competitive position
- Pricing below competition
- Pricing above competition
- Price lining
- Multiple pricing
- Service components
- Material costs
- Labor costs
- Overhead costs

The key to success is to have a well-planned strategy, to establish your policies, and monitor prices and operating costs constantly in order to ensure profits. Even in a franchise where the franchiser provides operational procedures and materials, it is a good policy to keep abreast of the changes in the marketplace, because these changes can affect your competitiveness and profit margins.

Advertising and Public Relations

Many owners of retail beverage outlets operate under the mistaken concept that the business, its products, and service will promote itself, and end up channeling money that should be used for advertising and promotions to other areas of the enterprise. Advertising and promotions, however, are the lifeline of a business and should be treated as such. We have devoted a whole chapter to marketing and promoting your coffee, espresso, and tea shop (*see Chapter 16: Internal Marketing: How to Keep Customers Coming Back to Your Establishment*).

Develop a plan that uses advertising and networking as a means to promote your specialty beverage business. Create short, descriptive copy (text material) that clearly identifies your beverages, services, prices, and your shop's location. Use catchy phrases to arouse the interest of your readers, listeners, or viewers. In the case of a franchise, the franchiser will provide advertising and promotional materials as part of the franchise package; you may need approval to use any materials that you and your staff develop. Even if this is not the case, as a courtesy, allow the franchiser the opportunity to review, comment on, and, if required, approve these materials before using them. Make sure the advertisements you create are consistent with the image the franchiser is trying to project. Remember, the more care and attention you devote to your marketing program, the more successful your coffee, espresso, and tea shop will be.

Business Plan: Section 3 The Management Plan

Managing a business requires dedication, persistence, the ability to make decisions, and the ability to manage both employees and finances. Your overall management plan, along with your marketing and financial management plans, sets the foundation for the success of your business.

Your employees are your most important resources and will play an important role in the total operation of your business. Consequently, it is imperative that you know what skills you do and do not possess since you will have to hire personnel to supply the skills that you lack. Additionally, it is important that you know how to manage and treat your employees. Make them part of the team. Keep them informed of any changes and ask for their feedback. Employees oftentimes have excellent ideas that can lead to new market areas or improvements of existing products or services that can improve your overall competitiveness.

Your management plan should answer questions such as:

- How does your background/business experience help you in this business?
- What are your weaknesses, and how can you compensate for them?
- Who will be on the management team?
- What are their strengths/weaknesses?
- What are their duties?
- Are these duties clearly defined?
- If a franchise, what type of assistance can you expect from the franchiser?
- Will this assistance be ongoing?
- What are your current personnel needs?
- What are your plans for hiring and training personnel?
- What salaries, benefits, vacations and holidays will you offer? If a franchise, are these issues covered in the management package the franchiser will provide?

If your business is a franchise, the operating procedures, manuals, and materials devised by the franchiser should be included in this section of the business plan. The franchiser should assist you with managing your franchise. Take advantage of their expertise and develop a management plan that will ensure the success of your franchise and satisfy the needs and expectations of employees, as well as those of the franchiser.

Business Plan: Section 4 The Financial Management Plan

Each year thousands of potentially successful businesses fail because of poor financial management. In 2010, 6.6 percent of the specialty coffee shops closed according to the Specialty Coffee Association of America". As a coffee, espresso, and tea shop owner, you will need to identify and implement policies that will lead to and ensure that you will meet your financial obligations.

To manage your finances effectively, plan a sound, realistic budget by determining the actual amount of money needed to open your shop (start-up costs) and the amount needed to keep it open (operating costs). The first step to building a sound financial plan is to devise a start-up budget. Your start-up budget will usually include such one-time-only costs such as major equipment, utility deposits, down payments, etc.

Start-Up Budget

- Personnel (costs before opening)
- Occupancy
- Equipment
- Supplies
- Salaries/Wages
- Income
- Payroll expenses
- Legal/Professional Fees
- Licenses/Permits
- Insurance
- Advertising/Promotions
- Accounting
- Utilities

An operating budget is prepared when you are actually ready to open for business. The operating budget will reflect your priorities in terms of how you spend your money, the expenses you will incur and how you will meet those expenses (from income). Your operating budget should also include money to cover the first three to six months of operation. It should allow for the following expenses:

Operating Budget

- Personnel
- Rent
- Loan payments
- Insurance
- Depreciation
- Advertising/Promotions

- Legal/Accounting
- Supplies
- Salaries/Wages
- Dues/Subscriptions/Fees
- Repairs/Maintenance
- Miscellaneous expenses
- Payroll expenses
- Utilities
- Taxes

Additionally, the financial section of your business plan should include any loan applications you have filed, a capital equipment and supply list, balance sheet, break-even analysis, pro forma income projections (profit and loss statement), and pro forma cash flow. The income statement and cash flow projections should include a three-year summary, detailed by month for the first year and detailed by quarter for the second and third years.

The accounting system and the inventory-control system you will be using are also generally addressed in this section of the business plan. If a franchise, the franchiser may stipulate in the franchise contract the type of accounting and inventory systems you may use. If you develop the accounting and inventory systems yourself, seek the input of a financial adviser; he or she can assist you in developing this section of your business plan. The following questions should help you determine the amount of start-up capital you will need to purchase and open a franchise:

- How much money do you have?
- How much money will you need to purchase the franchise?
- How much money will you need for start-up?
- How much money will you need to stay in business?

Other questions that you will need to consider are:

- What type of accounting system will you use? Is it a single- or dual-entry system?
- What will your sales and profit goals be for the coming year? If a franchise, will the franchiser set your sales and profit goals? Or, are you expected to reach and retain a certain sales level and profit margin?
- What financial projections will you need to include in your business plan?
- What kind of inventory-control system will you use?

Your plan should include an explanation of all projections. Unless you are thoroughly familiar with financial statements, get help in preparing your cash flow and income statements and your balance sheet. Your accountant or financial advisor can help you accomplish this goal.

Legal Forms of Business

Types of Business Organizations

When organizing a new business, one of the most important decisions to be made is choosing the structure of the business. Factors influencing your decision about your business organization include:

- Legal restrictions
- Type of business operation
- Capital needs
- Tax advantages or disadvantages
- Liabilities assumed
- Earnings distribution
- Number of employees
- Length of business operation

The advantages and disadvantages of sole proprietorship, partnership, corporation, and the new hybrid limited liability company are listed below:

Sole Proprietorship

This is the easiest and least costly way of starting a business. A sole proprietorship can be formed by simply finding a location and opening the door for business. There are likely to be fees to obtain business name registration, a fictitious name certificate, and other necessary licenses. Attorney's fees for starting the business will be less than those of the other business forms because less preparation of documents is required and the owner has absolute authority over all business decisions.

Partnership

There are several types of partnerships. The two most common types are general and limited partnerships. A general partnership can be formed simply by making an oral agreement between two or more persons, but a legal partnership agreement drawn up by an attorney is highly recommended. Legal fees for drawing up a partnership agreement are higher than those for a sole proprietorship, but may be lower than incorporating. A partnership agreement could be helpful in solving any disputes. However, partners are responsible for the other partner's business actions, as well as their own.

Corporation

A business may incorporate without an attorney, but legal advice is highly recommended. The corporate structure is usually the most complex and is more costly to organize than the previous two business forms. Control depends on stock ownership. Records must be kept to document decisions made by the board of directors. Officers of a corporation can be liable to stockholders for improper actions. Liability generally is limited to stock ownership, except where fraud is involved. You may want to incorporate as a "C" or "S" corporation.

Limited Liability Company (LLC)

An LLC is not a corporation, but it offers many of the same advantages. Many small-business owners and entrepreneurs prefer LLCs because they combine the limited liability protection of a corporation with the "pass through" taxation of a sole proprietorship or partnership. LLCs are now available in all 50 states and Washington, D.C. If you have other questions regarding LLCs, be sure to speak with a qualified legal and/or financial advisor.

Choosing a Name

This is one of the most exciting pre-opening activities you will do: naming your new specialty coffee shop! Think about the image you want to create. What is the ambiance of your store? What makes it special?

After you have selected your name, you will want to look into having it registered. After all the work and attention you have given to this detail, you do not want to have someone else come along and use the same name later on. In general, if you are going to do business in a state under a name other than your own personal name, you will need to check with your state's attorney general's office to see if you need to register. You can find these offices online. They often provide a good deal of information concerning how to register for a name. If you need some help finding this office, visit State and Local Government on the Net at **www.statelocalgov.net**.

You also might want to trademark your name to protect it. You can trademark on a national or statewide level. To register your coffee, espresso, and tea shop's trademark, contact the secretary of state's office in your state, or visit the United States Patent and Trademark Office at **www.uspto.gov**. They also have a search engine (TESS) that can help you determine if the name already has been trademarked.

Marketing Research: Identifying Your Target Market

Research has revealed that the major consumers of gourmet coffees and teas are adults who have attained high levels of formal education, as well as sophisticated teens entering higher education. The latter group, in particular, is driving the market for espresso, cappuccino and latté coffee consumption. According to a study by the National Coffee Association, 76 percent of all adult coffee drinkers started drinking coffee by age 24. Significantly, there is no statistical correlation between gourmet coffee and tea consumption and income levels. The growing trend to purchase small and frequent indulgences, such as a quality cup of coffee or tea, transcends all income streams.

Identifying your target audience, however, is a complex issue that requires gathering information to help you choose the best site for your coffee, espresso, and tea shop, develop your business, plan promotions, and set prices that will entice your target audience.

Essentially, you need to consider five main factors when conducting marketing research for your potential outlet: population and education, competition, product or service market match, desire, and income.

Your local census bureau or chamber of commerce can provide the necessary information and statistics. Other useful sources of information include the Small Business Administration (SBA), the Encyclopedia of Associations at your local reference library, which lists the names and addresses of the relevant trade associations for the coffee and tea industries, the annual survey of purchasing power published by *Sales and Marketing Magazine*, real estate companies, local newspapers, city officials, and personal observations.

Suppliers of coffee- and tea-making equipment, as well as wholesale coffee and tea merchants, are another good source of information. They can provide up-to-the-minute guidelines on current and local trends.

Industry Research

To know whether your idea has marketing potential, you need to be knowledgeable about the specialty coffee industry. There are many good sources to gather information on the industry.

National Coffee Association of U.S.A. (www.ncausa.org). This organization offers many benefits of being a member. Some of these benefits include:

- Access to market research on coffee consumption
- Education series programs, webinars, networking, and product knowledge available at the annual convention and coffee summit
- A monthly newsletter, *The Coffee Reporter*, containing information on the global coffee industry, ICO average indicator prices, retail prices, NCA activities, and developments in the retail, food service and manufacturing sectors of the U.S. coffee industry

National Coffee Drinking Trends (published by NCAUSA). This report tracks coffee consumption in the United States. Including information such as:

- The percent of the population that drinks coffee
- Number of cups drank per day (per capita and per coffee drinker)
- Percentage of type of coffee beverage consumed
- Daily coffee consumption by time of day

Specialty Coffee Association of America (www.scaa.org). This organization also offers many benefits of membership including training and education opportunities such as cupping workshops, brewing and espresso labs, roaster training, the latest facts and figures to proprietary research studies, free subscriptions, mailing lists, and SCAA's Annual Conference & Exhibition.

International Coffee Organization (www.ico.org) is the primary intergovernmental organization for coffee. The ICO's mission is to strengthen the global coffee sector and promote its sustainable expansion. On its website, the ICO provides statistical information about the coffee produced in various countries and regions, including the types, harvest season and preparation methods used.

Bellissimo Coffee Advisors (www.coffeebusiness.com). Bellissimo operates the American Barista & Coffee School and offers many excellent resources for the specialty coffee shop owner, including advice on writing your business plan, FAQs on opening a coffee business, and consulting services.

Coffee Universe (coffeeuniverse.com). The revitalized focus of Coffee Universe is on bringing the coffee drinking consumer news, information, and insights from the world of coffee. The site design has been updated, and the focus has been re-dedicated to everything coffee related. It showcases articles for everyone who enjoys coffee — from the occasional drinker to the long-time professional.

beantrends.com. Beantrends.com collects the most important and up to date information about the current trends when it comes to coffee beans. The site features articles, new ideas, and coffee recipes.

Planet Tea (www.planet-tea.com). This offshoot of Bellissimo Coffee Infogroup offers comprehensive tea information from some of the tea industry's foremost authorities and consultants. In addition, you will find feature articles, preparation advice, and health benefits.

Subscribe to industry trade magazines. Trade magazines, such as *Restaurant Hospitality* and *Restaurants and Institutions*, can be found on the Web at **www.restauranthospitality.com**. Such publications contain a great deal of information on the hospitality industry and can be helpful with everything from coming up with a concept to locating a new dishwashing machine. You should also study industry-specific literature such as the online magazines *Fresh Cup Magazine* (**www.freshcup.com**) and *Coffee Review* (**www.coffeereview.com**). *Fresh Cup Magazine* offers in-depth analysis of the specialty coffee and tea industries and links for suppliers and general coffee information. *Coffee Review* buying guide offers coffee reviews, a coffee reference section, blogs, and articles on coffee.

Join **www.restaurantowner.com,** an online community of thousands of independent restaurant operators. For a $99 one-time registration fee plus $12.99 per month, you can have access to information and training. You also have access to a library of forms, spreadsheets, operating templates, and other business and operational tools.

Network

The food service industry is not the easiest industry in which to network, but there are some options. Joining one of the organizations mentioned above is a good way to get started.

Joining the National Restaurant Association (**www.restaurant.org**) is also a good idea. This group offers many resources for food service entrepreneurs including a sample feasibility study that may be helpful in creating your own. (A feasibility study looks at your business and analyzes its ability to be a success and be profitable. In order to make a profit in your restaurant, you must know what prices to charge.) To obtain information on membership, write to:

National Restaurant Association
2055 L St., NW
Washington, DC 20036
202-331-5900

Other networking ideas include:

- **Enroll in a culinary program.** Many of the students in a culinary program will be starting out in the restaurant business, but other students will be entrepreneurs and food service professionals brushing up on their skills. Get to know some of these people. You may even consider forming your own networking group.
- **Join the chamber of commerce.** Joining your local chamber of commerce offers an excellent opportunity for networking and meeting business professionals in the restaurant industry as well as other industries.
- **Take the initiative.** Form your own organization! Contact area restaurateurs and see if they would be interested in forming a local organization.

Keep Up with Industry Trends

If you are going to own a restaurant, you will need to "keep up with the Joneses." Make sure you are aware of current food and beverage trends so you are not left behind.

- Look at the National Coffee Association's National Coffee Drinking Trends and the National Restaurant Association's current Restaurant Industry Forecast. These documents will be helpful in deciphering Americans' current eating and drinking trends.
- Become familiar with your specific segment of the industry. Along with generally being knowledgeable about the hospitality industry, you need to know your specific segment of the industry. Check out the resources listed above and do a Web search to locate specific resources for the specialty coffee industry.

- Drink out often. See what other specialty coffee shops are doing. What works for them and what does not? You can learn from your competitors' successes and mistakes!
- Subscribe to magazines such as *Gourmet* and *Bon Appetit*. These magazines are designed for the public and will help you define current food and beverage trends.

Selecting a Site for Your Coffee, Espresso & Tea Shop

After determining a likely area best suited for your coffee, espresso, and tea shop, be sure to obtain as many facts as you can about it; e.g, How many similar shops are located in the area? Can you find out something about their sales volume? Since retail specialty beverage establishments attract primarily local inhabitants, what is the population of the area? Is the trend of population increasing, stationary or declining? What do they do for a living? Are they predominantly highly educated, executives, clerks, laborers, or retired persons? Are they of all ages or principally older, middle-aged or young?

Check whether your site is located near a large office tower, in a prosperous residential area, near supermarkets, service stations, a university campus or a health and fitness facility — all of which are likely to provide a regular source of customers for your coffee, espresso, and tea shop.

Also, the zoning ordinances, parking availability, transportation facilities, and natural barriers, such as hills and bridges, are important in considering the location of your shop.

If the United States Census Bureau has developed census tract information for the area in which you are interested, you will find this especially helpful; the Census Bureau website is located at **www.census.gov**. This information can be valuable in measuring your market or service potential. Use the score sheet on the next page to help in determine the best site location:

Competition

Once you've narrowed down your location choices, you'll want to take a good, long look at the competition. Information on competition may be harder to access than demographics, but be creative here and you will probably end up with a lot of information. Your best source for information on the competition may be simply to visit competitors' establishments.

LOCATION ASSESSMENT WORKSHEET

Circle your grade for each factor: "A" for excellent, "B" for good, "C" for fair, and "D" for poor.

PROPERTY LOCATION:

1. Located in a good spot for the market	**(A)** B C D
2. Merchandise or raw materials readily available	**(A)** B C D
3. Nearby competition situation	A B C **(D)**
4. Transportation availability and rates	A B **(C)** D
5. Proximity to area attractions (hiking trails, Amish country, wine country, museums, etc.)	A **(B)** C D
6. Quality of available employees	A B **(C)** D
7. Prevailing rates of employee wages	A B **(C)** D
8. Parking facilities	**(A)** B C D
9. Adequacy of utilities (sewer, water, power, gas)	A **(B)** C D
10. Traffic flow	**(A)** B C D
11. Taxation burden	A B **(C)** D
12. Quality of police and fire protection	A B **(C)** D
13. Housing availability for employees	A B **(C)** D
14. Environmental factor (schools, cultural, community activities, enterprise of businesspeople)	**(A)** B C D
15. Physical suitability of building	A B C **(D)**
16. Type and cost of building/business	A **(B)** C D
17. Proven for future expansion	A **(B)** C D
18. Estimate of overall quality of site in 10 years	A B **(C)** D

Competitor Survey

An easy (and fun) way to find out about what the competition is up to is to be a "secret shopper." Visit your competitors and have a cup of coffee or buy a pound to take home. Look at the prices and service. How is the coffee? Do they serve other beverages? Do they serve food? Do they offer anything unique? What is their seating capacity? What is the atmosphere? How busy are they? When are their busy periods? Using a simple survey like the one on the next page can help you track competitor information.

Other ways to find information on competition include the following ideas:

- **Telephone book.** You can at least get a count and the location of your competitors.
- **Chambers of commerce.** These often keep a list of area businesses. Remember, however; it often only includes businesses that are members rather than all the businesses in the area.
- **Trade magazines** can be sources of competitor information, especially if there are regional trade magazines.
- **Local newspapers.** You can get a sense of the competition from advertisements and job classifieds. Many papers also have a weekly entertainment section that may list a number of the coffee, espresso, and tea shops in town with information on their prices and menus.

Laws, Regulations, and Licenses

When a person starts a business, he or she needs to learn about the federal, state and local regulations affecting that business; there may be zoning laws to consider, licenses to purchase and inspections to pass. The federal government has many resources a new business owner may find helpful. The U.S. Business Advisor website, **www.business.gov**, for example, offers resources such as:

- A business resource library
- The Small Business Administration's start-up adviser
- Online counseling
- Information on financial resources
- Links to laws that affect various industries

COMPETITION SURVEY

Competitor name: _____

Location: _____ Estimated square footage:_____

What are the major roads in the vicinity? _____

Is there a sign? ❏ yes ❏ no   How much parking? _____

What are the operating hours? _____

Is it a freestanding building? ❏ yes ❏ no   In a mall? ❏ yes ❏ no

What is the general appearance of the building exterior?_____
_____
_____

What is the general appearance of the building interior?_____
_____

Describe the dining areas (are there booths, tables, type of tablecloths, etc.): _
_____
_____

Number of weekly customers:

Mon _____ Tues _____ Wed _____ Thurs _____ Fri _____ Sat _____ Sun _____

What coffee beverages do they offer?_____

Do they sell coffee by the pound? ❏ yes ❏ no

Do they do their own roasting? ❏ yes ❏ no

Do they serve alcohol? ❏ yes ❏ no

Do they offer food? ❏ yes ❏ no

Delivery? ❏ yes ❏ no

Catering? ❏ yes ❏ no

What is the seating capacity?_____

How quickly do they turn over tables? _____

What are their prices? _____
_____

Do they offer entertainment? _____
_____

Other federal websites that have information you might find useful are:

- The Small Business Administration's website has information about laws and regulations that affect small businesses at **http://archive.sba.gov/index.html**.
- The IRS also offers information for small business owners on their website at **www.irs.gov/businesses**.
- The U.S. Department of Labor has a Web page that focuses on helping small business owners comply with that department's rules at **www.osha.gov/dcsp/smallbusiness/index.html**. Their elaws° webpage also provides employment laws assistance to small business owners (**www.dol.gov/elaws**).

Many states' departments of development offer one-stop shopping for new entrepreneurs, such as Ohio's 1st Stop Business Connection (**http://development.ohio.gov/1ststop/onestop/index.cfm**). This site takes you through the steps to create a business information kit that contains all the forms and copies of the state regulations you will need for your business enterprise for free. You can find out whether your state has a state agency such as the Ohio's 1st Stop by contacting your local economic development center, chamber of commerce, or small business development center.

For any local regulations that may affect your business, you should check with your chamber of commerce and your local Equal Employment Opportunity Commission (EEOC) office for information. You can contact the U.S. EEOC for help in finding your local office. They can be reached at 800-669-4000, or visit **www.eeoc.gov/field/index.cfm** for a list of field offices.

State Registration

Contact the secretary of state's office as early as possible to discuss your plans for opening a new business. Each state has different regulations. This office will be able to describe all of the state's legal requirements and direct you to local and county offices for further registration. There is generally a fee required for registering a new business; most often, it is less than $100. The city, county and/or state agency will most likely run a check to make certain no other businesses are currently using your particular business name. You also may be required to file and publish a fictitious name statement in a newspaper of general circulation in the area. You must renew this fictitious name periodically in order to legally protect it.

Should your state have an income tax on wages, request all pertinent information from the state department of labor or taxation. This would include all required forms, tax tables and tax guides. Also, contact the state department of employee compensation for their regulations and filing procedures.

City Business License

Check with the city business development department at your nearest city hall for a complete list of relevant registration requirements. Most states, cities, and provincial organizations require business name registration as well as a permit to operate a business. Your application will be checked by the zoning board to make certain that the business conforms to all local regulations. Purchasing an existing specialty beverage business will eliminate most of these clearances.

Sales Tax

Contact the state revenue or taxation agency concerning registry and collection procedures. Each state has its own methods of taxation on the sale of beverage and food products. Most states that require collection on food and beverage sales also require an advance deposit or bond to be posted against future taxes to be collected. The state revenue agency often will waive the deposit and accept instead a surety bond from your insurance company. The cost of this insurance is usually around 5 percent of the bond.

Sales tax is only collected on the retail price paid by the end user. Thus, when purchasing raw food products to produce menu items, it will not be necessary to pay sales tax on the wholesale amount. However, you must present the wholesaler with your sales tax permit or number when placing orders and sign a tax release card for their files. A thorough investigation into this area will be required to meet your particular state's requirements.

Certain counties and/or cities may also assess sales tax in addition to the state sales tax. This entire issue needs to be thoroughly researched, as an audit in the future could present you with a considerable tax liability.

Health Department License

The health department should be contacted as early as possible. A personal visit to discuss your plans and their needs would be in order. It would be to your advantage to show cooperation and compliance from the very beginning. The health department can and will close your facility until you comply with its regulations. Before opening, the health department will inspect the property. If the facilities pass the thorough inspection, they will issue the license enabling the shop to open. The cost of the license is usually less than $50. Should they find faults in your facility, you will be required to have them corrected before they will issue a license. Periodically during the year, the health department will make unannounced inspections of the premises. You must have all violations rectified before the next inspection.

Although the health department can at times seem like a terrific nuisance, they really are on your side; their goals and yours are the same. Many states now have laws requiring that at least the manager — and in some states, the entire staff — goes through and passes an approved health and sanitation program. The most common approved program is the ServSafe program developed by the NRA Educational Foundation. The ServSafe products include instructor guides, answer sheets, instructor slides, manager training, food-safety CD-ROMs, and instructor tool kits.

Fire Department Permit

A permit from the fire department, also referred to as an occupational permit, will be required before opening. As with the health department, contact the fire department as early as possible, preferably in person, to learn of their regulations and needs. Based upon the size of the building, the local and national fire code and the number of exits, the fire inspector will establish a "capacity number" of people permitted in the building at any one time. Follow the guidelines strictly, even if this means turning away customers because you have reached capacity.

Building and Construction Permit

Should you plan to do any renovations to the shop that are going to change the structural nature of the building, you may need a local building permit. Building permits are generally issued from the local building and zoning board. The fee is usually around $100, or it may be based on a percentage of the total cost of the project. Once the plans are approved, a building permit will be issued. The building inspector will make periodic inspections of your work at various stages of completion in order to ensure that the actual construction is conforming to the approved plans.

Sign Permit

Many local city governments are beginning to institute sign ordinances and restrictions. These ordinances restrict the sign's size, type, location, lighting, and the proximity of the sign to the business. The owners or managers of a shopping mall or shopping center may further restrict the use and placement of signs.

State Liquor License

Many states do not allow the sale of liquor in coffee and tea shops. Certain states vary the restrictions on sales of alcoholic beverages by county. A license to sell liquor in some states may cost but a few hundred dollars; in others, a license can cost upwards of $100,000. Several states are on quota systems and licenses are not even available. Certain counties in some states prohibit liquor sales entirely. A thorough investigation concerning your particular state, possibly with your lawyer, is in order.

Federal Tax Identification Number

All businesses must have a Federal Tax Identification Number. This number will be used to identify the business on all tax forms and other licenses. To obtain a Federal Identification Number, apply online at **https://sa2.www4.irs.gov/modiein/individual/index.jsp**. Also, at this time, request from the IRS the following publications, or download them via the Internet from **www.irs.gov**:

- Publication 15, Circular E "Employer's Tax Guide."
- Several copies of Form W-4, "Employee Withholding Allowance Certificate." Each new employee must fill out one of these forms.
- Publication 334, "Tax Guide for Small Businesses."
- From the Occupational Safety and Health Administration (**www.osha.gov**), request free copie sonline of "All About OSHA" and "OSHA Handbook for Small Businesses." Depending upon the number of employees you have, you will be subject to certain regulations from this agency. Their address is: OSHA, U.S. Department of Labor, 200 Constitutional Avenue NW, Washington, D.C. 20210.
- From the Department of Labor (**www.dol.gov**), request a free copy of "Handy Reference Guide to the Fair Labor Act." You can contact the Department of Labor at: Department of Labor, 200 Constitutional Avenue NW, Washington, D.C. 20210.

Opening a Bank Account

Opening a business bank account is a great deal more important than it may at first appear. If you received your financing through a local commercial bank, it is advisable to also use this bank for your business account, if it fills all your needs.

Whichever bank you decide to use, it is important that it can provide you with the following services:

- Night deposits
- A line of credit to certain suppliers
- All credit card services (if needed)
- Change service (coins, small bills)
- Nearby location for daily transactions

It is very important that you get to know all the bank personnel on a first-name basis, particularly the manager. Their assistance in obtaining future loans and gaining credit references will be invaluable. If it provides all your needs, it is suggested you use a smaller bank. Your account will mean a lot more to them than at a larger bank.

Take plenty of time to shop around for the bank that will serve you the best. Banks specialize in different services. Look at what they charge for each transaction and all other service charges. Compare very closely the handling charges on charge card deposits. A small percentage of thousands of dollars spread over a couple of years adds up to a great deal of money. Look at the whole picture very carefully. After you have selected a bank, you should order:

- Checks
- Deposit book
- Coin wrappers for all change
- Deposit slips
- Night deposit bags and keys
- Small bank envelopes

Insurance

Insuring a coffee and tea shop properly is similar to the coverage of any business enterprise where members of the public are in frequent attendance. Liability protection is of the utmost concern. Product liability is also desirable, as the consumption of food and beverages always presents a potential hazard. A discussion with your insurance agent is needed to determine under which insurance coverage you should be placed. Any written policy, however, should contain a basic business plan of fire/theft/liability/workers' compensation.

You may want to check with any professional organization you are a member of (such as the Specialty Coffee Association of America), and see if they offer special rates or can refer you to an insurance agent with experience in insuring coffee stores.

- **General Liability:** Covers negligence causing injury to customers, employees, and the public
- **Replacement Cost Endorsement:** Provides for full reimbursement for the actual cost of repair or replacement of an insured building
- **Vandalism:** Covers loss or damage caused by vandalism or malicious mischief
- **Glass Insurance:** Covers replacement to show windows, glass counters, mirrors, and structural interior glass broken accidentally or maliciously
- **Sprinkler Damage:** Insures against all direct loss to buildings or contents as a result of leakage, freezing or breaking of sprinkler installations
- **Flood Insurance:** Flood insurance is written in areas declared eligible by the Federal Insurance Administration. Federally subsidized flood insurance is available under the National Flood Insurance Program
- **Earthquake Insurance:** Covers losses caused by earthquakes
- **Contents and Personal Property Damage:** Covers general property and replacement costs
- **Fire and Theft Liability:** Covers the buildings and all permanent fixtures belonging to and constituting a part of the structures. Coverage usually includes machinery used in building services such as air-conditioning systems, boilers, elevators, etc. Personal property also may be covered.

- **Extended Coverage Endorsement:** Covers property for the same amount as the fire policy against damage caused by wind, hail, explosion, riot, aircraft, vehicles, and smoke.
- **Business Interruption Insurance:** Covers indirect loss from fire or theft that can be greater than the direct loss.
- **Workers' Compensation Insurance:** Mandatory in most states, workers' compensation insurance covers loss due to statutory liability as a result of personal injury or death suffered by an employee in the course of his or her employment. Be certain to obtain all the information that pertains to your particular state.

Etc.

A coffee tree can flower eight times in one year, depending on rainfall. When it is in bloom, the coffee tree is covered with 30,000 white flowers that begin to develop into fruit after 24 to 36 hours. Coffee cherries turn from yellow to orange and then bright red, six to eight months after flowering. — www.justaboutcoffee.com

Organizing Pre-Opening Activities

Opening a coffee and tea shop, or any business for that matter, is a great test of anyone's organizational and managerial abilities. It is imperative that communication be maintained with your key personnel. The best way to do this is to keep a written record of the assignments that need to be completed, who the assignments are delegated to, and when they must be completed. Allow plenty of time for assignments and projects to be accomplished. Delegate responsibilities whenever possible, but above all else, keep organized! Maintain a collective composure, and deal with people and problems on a level and consistent basis, and you will be off to a great start.

First Priorities

Suggested items that must be completed well ahead of opening date are:

1. List the shop's name and number in the phone book and yellow pages.

2. Order and install an employee time clock or appropriate software.

3. Allow shipping and lead time for nonperishable items:
   - Coffee- and tea-making equipment including espresso machine, grinders, dosers, drip brewer, boilers, tea brewers, milk steamers, frothers, display equipment, etc.

- Cleaning, water treatment, and sanitation units
- Cash registers, cash-handling equipment, and accounting software
- Drop safe for office
- Coffee and teacups, teapots, other chinaware, and silverware, utensils, etc.
- Tables, chairs, drapes, linen, napkins, and table settings, etc.
- Staff uniforms
- Printing: menus, stationery, business cards, etc.

4. Develop a list of all construction projects. It should include who is completing them and when they will be completed, plus a list of materials needed.

5. Set up a large calendar on the wall with deadlines, when deliveries will be expected, construction projects finished, equipment installed, meetings, and, of course, the opening date.

6. Contact the art galleries or artists' groups in your area. They may be able to supply you with artwork to be displayed in the shop on a consignment basis.

Additional Pre-Opening Activities — Payroll

Several people will be on the payroll before the opening date. You will need the assistance of personnel to assemble chairs, do odd painting, hang picture, and do anything required to be ready for the opening date. Many of these temporary employees may be used for various jobs in your shop after opening. A time clock certainly should be used during this period for better control. Overtime must be monitored carefully and, if possible, avoided. This will require a great deal of organization of assignments and scheduling.

Many of these jobs will be boring and tedious. Compensate these employees well for their efforts. Having a free espresso would certainly be greatly appreciated!

In most beverage outlets, an internal bookkeeper calculates and prepares the payroll. We highly recommend the use of QuickBooks computer software, Peachtree or other competing software for payroll processing. Additionally, QuickBooks will be very useful in other parts of your business and in your business planning. QuickBooks is located online at **www.quickbooks.com**, and Peachtree at **www.peachtree.com**.

However, like many companies, you may prefer to use a computerized payroll service or your accountant. Using a computerized payroll service is highly recommended. Look ahead to the section on payroll preparation in Chapter 17: Internal Bookkeeping: Accounting for Sales and Costs.

Pre-Opening Promotion

The most important part of your specialty beverage business venture, along with location and sufficient capital, is marketing your products and services. Your marketing and promotion plans for your coffee, espresso, and tea shop are an important part of your business plan.

There is a definite distinction between promotion and advertising. Promotion involves creating an interest in a new project, usually at little or no cost.

As soon as possible, put up the new shop sign or a temporary sign explaining briefly the name of the new establishment, the type of beverage outlet, hours of operation, and the opening date. People by nature are most interested in what is occurring in their neighborhood; give them something to start talking about. This is perhaps the best and least expensive promotion you can do.

Described below are some pre-opening promotional ideas:

- Emphasize the benefits to the community of your new coffee, espresso, and tea shop. Meet with the advertising representatives for the local papers. Determine advertising costs and look into getting a small news story published describing the shop.

- Take a tip from the Starbucks® professionals who, in the lead-up to the opening of a new outlet, always organize a "press preview" opportunity, and invite local politicians or media personalities to enthuse about their unique products and services. Follow their lead; encourage local dignitaries to try their hand at operating your state-of-the-art coffee- and tea-making equipment.

- Have plenty of the shop's business cards on hand as soon as possible; they are a great source of publicity.

- Join the Better Business Bureau® and the local chamber of commerce. Besides lending credibility to your organization, they often can supply you with some very good free publicity.

- When you place your employment ad in the classified section, always list the type of coffee and tea shop, as well as location. This inexpensive classified advertising will help spread the word.

Selecting Coffee and Tea Suppliers

The suppliers you choose can make or break your specialty beverage venture, so it is in your best interest to view them as your long-term business partners. The perishable nature of coffee and tea ingredients, more so than any other retail beverages, requires precision timing for deliveries in order to ensure optimum product quality. Coffee and tea retailers are highly dependent upon their chosen suppliers doing what they say they are going to do.

The range of suppliers of renewable products as well as equipment will depend on the scope of your particular coffee and tea shop, but of primary concern will be the suppliers of your espresso equipment, including your espresso machine, grinder, brewer and tea-brewing equipment. Choosing the most reliable suppliers of coffee and tea-making equipment is, therefore, central to the future success of your business. Any delay in supplying the necessary machines and equipment, or in servicing malfunctioning equipment, can cost you dearly. So take time to source suppliers who will work with you; you need purveyors of both renewable products and equipment that are aware of the bigger picture.

When making initial contact with potential suppliers, try to:

- Evaluate their response as soon as they answer the phone. Are they professional and friendly, and do they appear to take a personal interest in your business?

- Ask potential suppliers how they will add to the success of your specialty beverage operation, beyond just supplying products and services. For example, will they provide you with drinks recipes or perhaps give you a practical demonstration of how to get the best from your espresso machine?

- Assess whether they try to put pressure on you to make a decision or focus too heavily on price; both are telltale signs that they are not listening to your specific requirements.

Approximately six to eight weeks before the scheduled opening date, it will be necessary to contact all the local suppliers and meet with their sales representatives. Make certain each sales representative understands that quality products are your top consideration. Competition is fierce among both sales representatives and suppliers. Let each know you are considering all companies equally. Never become locked into using only one purveyor. Shop around, and always be willing to talk with new sales representatives.

Important points to consider when choosing coffee and tea suppliers include:

- Quality of products. Accept nothing but A-1.
- Reliability

- Delivery days. All deliveries should arrive at a designated time.
- Is the salesperson really interested in your business?
- Do they seem to believe in what they are selling?
- Billing terms (interest, credit, etc.)
- Is the company local (for emergencies)?
- From the first meeting with the sales representative, you should obtain:
  - Credit applications to be filled out and returned
  - Product lists or catalogs describing all the products
  - References from the restaurants they are currently servicing in the area. Check them out!

You should supply them with a list of the products you will be purchasing, with estimates as to the amount of each item you will be using every week.

Emphasize to the sales representative that price is certainly an important consideration, but not your only one, when selecting a supplier. Point out to the sales representative the other concerns you have about using their company. Indicate that you do intend to compare prices among the various companies but would not necessarily switch suppliers due to a one-time price undercutting. Loyalty is important to sales representatives; they need to expect that order from you each week. But at the same time, let them know they must be on their toes in order to earn your business.

Most companies offer a discount for bulk purchases. Keep this in mind when comparing prices and suppliers. Choosing a supplier is often a difficult task, with so many variable factors to consider. Begin to analyze these problems in terms of the overall picture, and your purchasing decisions will consistently become more accurate.

Installation of Coffee- and Tea-Making and Related Equipment

The U.S. specialty coffee and tea industry is relatively young, and retailers of up-market beverages are constantly having to familiarize themselves with the changing complexities of their business. The same applies to the suppliers and installers of specialty coffee- and tea-making equipment that also have to negotiate an ongoing learning curve. We recommend, therefore, that you build in extra lead time for the ordering and installation of your specialized equipment.

Milk Dispensers/Ice Cream Freezers

In the flurry of pre-opening activity, do not forget to organize any additional pieces of equipment necessary for the smooth running of your operation, such as milk dispensers and cream freezers. Many suppliers offer contracts for the use of equipment that are worth considering when you also guarantee to purchase their products exclusively. Ice cream freezers, milk dispensers, and various other kitchen equipment, such as water boilers, are available on contract. Your sales representative will have all the information about the necessary equipment. These arrangements may be very beneficial for small coffee and tea shops that have limited capital. Whatever your financial situation, do a thorough, careful investigation into the terms of the service contract.

Organizing Public Utilities

Notify public utility companies of your intention to be fully operational by a certain date. Allow plenty of lead time for completion. Some of these companies may require a deposit before they will provide service. Every company and city has different policies, so be sure to investigate yours thoroughly.

Phone Company

Two external phone lines are recommended, with some sort of intercom, handheld radio system, and/or paging system throughout the shop so you can speak from your position to key areas for any information that you may need to communicate. A discussion with your local phone company business office about your needs will reveal your many options. You also may wish to consider the installation of a music intercom paging system. Above all, be sure to place local emergency numbers at all phones.

Gas and Electric Companies

All major items of equipment need special hook-ups that can only be completed by trained technicians of either the gas or electric company, or by authorized representatives. They should be contacted as early as possible to come and evaluate the amount of work required. In many cases, they will need to schedule the work several weeks ahead of time.

Many gas and electric companies offer service contracts for purchase. If available, it is highly recommended that you purchase them. Equipment that is maintained to manufacturers' specifications will last longer and operate more effectively and efficiently. Set up a loose-leaf binder to contain all the information on your equipment and its maintenance schedules. Included in this binder should be warranties, copies of receipts, brochures, equipment schematics, operating instructions, maintenance schedules, parts lists, order forms, past service records, manufacturers' phone numbers, a chart showing which circuit breaker operates each piece of equipment, etc. Keep this manual up to date from the very beginning. Become aware of your equipment's needs and act accordingly. Train your employees thoroughly in the proper use of all equipment, and it will serve the establishment well for many years.

Water

Running a specialty beverage operation means that you cannot take any risks with the standards of water supply to your brewing equipment; the quality and purity of the water that goes into your tea and coffee is of vital importance to the overall success of your business.

Water is different in all parts of the country due to the type of chemical particles it contains. Water that has been subjected to a chemical treatment plant may contain a high level of chlorine. Bear in mind that the chemical particles in the water can have a particularly bad effect in the brewing of fresh coffee and tea. Your state's department of natural resources can give you information concerning the water's chemical makeup in the local area.

Several companies now have filtering devices on the market that attach directly to the water supply lines. Discuss your particular situation with your state's department of natural resources and the sales representative for your coffee and tea suppliers.

Securing Other Essential Services

Locksmith

A registered or certified locksmith must be contacted to change over the locks as soon as you occupy the shop building and at intervals thereafter. Also, ensure that the locksmith periodically changes safe combinations.

Fire and Intrusion Alarms

Every beverage and food outlet should have two separate alarm systems. A system for fire, smoke and heat detection, and one for intrusion and holdup. As a side note, the installation of an alarm system will increase the value of the property, and a 24-hour monitored system may make you eligible for a rate reduction of 5 to 10 percent with your insurance company on the insurance premium.

Dishwasher Chemical Company

Contact all the dishwasher chemical suppliers in the area and meet with their representatives. In most areas, four to five companies will be able to provide the dishwasher with the service it requires. Several of these companies will monitor the entire system, making sure the machine and staff are working together for maximum efficiency. Clean cups, saucers, and serving accessories are an absolute necessity for any beverage outlet. Do not gamble on the outcome by not using an expert.

Sanitation Service

In most counties, a private business must provide its own garbage pickup. Receive quotes from all the sanitation companies in the area. Prices may vary considerably depending upon who purchases the dumpsters. You may wish to get advice from your local health department to help you make your selection.

Parking Lot Maintenance

Parking lots will need periodic maintenance besides the daily duty of light sweeping and picking up of any trash. Painting new lines for the parking spaces should be done annually. Blacktop surfaces will also require a sealant to be spread over the surface periodically. Winter climates will require snow removal and possibly salting and sanding of the lot. Most of these services may be purchased under contract.

Plumber

A local plumber will be needed to handle any miscellaneous work and emergencies that may occur. The plumber must provide 24-hour emergency service. Make every effort possible to retain the plumber that did the original work on the building.

Electrician

As with the plumber, it would be a great advantage to retain the original electrician who worked on the premises. An electrician will be needed when equipment is installed or moved. If it has not been done already, the electrician should check and label all the circuits and breakers in the building. The electrician also should be on 24-hour emergency service.

Refrigeration Service

The most important consideration when choosing a refrigeration company is how fast they can respond to emergencies. The company must have 24-hour service.

Exterminator

Exterminators must be licensed professionals with references from other similar beverage outlets they service. You may wish to consult the health department for their recommendations. Exterminators can eliminate any pest-control problems such as rats, cockroaches, ants, termites, flies, etc. The company selected should be signed to a service contract as soon as possible. This is not an area to cut corners or try to do yourself; it will not pay in the long run.

Plant Maintenance

If your coffee, espresso, and tea shop contains large, expensive plants, you may need the services of a plant maintenance company. A professional plant-care person can provide all the necessary services to protect your investments: watering, pruning, transplanting, arranging, etc. Contact plant-care companies in the area to get their opinions, quotes, and references.

They must be made aware that they are working in an environment where toxic sprays may be used only with the approval of the health department and, even then, very cautiously.

Outside Landscaping

You may wish to have the exterior areas of the shop professionally designed and landscaped. An appealing exterior is at least as important as the interior. Contact local landscapers to get their opinions, designs, quotes, and references.

Ventilation Cleaning Service

Contact a company that specializes in the cleaning of ventilation systems. They should appraise and inspect the whole ventilation system before opening. Usually, twice-a-year cleaning is required.

Heating and Air-Conditioning

You will need the services of a company that can respond 24 hours a day, at a moment's notice. Losing the heating system in the winter or the air-conditioning in the summer will force your business to close. Make certain the company is reliable with many references. Heating and air-conditioning systems need regular service and preventive maintenance to ensure they function at maximum efficiency. Energy and money will be wasted if the system is not operating correctly. A service contract should be developed with these companies to ensure the machines are being serviced to the manufacturers' schedule. Keep the contract and all additional information in the equipment manual previously described.

Janitorial and Maintenance Service

Depending upon the size and operating hours of your establishment, you may wish to use the services of a professional cleaning company. This would be highly recommended. The maintenance service company selected must have impeccable references. The company should be insured against liability and employee pilferage (employees should be bonded). The cleaning service usually arrives during the night after closing time. They will clean and maintain the areas previously agreed upon in the service contract and their work is guaranteed. Cleanliness also has an important effect upon your employees. A spotless shop will create the environment for positive employee work habits.

Florist

Should you decide to have fresh cut flowers, you will need to contact a local florist. Each week the florist will set aside a selection of cut flowers of your choice. Many coffee and tea shops use only a single flower or rose in a long-stem vase with some fern for backing. Should you decide to do this, make sure there is a large supply of backup flowers. Some customers will take them home when they leave. Adding fresh water with a little dissolved sugar or a chemical provided by the florist to the vases every day will keep the flowers fresh-looking for a week or more.

Linen Service

If your aim is to create the ambience of a traditional, British-style tea shop, then quality linen tablecloths and matching napkins will add that finishing touch. Linen must be spotless and wrinkle-free. A poorly folded or soiled tablecloth will make a lasting negative impression on the customer. Ask several laundry companies for "package" quotations for cleaning and pressing your table linen, staff uniforms, serving towels, aprons, and other high-turnover linen items. They will pick up dirty linen and leave clean, ready-to-use items, ensuring they have left enough linen to carry you through until the next delivery.

If you decide to do your laundry in-house, you may wish to consider investing in table linen made from Visa® material. Visa requires no ironing or pressing when washed and dried. The material is ideal for tablecloths and napkins. Visa is extremely strong and durable. Perhaps the only disadvantage it may have over conventional material is that water tends to bead on it, rather than absorb into it. The napkins are smoother and more likely to slide off one's lap than conventional cloth.

Music

Music in the background sets the mood and enhances the atmosphere. Music is a very important part of any café-style experience. The most inexpensive way to provide a music system for your shop is to set it up yourself. Contact a local stereo dealer. After examining the acoustics in the building, they will be able to suggest a system that will meet your needs best. Take care to camouflage the speakers into the surroundings. The speakers should have individual volume controls for each area. CDs, using multiple-CD changers, with the type of music that befits the desired atmosphere will add to the café culture ambience and buzz. A radio station should never be used.

Music Licensing

If you are interested in playing recorded music in your coffee, espresso, and tea shop, you will need permission (a license) to play CDs, records, or tapes in your establishment. Although most people buy a CD or tape thinking it is then their property, there is a distinction in the law between owning a copy of the CD and owning the songs on the CD.

When you buy a CD or tape, the purchase price only covers use for your private listening, similar to the "home" use of "home videos." When you play these CDs or tapes in your shop, it becomes a public performance. Songwriters, composers, and music publishers have the exclusive right of public performance of their musical works under U.S. copyright law.

There are two licensing agencies in the United States: ASCAP® and BMI®. You can contact ASCAP at 800-505-4052, **www.ascap.com**; and BMI at 212-220-3000, **www.bmi.com**. We highly recommend that you contact both ASCAP and BMI to ensure your compliance.

Ordering China, Glassware, Flatware, Utensils, and Miscellaneous Items

As a general guideline, you are likely to need 8-, 12- and 16-ounce sizes of coffee mugs; 8-ounce cappuccino cups with saucers; espresso cups and saucers; double-espresso cups with plates; demitasse cups and saucers; other specialty coffee cups; bone china tea cups and saucers for serving tea; plus a range of different-sized glasses for cold drinks and juices. If you also sell alcoholic beverages, you will need to serve them using the appropriate glassware, such as brandy and liqueur glasses and 0.5-, 1- and 1.5-ounce shot glasses.

Additionally, you will need to purchase a range of matching china plates and bowls and silverware, in line with your side-snacks and dessert menus. Pay particular attention when choosing the design of the dessert plates, dishes, and parfait glasses. Remember, presentation often will result in impulse orders for an extra portion of dessert, so it pays not to scrimp on the purchase of eye-catching dessert-ware.

Bear in mind that breakages will be highest for key items of chinaware, such as espresso cups and dessert plates; order extra stock accordingly. Also, keep in mind that dishwashers and other machines all work at different speeds and that not maintaining enough stock will slow down service. Too much stock, however, will cause you to store items in the shop, tying up cash. Figures will need to be adjusted depending on the menu and how many uses you can have for the same piece of china or flatware.

Apart from standard flatware for serving snacks and desserts, you also will need to stock up on specialty flatware such as small espresso spoons, long latté spoon,s and large spoons for scooping foam.

Do not overlook the importance of attractive containers for your countertop or refrigerated food displays. For example, if you are trying to promote your signature "hand-baked" pastries and muffins, you will need to invest in attractive display chinaware, cake plates, or baskets.

Other miscellaneous items and utensils you may need to purchase before opening your coffee, espresso, and tea shop include:

- Knockbox for used coffee grounds
- Cinnamon and nutmeg shakers
- Baskets for individual creams and sugars
- Espresso pourers
- Cream thermos
- Dessert or cake servers
- Dry and wet measuring cups
- Multi-level rack for syrups
- Honey dispensers
- Steam milk thermometers
- Steaming pitchers (32- to 48-oz.)
- Muffin tongs
- Cutting boards
- Measuring spoons

- Prep knives
- Ice cream scoops
- Plastic sealable containers
- Steel scoops for green coffee
- Whipped cream dispenser (with extra chargers)
- Cookie flippers
- Chocolate graters
- Bean blending containers
- Individual teapots and tea cozies

Worksheets

The following worksheets, provided courtesy of the Small Business Administration, will aid the coffee and tea shop manager greatly in estimating start-up costs and expenses.

How Much Money Do You Need?

To help you estimate the amount of financing you will need to get your venture off the ground, use the following checklist. Keep in mind, however, that not every category applies to your specific business. Estimate monthly amount.

MONTHLY COSTS WORKSHEET

WAGES

Salary of owner/manager (if applicable)	$
All other salaries and wages	$
Taxes, including Social Security	$

PROPERTY

Mortgage/property taxes	$
Maintenance (facilities/equipment)	$
Insurance	$
Interest	$
Leases (equipment/furniture/etc.)	$
Fixtures/equipment/furniture	$
Remodeling	$
Installation of fixtures/equipment/furniture	$

UTILITIES

Telephone	$
Utilities	$
Deposits with public utilities	$

MISCELLANEOUS

Advertising	$
Advertising and promotion for opening	$
Delivery expenses	$
Supplies	$
Legal and other professional fees	$
Dues/subscriptions	$
Inventory purchases	$
One-time start-up costs	$
Starting inventory	$
Licenses and permits	$
Accounts receivable	$
Miscellaneous	$
Cash reserve/operating capital	$
Other	$
TOTAL	$

*Your total amount will depend upon how many months of preparation you want to allow for before actually beginning operations.

FURNITURE & FIXTURES WORKSHEET

If you plan to pay for an item in full, leave the Amount Down and Monthly Payment columns blank, and list the price in the Total column.

ITEM	AMT. DOWN	MONTHLY PAYMENT	TOTAL
Counters			
Storage shelves			
Display stands/tables			
Cash register			
Safe			
Window display fixtures			
Special lighting			
Outside sign			
Delivery equipment			
Bathroom equipment			
Computer			
Software			
Kitchen equipment			
Kitchen utensils			
Dining furniture			
Dinnerware			
Other			
Other			
Other			
Other			
	TOTAL DOWN PAYMENT	**TOTAL MONTHLY PAYMENT**	**TOTAL**

Business Logo and Business Cards

Once you have come up with a name for your coffee shop, you will want to develop a logo. A logo should include your store's name and an image that represents it. Many shop owners use a sketch, drawing, or photo of the store itself. You will need to consider the font or typeface for the lettering and colors. Because this will be such an integral piece of your marketing, do not scrimp. Look into hiring a professional to design your logo. You will probably put the logo on every single piece of your marketing items, so you want this to look good!

Business Cards

Long before you open, you will want to design and produce your business cards. These can be a fairly inexpensive and convenient way to market your new shop. There are many good design programs out now so that you could try to design these by yourself. You do want to make sure these look professional, though, so even if you do most of the work yourself, you may want to employ a graphic design for artistic input.

Whether you use a designer only as a consultant or for the whole project, there are many sources for finding these artistic individuals. If you have an area college with an art program, you might try contacting the school to see if anyone is interested in bulking up his or her portfolio. Many of these students are entirely capable of producing professional designs even though they have not had much on-the-job experience.

Many designers also do freelance work. Contact one of the professional design organizations, such as the American Institute of Graphic Arts (AIGA), to see if they can provide you with a directory of freelancers. The AIGA can be contacted at: AIGA, 164 Fifth Avenue New York, NY 10010, 212-807-1990, **www.aiga.org**. Also, look at **www.sologig.com** for freelancers. If you are designing your own business card, be sure to keep the following design principles in mind:

- Alignment
- Contrast
- Repetition
- Proximity

Contrast needs to be obvious or it might look like a mistake. For instance, you can bold all your headers in a brochure and keep all the other text as regular text.

You also can unify a design and create contrast with repeating graphic elements. Think about using bullet lists, for example.

Alignment communicates connection between the elements of your design. When designing a business card or brochure (or any other promotional piece), think about the paper as a grid and place your elements on the grid, trying to balance them and create a pleasing design for the eye. Do not be too constricted by the grid; be bold and place some elements outside of it (angle a picture of your shop, for example) to create visual interest.

Proximity creates a focus for your business card by creating relationships between elements. After you have designed a card, try the squint test. Hold the piece at about arm's length. If all you see is gray, you need to work on proximity.

Try to use these elements in all your graphic designs. Also, think about color. Two- and four-color jobs are more expensive to print, while a nice, clean black and white design might serve just as well.

Because a business card is so small, you want to make sure you do not try to include too much information, and it is very important for it to be eye-catching (otherwise the person you hand your card to is just going to throw it to the back of their desk drawer with all the other business cards in there). Remember, simplicity is often best. Use an image for the focal point of your card and make sure to include pertinent information such as the store's name, address, phone numbers, website, and email addresses. Once you get all this information on the card, there is little room for anything else.

While many people prefer the simplicity of a 1- by 2-inch card because it fits easily into cardholders, others prefer a folded card because it draws people's attention and seems a little more sophisticated.

Poynter.org has several helpful design pages you might want to investigate on color (**www.poynter.org/how-tos/newsgathering-storytelling/visual-voice/12711/understanding-color**), elements of typography (**www.poynter.org/how-tos/newsgathering-storytelling/visual-voice/17140/elements-of-typography**) and using a grid for design (**www.poynter.org/how-tos/newsgathering-storytelling/visual-voice/12369/the-grid-the-structure-of-design**).

Illustrations

You may want to use a photo or original drawing for the main artwork or logo on printed materials for your business cards, brochures, and other advertising pieces, but you may want to use other illustrations at times. How do you find these and what are the rules on using someone else's original material? Most prepared artwork is copyrighted, and you cannot use it without permission. With art, many times you will see the copyright (©) or trademark (™) symbol indicating this. If you do not see one of these marks, however, it does not mean the piece is not copyrighted. You will need to track down the person who owns the copyright and ask permission to use the piece. It is always a good idea to have this permission in writing in case of any future misunderstandings. A good place to start looking for copyright ownership is the U.S. Copyright Office at **www.loc.gov/copyright**. The Copyright Clearance Center, Inc. (**www.copyright.com**) is also a good resource. You may be able to easily acquire permission through the service offered on this site. You can also go to the United States Patent and Trademark Office's Web site at **www.uspto.gov** to look for images that have been trademarked. Finally, if the image is in a published source, you can contact the publisher to inquire about permission. When acquiring permission, keep in mind that there is often a fee for usage. This fee can be as low as $10 or as high as several thousand, depending on the image.

Graphic images websites such as iStockphoto® (**www.istockphoto.com**) and ThinkStock® (**www.thinkstockphotos.com**) are good sources for purchasing professional images.

There are some good free sources of images as well. You might find something you can use in one of Dover Publications' clip-art books. They offer everything from books of nautical illustrations to Victorian house designs to herbs and plants. You can order any of their publications from their website at **http://store.doverpublications.com**. These books are generally in the $20 price range. Other Internet sources include clipart.com™ (**www.clipart.com**), which has dozens of coffee images available to subscribers on its website.

If you are going to use a photo of your shop, you would do well to have a professional photographer take the shot. You want the image to look professional on your literature. However, many of the new digital cameras do just as good a job, and if you have the equipment and are inclined to try, you can shoot a high-quality photo yourself.

Paper and Color

Different colors can evoke different emotions, so choose the colors for your marketing literature with careful consideration. There are probably thousands of choices of paper when you consider all the variables. There are colored papers, textured papers, coated papers, and different paper weights. When designing a brochure or business card, you will want to use a weight heavier than regular writing paper, probably something in the 60-pound-cover or higher range. While coated papers are more expensive than uncoated, you also might want to consider using a coated paper because the ink does not seep into the paper when printed and colors are much brighter and crisper since type and images do not bleed at the edges, as is the case with uncoated papers.

Also, keep in mind that cover paper and colored ink are more expensive than letter-weight paper and black ink. But when it comes to these key advertising pieces, you should not skimp; you want to catch the potential guest's eye and attract them to your coffee shop.

When it comes to printing your cards, check local printers, and compare prices. You will probably find a wide range of prices for the same service. You might find that a particular printer already has the paper or ink you want in stock from another job, so you might be able to get a discount. Even if they have a similar paper and would give you a discount, consider it; if the paper is similar enough to the one you wanted, it will not detract from the finished piece, and you could see a nice chunk of savings!

If you do not hire a professional designer, there also are many software programs you can use to design your our business cards and brochures. Many are easy to use, professional looking, and could save you a quite a bit on printing costs!

- CAM Development — **www.camdevelopment.com**
- Avanquest® — **www.avanquest.com/USA/Business-Card-Factory-Deluxe-4.0**®

You can design and purchase business cards and other printed material for your shop online at such sites as Vistaprint® (**www.vistaprint.com**), 123Print® (**www.123print.com**), and Zazzle® (**www.zazzle.com**) using their professional templates.

You also can check with our local office supply store, such as Staples® or Office Depot for other software programs.

What to Do with Your Business Cards and Other Marketing Pieces

Now that you have all these beautiful marketing pieces, what do you do with them? Be creative when thinking about distributing your cards and brochures. Are there any local attractions that would let you drop off a stack, such as an area museum? Is there a college in the area? Check with the alumni association and office that deals with new students; they might have a way for you to get your brochures out to the public. If you are a member of the chamber of commerce or a local tourist office, try them as well. Area event planners and music venues may be other good sources.

Etc.

The first European coffee was sold in drugstores in 1615 as a medicinal remedy. The first coffee house opened in Berlin in 1721. —**www.discountcoffee.com/coffee-trivia**

3

The Basics of Buying a Coffee, Espresso & Tea Shop

As mentioned in the introduction to this manual on *How to Open a Financially Successful Coffee, Espresso & Tea Shop*, the consumption of specialty coffees and teas outside the home is at an all-time high, with new European-style coffee and tea shops opening daily across the United States. But, as competition is cutthroat in this growing segment of the beverage industry, it is doubly important that you choose a site that offers long-term potential for building your profit margins and staying ahead of the competition.

Choosing the Best Location

Your choice of location will depend on a number of practical considerations, including available budget and findings from your market research about potential customer profiles, demographics, local competition and traffic patterns. Other, more subjective factors, such as your "vision" and perceived image of your establishment, will also play a part in your final decision.

One of the most important (and often overlooked) factors to have in mind when selecting the ideal location for your coffee, espresso, and tea shop is the volume of foot traffic that passes by your shop. Retail coffee and tea outlets depend on impulse, "walk-in" trade for their day-to-day survival. Available flow of foot traffic should, therefore, be central to your decision about where to locate your shop.

Here are a few possible sites that are likely to generate foot traffic and, thus, potential customers for your coffee, espresso, and tea shop:

- University campus
- Supermarket
- Large office block
- Municipal building
- Transit center
- Train station
- Busy sidewalk
- Gym or fitness center
- Theater
- Convention center
- Shopping mall
- Service station
- Hospital or medical center
- Bookstore
- Bus stop
- Airport
- Library
- Concert hall
- Art gallery

Before you start looking at specific sites, you will want to consider what type of operation you want.

Lease vs. Own

You may want to consider leasing rather than buying a location for your restaurant. You may be able to lease a building with less money up front. It will be easier to start your new restaurant, and there may be certain tax advantages to leasing. Additionally, if the time ever comes when you want to move, you would not have all the costs associated with selling the building.

You should look at the following items in a commercial lease:

- Length of lease. Many commercial leases go for five or ten years, rather than a single year.
- Rent rate and timing of rent increases
- Whether the rent includes insurance, property taxes, and maintenance costs (called a gross lease), or whether you will be charged for these items separately (called a net lease).
- The amount of the security deposit and conditions for its return
- The square footage of the space you are renting
- How improvements and modifications will be handled and who will pay for them. Pay specific attention to sign specifications.

- Who will maintain and repair the premises?
- Whether there is an option to renew the lease or expand the space
- How the lease may be terminated, including notice requirements, and penalties for early termination

Commercial leases are different from residential leases. If you have rented an apartment, that does not mean you know what you are getting into. Commercial leases do not fall under most consumer protection laws. For example, there are no caps on security deposits or rules protecting a tenant's privacy. Commercial leases usually are customized to the landlord's needs, but they can be subject to more negotiation between the business owner and the landlord. Because there is no standard lease form, you must be sure to read each lease agreement you look at carefully. It probably would be wise to have your lawyer look at the lease as well.

- **Lease breaking.** Unlike a residential lease where if you break the lease, you simply forfeit your security deposit, commercial leases are contracts, and if you break it, more than your security deposit may be at stake. Pay close attention to these terms in the lease agreement.

- **Future growth.** Think before you enter into a lease agreement, and make sure it fits your current and future business needs. Especially consider where you think your business will be in the future if you are entering into a long-term lease agreement. Make sure the lease covers your ability to make the necessary modifications your building may need now or five years down the road.

- **Signs and competition.** Also, make sure you are able to put up a sign. If you lease in a large commercial complex, make sure the lease includes some competition safeguards for you. You do not want to open your coffee shop and see the landlord rent the space next door to another coffee shop two months later!

- **Leasing broker.** You may want to engage a leasing broker to help you locate business leases. A leasing broker works much the same way as a real estate broker: they will do a great deal of the legwork for a fee.

Existing Operation

Other opportunities to buy operations that are not franchises exist. Again, this would require less capital at the start of your venture because, in many cases, when someone sells an existing operation, this includes all the equipment as well. You need to be careful if you are considering buying an existing operation; you do not want to buy one that is a failing business.

Check the financial records. You will want to look at the company's financial records from the past several years to get a good sense of the company's financial health. While you may be able to breathe some life back into the business, do not expect miracles.

Why are they selling? Do some sleuthing to find out why the seller is selling and what the word on the street is about the location. Be on site for a few days and see what happens at the operation now. Finally, make sure the location is a good one for your operation.

Existing operations for sale can be found in the classified section of newspapers and in trade publications. Also look at BusinessesForSale.com at **www.businessesforsale.com**, and TheBizSeller at **www.thebizseller.com**.

New Building

The good thing about new buildings is that you do not have to go in immediately and do remodeling or updating. Newer buildings also will be up to code. If you are buying a site to build a structure, you may find this Web address useful: **www.firstsourceonl.com**. After registering as a user, you can enter information on the type of structure you want to build, the gross square feet you need, and the zip code, and the program will provide you an itemized cost estimate. You can find a database for building codes for most major cities on this same website.

Existing Building

Older buildings often have more character than new buildings. You may also be able to benefit from a tax break with some older buildings. Since 1976, there have been provisions in the federal tax code to benefit taxpayers who own historic commercial buildings. These buildings are structures that are listed on the National Register of Historic Places, in national historic districts, in local historic districts, or are National Historic Landmarks. This tax credit has gone a long way in helping cities revitalize historic areas. Currently the tax benefit to the owner is a 20 percent tax credit. For further information on this tax credit, visit the Internal Revenue Services' website at **www.irs.gov** or Federal Historic Preservation Tax Incentives, National Park Service (**www.nps.gov/tps/tax-incentives.htm**), 1201 "Eye" Street, NW, 6th Floor Washington, DC 20005. They can be reached by email at NPS_TPS@nps.gov or by phone at 202-513-7270.

Type of Facility

You also will need to consider whether you want your specialty coffee shop to be a freestanding structure or part of a strip mall or shopping center. Consider the advantages and disadvantages of each type of location. Will tourists be a significant part of your business? You may want to consider locating in a theme/historical shopping area, such as Albuquerque's Old Town. On the other hand, many popular coffee chains are located in strip malls, marketing to the local population of shoppers.

Think about the competition and nearby businesses. If you choose to be part of a shopping area, you are likely to attract customers from the other business areas. However, there also may be more competition in such an area than if you own a freestanding location. You may find more space and parking constraints in a shopping area location.

Think about your customer profile. Also, consider whether to locate in the urban center or the suburbs of the community. Does your customer profile tell you your customers will be businesspeople? You will do better in the urban center where more businesses are likely to be located.

Strip-Mall Locations

If you decide to locate in a strip mall, there are three positions your store can be in: 1) detached from the other buildings, 2) attached to the other stores in the strip mall, and 3) at one of the ends of the line of attached buildings.

- **Freestanding building.** In general, the freestanding building may be the best and most visible option. Of all the attached stores, the ones at the ends produce more sales than those in the middle, and usually one end has higher visibility.

- **Middle locations.** The middle stores in a strip mall are more problematic. When you are housed in one of these, you become one of the crowd, and it is hard for the potential customer to notice you. On top of this, many lessors will have restrictions on signs, so you may not be able to differentiate yourself with your store's sign. There may be other ways to distinguish yourself, however, depending on your lease agreement. You may be able to put tables outside, or a sandwich board listing specials. Perhaps you can use piped out music to attract customers, or put one of your servers on the sidewalk with samples.

- **Center locations.** If your restaurant is located right in the center, you may have greater visibility due to the architecture of the building. Also, be sure to pay attention to any anchor stores in the mall, such as major department stores; you will have higher visibility located next to one of these.

- **Other strip malls in vicinity.** Finally, if you decide to locate in a strip mall location, pay attention to other shopping venues in the area. Generally, where there is one strip mall, there is another. Be sure that you are not locating your coffee shop in a secondary location. Pay attention to how visible your location will be to someone driving by. Can they pick you out of all the other options they are seeing? Also, try to find out from the owner if there are plans to build any buildings in the lots in front of your strip mall, obscuring your visibility in the future. In addition, think about where you want to take your operation in the future. If you are planning to expand in five years, a strip mall location may not be the best choice because it could limit or eliminate your expansion plans.

Shopping Mall Locations

If you decide to look at shopping mall locations, you also will want to do your homework.

- **Visit the mall.** Find out what stores are already there and what new stores have plans to open. Find out what you can about square footage, and pay attention to peak shopping hours and the customer mix.
- **Notice where the larger stores are located**, such as department stores. A location near one of these would be ideal.
- **Stay away from dead-end corridors.** Customers tend not to go exploring in a mall if they do not see much activity down the corridor.
- **Food courts.** Many of the malls nowadays have food courts. You may want to consider locating your coffee store in one of these. Be aware, however, that this will limit what you can do. Operations in food courts are typically small, so you may have to serve a limited menu due to the space and equipment constraints. Naturally, this may affect your sales and ability to make profits.

Theme Centers

Many cities have areas in town devoted to historic or other themes. Albuquerque, for example, has Old Town. Columbus, Ohio, has Germantown. Depending on the theme of your shop, it might be appropriate to locate in one of these centers. Look at your shop's concept. Would it contribute to such an area?

Look at the other stores. Notice what the other shopping and entertainment venues are in the center. Would you benefit from having them as neighbors? Even if you are a Mexican restaurant, the historic center of Albuquerque may not be the best location for you; if your customers tend to be residents, you will attract more customers from a strip mall or freestanding location.

Freestanding Locations

Freestanding locations have their good and bad points as well. If you are located in such a facility, you may not have the benefit of business created by nearby stores. On the other hand, you do have more flexibility with how you use your space, and you have a greater ability to expand your operation than if you are in a mall or part of a strip mall. You also do not have to worry about regulations that might govern what type of sign you can use, and you do not have to share your parking space.

Cart

According to Bellissimo Coffee Infogroup, at **www.espresso101.com,** starting up and initially stocking a coffee cart business costs around $20,000 to $25,000, as compared to starting a sit-down space which can cost as much as $200,000 to $375,000 to start up. If you are just beginning your business and have limited funds, you may want to consider a cart rather than a piece of real estate. Naturally, you would not have the same amount of room, so your drink and food menu would be more limited. On the plus side, you would not be tied to one location, so you and your cart could go to the sales. If there is a special event, you could be there. Or, if there is a college in your town, you could park there during the week and find another suitable location for sales on the weekends. Remember to check with your local government about permits and if there are certain areas vendors are not allowed. Also, keep in mind the weather. A cart in Florida may be able to be more financially successful than one in Minnesota simply due to weather conditions.

Facility Requirements

You also need to think about the type of space and design requirements for your site. Break the operation up into front-of-the-house and back-of-the-house to figure out what you need in both areas.

How much space do you need? According to facility experts, dining will take up the majority of your space. This is followed by kitchen and prep space, and then storage space. Usually, space breaks down as follows: dining space is 40 to 60 percent of total facility; kitchen space is 30 percent; storage and the administrative office take up the remaining space. About 12 percent should be allotted for actual food preparation; the remainder of the production space will be for dishwashing, trash, and receiving. If you are starting from scratch, you may want to engage the services of an architect or restaurant design consultant to help you design your space, but the services of these professionals can cost several thousand dollars.

How much room do you need for dining? Check your sales forecast to determine dining room needs. How much room do you need for dining? Let's say your sales forecast tells you that you have the potential to make $4,000 a week, serving 400 people weekly. You plan to be open 6 days a week and you estimate you can turn your tables once a night, so you need to be able to fit approximately 35 patrons at a time (400 people ÷ 66.66 people; 66.66 people ÷ 2 table turns = 33.33). For dining, you will need about 15 to 18 square feet per customer per table; therefore, you will need approximately 630 square feet for dining. Remember, this does not take a bar, lobby, hostess area, coatroom, or restrooms into consideration.

What do you need for bar space? If you have a bar, you should have about one bar seat for every three dining seats. Allow 2 square feet for bar stools and chairs and about 10 to 12 square feet per customer at a table.

Coffeehouse space needs will vary depending on whether or not you are serving food. If you are, your space needs will be similar to a sandwich shop because you will probably be serving fare that requires similar equipment. You may want to have additional space for a coffee bar, espresso machine, and coffee accessories. You also may want to include a retail area. In general, between 800 and 3,000 square feet should take care of your needs.

Now that you have picked the community in which to locate your restaurant and you have decided on the type of facility that will work for you, you must pick the specific site. What are the elements of a successful location for your operation? In a restaurant, the most important factor in sales is going to be how you can draw in the customer. Specific site characteristics have more effect on this than the previously mentioned factors.

Site Characteristics

Now that you have narrowed your search down to a few locations, you need to compare these locations to determine which one is the best. Here are some factors you need to consider in this comparison:

- **Visibility.** How easy is it to see the location for the customer? You will get maximum visibility if you are located on the far corner of a main road intersecting a secondary road. You also should try to find a level location. This will enhance your visibility, and it will make it easier for drivers to get in and out of your parking lot, particularly in the winter when there may be ice and snow. Try to avoid dead-end and one-way streets.

- **Parking.** How much parking is there? The Urban Land Institute (**www.uli.org**) and International Council of Shopping Centers (**www.icsc.org**) lists standard ratios of parking needed for shopping centers. They suggest that there should be at least 2.2 square feet of parking for every square foot of shopping center space. For supermarkets, they suggest at least 3 square feet of parking for every square foot of supermarket space. You may want to look at this; it may help you make some estimates on the amount of parking you would need. In areas with little parking or areas with higher crime rates, you may want to consider using valet parking.

- **Ingress/Egress.** How easy is it to get into the parking lot and leave the parking lot? Look at the roads in front of a possible location. Are there medians? These can make turning into your parking lot a problem. What about traffic lights? If you are on a busy road and your site is located on a corner without a light, customers may find it difficult to get into your parking lot as well.

- **Accessibility.** How easy is it for your customers to get to the location from their homes and/or businesses? One of the things you will want to do is drive the trade area. Get in your car and drive from various points to your possible location. How long does it take you to get there? If you are going to be serving lunch, drive during the lunch hour. Serving dinner? How long does it take to get to the location during evening rush hour?

- **Retail synergy.** How does the presence or absence of other retailers affect consumer traffic? When we use the word "competition," it usually has a negative connotation, but not all other business is competition. Synergism refers to the idea that you can increase business because of your proximity of other businesses.

- **Security.** How safe is the location perceived? Check with the local police department to see what types of security problems, if any, the neighborhood has experienced. Be sure to make your specific site safe with outside lighting as well.

Real Estate and Its Value

The real estate property value of a shop is often its most valuable feature. In many cases, the real estate is a bigger attraction to the buyer than the business itself. In fact, many shops are bought and sold without the real property being part of the operation. These are cases where the shop leases its property from a landlord who has no involvement in the business itself. "Real estate" is the land itself and any permanent improvements made on the land, such as utility connections, parking lots, buildings, etc. The value of real estate is one of the major assets that need to be calculated when determining a beverage and food service operation's value. Generally, there are three procedures for determining the value of a property: market approach, cost approach and income approach.

Market Approach

The market approach is based on the idea of substitution. Basically, this means that the value of a property is determined by comparing it with like pieces of property in similar areas. Since these comparable properties are usually not exactly the same as the property you are trying to value, you will need to make adjustments, which is a subjective process at best. At worst, it is impossible, because owners of similar properties are extremely unlikely to tell you the details of their businesses. For these reasons, the market approach generally is not used to estimate the value of a shop's real estate.

Cost Approach

The cost approach is based on the idea of replacement. In simple terms, the property is valued on what it would cost to replace it completely. To determine this, you must add the replacement costs of all the assets in your establishment. Obtain purchase prices for new equipment and assets that exactly match your existing ones. The cost approach is not widely used to estimate the value of a shop's real estate, but is used mostly by insurance companies while processing a claim.

Income Approach

The income approach bases its valuation on the anticipation of future income to be derived from the property. The real estate value, then, is the present value of the estimated future net income plus the present value of the estimated profit to be earned when the property is sold. This is the preferred approach when determining an accurate sales price for an income-producing property.

The Value of Other Assets

A retail outlet's assets are often broken down into three categories: real estate, other reversion assets, and the business. A reversion asset is one that retains its value regardless of the success or failure of the business, such as real estate, equipment, inventories, receivables, prepaid expenses (deposits, taxes, advertising, etc.), leasehold interest, licenses, and franchises. As these assets keep their value even if a business goes under, it is in an owner's best interest to own as many reversion assets as possible.

The business itself consists of everything the owner wishes to sell. Usually this means the furniture, fixtures, equipment, leasehold improvements, etc. It also may include tax credits, favorable operating expenses, customer lists, and name recognition. The price for a beverage and food service business is usually 40 to 70 percent of the operation's 12-month food-and-beverage sales volume. The seller usually will set the sales price at the high end of this percentage, and the prospective buyer will set it at the low end.

The purchase price will also be based on many other factors including:

- **Profitability.** Has the most influence on a shop's sale price and salability
- **Leasehold terms and conditions.** Term remaining and monthly lease payments will greatly affect sales price.
- **Track record.** Businesses need to show acceptable track records to entice buyers.
- **Other income.** Usually minimal for a beverage outlet, but includes rebates and interest on bank deposits
- **Below-market financing.** A small down payment by the buyer to ensure favorable rates for the balance
- **Personal goodwill.** If the existing staff agree to stay on, personal goodwill is not transferable upon sale.
- **Franchise affiliation.** If the shop is part of a large franchise, the sale price will increase significantly.
- **Number of buyers and sellers.** Buying peaks in early spring and summer affect selling price.
- **Contingent liabilities.** Previous owner commitments; e.g., coupons already issued, pension plans, etc.
- **Grandfather clauses.** Meeting fire, health, and safety codes that the previous owner may have avoided

Goodwill

Goodwill is the amount of money paid for a beverage and food outlet in excess of the current book value of the physical assets. Most buyers, however, look at excess earnings as attributable to positive goodwill and deficient earnings to negative goodwill. In order to compute the goodwill value, the shop's income statement from the past 12 months must be reconstructed. The sales volume is critical because the most likely sales price is tied into the previous 12 months' net food and beverage sales volume. The sales volume is doubly important because a seller will have to adhere to the figure supported in the sales reports. Buyers generally are not interested in hearing about phantom buried income or optimistic forecasts of future sales.

Terms, Conditions and Price

Potential buyers should be aware of the fact that, in most cases, sellers will determine likely sales price, terms, and conditions, and will then pad those somewhat to create room for negotiation and compromise.

As much as possible, anticipating every potential problem that may arise during negotiations will put sellers in a good position to offer solutions to a buyer's objections. It is a good idea for a seller to hire an attorney, accountant, or business broker when calculating a preferred sales price, terms, and conditions. As part of the negotiations, we recommend that the buyer incorporate attorney, accountant, or business broker transaction costs and fees into the price that he or she is offering. It is also good practice for the seller to enumerate all the assets included in the sale of the shop. At the very least, this will garner respect from potential buyers, and it may give the seller a leg up during initial negotiations.

Terms
The terms of sale are the procedures used by the buyer to pay the seller. A buyer usually is willing to accept a proposed sales price if the seller will accept the buyer's terms. A large down payment is likely to demonstrate the buyer's commitment to the long haul. In addition, a seller is more likely to grant favorable terms to a buyer making a substantial down payment because the financial risk is lessened.

Conditions
The seller and buyer will attach several conditions to most sales contracts. Sometimes they are separate agreements, but most of the time, they are part of the sales contract.

Determining Price from a Buyer's Perspective

Potential buyers must do a thorough financial analysis of the shop. They should study its current profitability carefully and use this information to determine its potential capacity for generating revenue. There is a very close relationship between a shop's current profitability and its likely sales price. Understandably, sellers are not particularly eager to divulge their financial records to buyers. However, if a seller is forthcoming with this information, it can signal to the buyer that he or she has nothing to hide.

It is a good idea for the buyer to hire an accountant to assist in this financial analysis. This will help determine whether the deal meets the buyer's investment requirements. Buyers also should consider hiring other specialists to work with contracts, unemployment compensation, insurance, and banking. Small Business Development Centers (SBDC) throughout the country offer free consulting services to businesses with fewer than 500 employees.

The buyers also should complete at least a rough market and competition survey before performing a financial evaluation. This will ensure the buyer's familiarity with the shop's location and will help when estimating future revenues and expenses. If the buyer is unfamiliar with the area, an independent consulting service can be hired to provide a useful survey.

A seller expects a written offer with price, terms, conditions, and an earnest money deposit before allowing a potential buyer to review confidential financial information. It must be agreed that the buyer can withdraw if he or she is unhappy with the financial records. This is because the earnest deposit is at risk unless the right to retract the offer is in place. When reviewing the seller's financial records, the buyer should expect that an independent CPA has never audited them. Auditing is a costly process, and most small coffee and tea shops do not do it unless they absolutely have to. A lucky buyer is one who is given audited financial statements.

Buyers need to reconstruct historical financial statements to show what they could have been, had the buyer been operating the business. This is usually done from only the previous year's statement. Patience is important here; this is a time-consuming process. If errors are made, the estimate of the business' sales price may be inaccurate. Sellers will tend to overestimate customer counts and check averages and underestimate utilities and other expenses. The inexperienced buyer should be wary when evaluating these numbers and may want to hire professional counsel.

Also, it is important to be aware that sellers usually will include only the financial details they initially want to reveal. Buyers should evaluate this information carefully, with special attention to the apparent net cash flow, before spending a lot of time and money on detailed analysis.

During this analysis, it is important to note that the typical beverage outlet purchase will not appear to generate enough money to provide sufficient cash flow, give the buyer an appropriate salary and ensure a return on the initial investment. Do not be put off too quickly, however. Solid analysis often reveals that a change in ownership can enhance an operation's profitability considerably.

This analysis should examine all relevant tax filings to determine the most likely annual sales volume that the shop will generate. The profit figures included in these filings will be used to determine an accurate sales price. Personnel records are crucial in determining if there have been any Department of Labor judgments against the current owner, or if there are any pending judgments that could impede the transfer of ownership. It is a good idea to meet with a Department of Labor representative to find out if the shop is currently under investigation.

Cost of equipment, beverages, food, and miscellaneous supplies are a specialty beverage business's biggest expenses. The potential buyer should take a random sample of cancelled invoices and check their consistency with the cost of goods sold and direct operating supplies expenses listed on the current income statement. Cancelled invoices are a good test of the current owner's purchasing skills. Potential buyers also should analyze balance sheets and income statements carefully. Balance sheets can reveal the anxiety level of a seller. As a buyer, it is important that you keep in mind that you are basing your price on current income, but purchasing the operation's future revenue-making ability; this is one of the most critical tasks the buyer will perform.

Initial Investment

Equally important as price, terms, and conditions is the total amount of money required to begin operating. Beverage outlets require significant amounts of cash when starting, and buyers must estimate as accurately as possible the total initial investment needed to get their businesses up and running in the way they envision them. One of the very appealing aspects of purchasing an existing shop is that many start-up costs are avoided. There are, however, a number of start-up costs even with transfer of ownership. Here are a number to be aware of:

- Investigation costs
- Transaction costs
- Deposits
- Legal fees
- Advertising
- Loan fees
- Insurance
- Distributorship fees
- Accounting fees
- Other prepaid expenses
- Locksmith
- Contingency funds

- Down payment
- Working capital
- Licenses and permits
- Renovations and new utensils
- Fictitious name registration
- Equity fees
- Franchise fees
- Pre-opening labor
- Other consulting fees
- Sales taxes
- Security

Strategies for Buying

Before contacting sellers, potential buyers should prepare a document that outlines for themselves their desired sales price, terms, and conditions. You also will need to consider the shop's investment yield, taxes, and the effect the business will have on your personal life. Basically, buyers should be looking for establishments that will meet their numbers and ones that they are going to be happy working at 12 to 14 hours a day. Buyers should prioritize their objectives and consider the trade-offs that must be made to attain them. Buyers generally want to accomplish the flowing objectives:

- **Best possible sales price.** Serious buyers and sellers compromise on the sales price, terms, and conditions in order to reach a mutually satisfying end. Buyers are usually willing to trade price for terms and conditions. Most buyers will draw the line at a sales price that exceeds the shop's replacement cost.
- **Reasonable down payment.** Most serious buyers are willing to maintain a 1:1 debt-to-equity ratio. Many buyers want to lower their down payments to reduce risk, and unfortunately, find themselves with businesses that cannot support their debt load.
- **Reasonable initial investment.** Serious buyers are willing to match dollars of debt equally with dollars of personal equity. Buyers do want most of their equity to go towards the down payment.
- **Maximum future profits.** Buyers are buying a shop's current financial performance but always are looking for the highest potential revenue-generating business.
- **Reduced possibility of failure.** Only one out of five established businesses that are purchased go under. That is much better than the four-out-of-five failure rate of new businesses.
- **Enhancement of borrowing power.** Most lenders prefer financing an existing, profitable operation to a new venture.
- **Minimizing tax liabilities.** Buyers need to be aware of the tax consequences of the shop they are buying. Both buyer and seller should work at minimizing taxes. The only way to ensure that this happens is for both parties to hire accountants.

Buyers, too, should develop a purchase plan that lists potential sellers, analyzes their motivations for selling, analyzes the businesses, and develops planned responses to counteroffers. Research into a seller's motivation is crucial here and can serve the buyer in a number of ways.

The following is a list of major seller motivations:

- Owners who want to retire

- Disillusioned owners who do not know how to remedy their problems
- Owners with tax problems
- Owners with other investment opportunities
- Owners with distressed properties and insufficient cash flow to fund remodeling
- Distressed owners with profitable operations, but troubled personal relationships

Once a buyer has responded to a sales solicitation, he or she will receive enough information to determine if the shop meets or exceeds investment requirements. The buyer should do more preliminary work to find out further specifics about whether a shop is a good business opportunity. One of the best indications is the shop's real property lease payment. If it is less than or equal to 6 percent of the shop's total sales volume, it is probably worth further investigation.

When a buyer decides to pursue more research, he or she should tour the facility, learn the lease highlights and other purchase options, and evaluate the neighborhood, competition, customer viewpoint, history of ownership, and the owner's reason for selling. After doing a deeper analysis of the shop, the buyer must once again determine if it meets his or her investment requirements. If so, an earnest money deposit and offer should be delivered to the seller in return for detailed information on the shop.

Financing

The typical offer and acceptance agreement includes several conditions necessary for the deal's completion. Most of these are met easily, but two are difficult to meet: the buyer's qualification for financing and the attainment of all necessary permits and licenses. As a buyer, you can do little if you do not qualify for permits, unless you need to fix only simple code violations to qualify. In the financing realm, however, the seller and buyer have more control and can adjust the final sales contract to suit the buyer's needs. Buyers should be aware that there is no bigger threat to their success than inadequate or inappropriate financing. Excessive debt burden is one of the most consistent reasons businesses go under.

SBA Financial Programs

The Small Business Administration (SBA) offers a variety of financing options for small businesses. Whether you are looking for a long-term loan for equipment, a general working capital loan, a revolving line of credit, or a micro-loan, the SBA has a financing program to fit your needs. These programs are discussed in detail on the SBA's website at **www.sba.gov**.

SBA Assistance

The SBA is the largest source of long-term small business financing in the nation. In order to determine whether you qualify or whether an SBA business loan best suits your financing needs, contact your banker, one of the active SBA-guaranteed lenders or an SBA loan officer.

The 7(a) Loan Guaranty Program

The 7(a) Loan Guaranty Program (**www.sba.gov/financing/sbaloan/7a.html**) is the SBA's primary loan program. The SBA reduces risk to lenders by guaranteeing major portions of loans made to small businesses. This enables the lenders to provide financing to small businesses when funding is otherwise unavailable at reasonable terms. The eligibility requirements and credit criteria of the program are very broad in order to accommodate a wide range of financing needs.

When a small business applies to a lending institution for a loan, the lender reviews the application and decides if it merits a loan on its own or if it requires additional support in the form of an SBA guaranty. The lender then requests SBA backing on the loan. In guaranteeing the loan, the SBA assures the lender that, in the event the borrower does not repay the loan, the government will reimburse the lending institution for a portion of its loss. By providing this guaranty, the SBA is able to help tens of thousands of small businesses every year get financing they could not otherwise obtain.

To qualify for an SBA guaranty, a small business must meet the 7(a) criteria, and the lender must certify that it could not provide funding on reasonable terms except with an SBA guaranty. The SBA can then guarantee as much as 85 percent on loans of up to $150,000 and 75 percent on loans of more than $150,000. In most cases, the maximum guaranty is $1 million. Exceptions are the International Trade, DELTA, and 504 loan programs, which have higher loan limits. The maximum total loan size under the 7(a) program is $2 million.

Friends and Relatives

Many entrepreneurs look to private sources such as friends and family when starting out in a business venture. Often, money is loaned interest free or at a low interest rate, which can be quite beneficial when getting started.

Banks and Credit Unions

The most common sources of funding, banks and credit unions will provide a loan if you can show that your business proposal is sound.

Borrowing Money

It is often said that small-business people have a difficult time borrowing money. This is not necessarily true. Banks make money by lending money. However, the inexperience of many small business owners in financial matters often prompts banks to deny loan requests. Requesting a loan when you are not properly prepared sends a signal to your lender. That message is: high risk! To be successful in obtaining a loan, you must be prepared and organized. You must know exactly how much money you need, why you need it, and how you will pay it back. You must be able to convince your lender that you are a good credit risk.

How to Write a Loan Proposal

Approval of your loan request depends on how well you present yourself, your business and your financial needs to a lender. Remember, lenders want to make loans, but they must make loans they know will be repaid. The best way to improve your chances of obtaining a loan is to prepare a written proposal. A well-written loan proposal contains:

General Information

- Business name, names of principals, Social Security number for each principal, and business address
- Purpose of the loan: exactly what the loan will be used for and why it is needed
- Amount required: the exact amount you need to achieve your purpose

Business Description

- History and nature of the business: what kind of business it is, its age, number of employees and current business assets
- Ownership structure: details of your company's legal structure

Management Profile

Provide a short statement about each principal in your business: include background, education, experience, skills, and accomplishments.

Market Information

- Clearly define your company's products as well as your markets.
- Identify your competition and explain how your business competes in the marketplace.
- Profile your customers and explain how your business can satisfy their needs.

Financial Information

- Financial statements: balance sheets and income statements for the past three years. If you are just starting out, provide a projected balance sheet and income statement.
- Personal financial statements on yourself and other principal owners of the business
- Collateral you are willing to pledge as security for the loan

How Your Loan Request Will Be Reviewed

When reviewing a loan request, the lender primarily is concerned about repayment. To help determine your ability to repay, many loan officers will order a copy of your business credit report from a credit-reporting agency. Therefore, you should work with these agencies to help them present an accurate picture of your business. Using the credit report and the information you have provided, the lending officer will consider the following issues:

- Have you invested savings or personal equity in your business totaling at least 25 to 50 percent of the loan you are requesting? (Remember, a lender or investor will not finance 100 percent of your business.)

- Do you have a sound record of credit-worthiness as indicated by your credit report, work history and letters of recommendation? This is very important.

- Do you have sufficient experience and training to operate a successful business?

- Have you prepared a loan proposal and business plan that demonstrate your understanding of, and commitment to, the success of the business?

- Does the business have sufficient cash flow to make the monthly payments?

Closing the Sale

Once buyer and seller have agreed on the particulars, they will commit themselves to a binding sales contract and transfer ownership. There are often lawyers, brokers, accountants, lenders, escrow agents, government officials, trade unions, family members, and other people involved in this transaction. It usually takes 30 to 60 days to finish the ownership transfer.

The close of escrow happens when all the documents necessary to complete the sale are recorded at the county recorder's office. This usually happens the morning after the closing date. The documents usually recorded include:

- Deed
- Mortgage or deed of trust
- Sales contract
- Bill of sale
- Request for notice

- Promissory note
- Other security agreements
- Options
- Assignments
- Notice of completion of work

If the new owner does not make payments on an assumable loan, the seller will want to be notified. If they have made the request for notification in advance — and made it part of public record — it will happen. The notice of completion of work is also included in these filings because many people will record guarantees and warranties to make sure there are no questions regarding their dates of expiration.

Etc.

Coffee comes from a tree or bush that bears cherry fruit. The coffee bean is the seed inside the cherry. If coffee was not such a valuable and tasty commodity we probably would see coffee cherries in the grocery store. The coffee cherry's taste is one of a very delicious tart fruit that some describe as light, honey, sweet, peachy, and watermelon.

—**coffeecupnews.org**

4

How to Invest in a Franchise

Many specialty beverage operators have been helped in getting a sound start and have expanded through investing in a franchise. In the specialty coffee, espresso and tea industry, national franchise opportunities include, among others, Bad Ass Coffee of Hawaii™ (**badasscoffee.com**), Barista Brava® (**www.baristabrava.com**), Barnies Coffee Kitchen™ (**barniescoffeekitchen.com**), Caffé Appassionato® (**www.caffeappassionato.com**), Dunkin Donuts® (**www.dunkinfranchising.com**), Joffrey's Coffee & Tea Company® (**www.joffreys.com**), Gloria Jean's Coffees® (**www.gloriajeans.com**), Port City Java (**www.portcityjava.com**), Seattle's Best Coffee® (**www.seattlesbest.com**), Starbucks (**www.starbucks.com**), and The Coffee Beanery® (**www.coffeebeanery.com**).

According to the U.S. Department of Commerce, buying a franchise is the average person's most viable avenue to owning a business. You may want to consider such an investment. Franchising can minimize your risk. It will enable you to start your business under a name and trademark that has already gained public acceptance. You will have access to training and management assistance from experienced people in the beverage industry. Sometimes, you can obtain financial assistance; this allows you to start your business with less cash than you would ordinarily need.

On the other hand, you must make some sacrifices when entering a franchise operation. You lose a certain amount of control of the business. You will no longer truly be your own boss in some situations. And, of course, you must pay a fee or share profits with the franchiser. This chapter will present some of the advantages and disadvantages of franchising and how to evaluate a potential franchise.

Definition of Franchising

Essentially, franchising is a plan of distribution under which an individually owned business is operated as though it were a part of a large chain. Products are standardized. Standardized trademarks, symbols, design elements, and equipment are used. A supplier (the franchiser) gives the individual dealer (the franchisee) the right to sell, distribute, and market the franchiser's product by using the franchiser's name, reputation, and selling techniques. The franchise agreement (or contract) usually gives the exclusive right to sell, or otherwise represent, the franchiser. In return for this exclusive right, the franchisee agrees to pay a sum of money (a franchise fee) or a percentage of gross sales or to buy equipment or supplies from the franchiser — often these options are variously combined.

Advantages of Franchising

As a franchisee, you have the luxury of starting a business with:

- **Limited experience.** You are taking advantage of the franchiser's experience — experience that you probably would have gained the hard way, through trial and error.

- **A relatively small amount of capital** and a strengthened financial and credit standing. Sometimes the franchiser will give financial assistance to enable you to start with less than the usual amount of cash. For example, the franchiser may accept a down payment with your note for the balance of the needed capital. Or, the franchiser may allow you to delay in making payments on royalties or other fees in order to help you over the "rough spots." With the name of a well-known, successful franchiser behind you, your standing with financial institutions will be strengthened.

- **A well-developed image** and consumer support of proven products and services. The goods and services of the franchiser, such as Starbucks for example, are proven and widely known. Therefore, your business has "instant" pulling power. To develop such pulling power on your own might take years of promotion and considerable investment.

- **Competently designed facilities, layout, displays, and fixtures.** The franchising company has designed effective facilities, layout, displays, and fixtures based upon experience with many dealers.

- **Chain buying power.** You may receive savings through chain-style purchasing of products, equipment, supplies, advertising materials, and other business needs.

- **The opportunity for business training.** You will receive continued assistance from experienced management in proven methods of doing business. You can normally expect to be trained in the mechanics of the beverage business and guided in its day-to-day operation until you are proficient at the job. Moreover, the franchiser provides management consulting services a on a continuing basis. This often includes help with recordkeeping as well as other accounting assistance.

- **National or regional promotion and publicity.** The national or regional promotion of the franchiser will help your business. Also, you will receive help and guidance with local advertising. The franchiser's program of research and development will assist you in keeping up with competition and changing times.

All of these factors can help increase your income and lower your risk of failure.

Disadvantages of Franchising

Franchising also has some drawbacks that must be considered:

- **Submission to imposed standardized operations.** You cannot make all the rules. Contrary to the "be your own boss" lures in franchise advertisements, you may not be your only boss. In addition, you must subjugate your personal identity to the name of the franchiser. Obviously, if you would like your operation to be known by your own name, a franchise is not for you. The franchiser exerts fundamental control and obliges you to: 1) conform to standardized procedures, 2) handle specific products or services which may not be particularly profitable in your marketing area, and 3) follow other policies which may benefit others in the chain but not you. This means that you forfeit the freedom to make many decisions — to be your own boss.

- **Sharing of profits with the franchiser.** The franchiser nearly always charges a royalty of a percentage of gross sales. This royalty fee ultimately must come out of the profits of the franchisee or be paid whether the franchisee makes a profit or not. Sometimes such fees are exorbitantly out of proportion to the profit.

- **Required purchases.** Merchandise, supplies, or equipment that the franchiser requires you to purchase might be obtained elsewhere for less. Additionally, you might pay more to the franchiser than other franchisees for the same services.

- **Lack of freedom to meet local competition.** Under a franchise, you may be restricted in establishing selling prices, in introducing additional products or services or dropping unprofitable ones, even in the face of insidious local competition.

- **Danger of contracts being slanted to the advantage of the franchiser.** Clauses in some contracts imposed by the franchiser provide for unreasonably high sales quotas, mandatory working hours, cancellation or termination of the franchise for minor infringements, and/or restrictions on the franchisee in transferring the franchise or recovering his or her investment. The territory assigned to the franchisee may overlap with that of another franchisee or may be otherwise inequitable. In settling disputes of any kind, the bargaining power of the franchiser is usually greater.

- **Time consumed in preparing reports required by the franchiser.** Franchisers require specific reports. The time and effort of preparing these may be inordinately burdensome. On the other hand, you should recognize that if these reports are helpful to the franchiser, they probably will help you manage your business more effectively.

- **Sharing the burden of the franchiser's faults.** While ordinarily the franchiser's chain will have developed goodwill among consumers, there may be instances in which ill will has been developed. For example, if a customer has been served a tepid espresso or received poor service in one outlet, that customer is apt to become disgruntled with the whole chain. As one outlet in the chain, you will suffer regardless of the excellence of your particular unit. Furthermore, the franchiser may fail. You must withstand the chain's mistakes as well as share the glory of its good performances.

Minority Participation in Franchising

A number of franchise systems have developed special programs for minority individuals who seek to go into business for themselves. One such program asks the minority individual for only a 2-percent down payment. The franchiser matches this with 98 percent financing and up to a year of training. Another program is a joint venture between a minority-owned business and an established franchising company. This joint venture is not a merger of the two companies. Rather, it is a plan whereby each company contributes an equal amount of dollars, but all responsibility for day-to-day operations is left with the minority-owned company.

Franchise Financing

There are a growing number of alternatives for individuals and investors who want to enter franchising or expand their current market position. More and more local and regional banks, along with national non-bank lenders, are offering franchise financing. Lending institutions have a greater appreciation for the importance of franchising in the marketplace, for its future growth and its stability as a distribution method.

For example, the International Franchise Association (**www.franchise.org**) lists more than 30 bank and non-bank franchise lenders in its Franchise Opportunities Guide this year. The U.S. Small Business Administration (**www.sba.gov**), which backed an agency record 61,689 small business loans totaling $30.5 billion in fiscal year 2011, works with local and regional banks to offer its guaranteed loan program to start-up franchisees.

Evaluating a Franchising Opportunity

A franchise costs money. One can be purchased for as little as a few hundred dollars, or as much as a quarter of a million dollars or more. Hence, it is vital that you investigate and evaluate carefully any franchise before you invest.

Beware of the "fast buck" artists. The popularity of franchising has attracted an unsavory group of operators. Sometimes known as "front money men," they usually offer nothing more than the sale of equipment and a catchy business name. Once they sell you the equipment, they do not care whether you succeed or fail. If you are promised tremendous profits in a short time, be wary.

The following checklist will aid you in selecting the right franchise. Check each question when the answer is "yes." Most, if not all, questions should be checked before you sign a franchise contract.

Questions to Answer Affirmatively Before Going into Franchising

Check if answer is yes, and tick the box to the left.

Questions to Ask About the Franchiser

- ❑ Yes ❑ No Has the franchiser been in business long enough (5 years or more) to have established a good reputation?

- ❑ Yes ❑ No Have you checked the Better Business Bureau, chambers of commerce, Dun and Bradstreet and bankers to find out about the franchiser's business reputation and credit ratings?

- ❑ Yes ❑ No Did the above investigations reveal that the franchiser has a good reputation and credit rating?

- ❑ Yes ❑ No Does the franchising firm appear to be financed adequately so that it can carry out its stated plan of financial assistance and expansion?

- ❑ Yes ❑ No Have you discovered how many franchisees are now operating?

❏ Yes ❏ No   Have you ascertained the "mortality" or failure rate among franchisees?

❏ Yes ❏ No   Is the failure rate small?

❏ Yes ❏ No   Have you checked with some franchisees and found that the franchiser has a reputation for honesty and fair dealing among those who currently hold franchises?

❏ Yes ❏ No   Has the franchiser shown you certified figures indicating exact net profits of one or more going operations which you have personally checked yourself?

❏ Yes ❏ No   Has the franchiser given you a specimen contract to study with the advice of your legal counsel?

Will the franchiser assist you with:

❏ Yes ❏ No   A management training program?

❏ Yes ❏ No   An employee training program?

❏ Yes ❏ No   Public relations program?

❏ Yes ❏ No   Obtaining capital?

❏ Yes ❏ No   Good credit terms?

❏ Yes ❏ No   Merchandising ideas?

❏ Yes ❏ No   Designing store layout and displays?

❏ Yes ❏ No   Inventory-control methods?

❏ Yes ❏ No   Analyzing financial statements?

❏ Yes ❏ No   Does the franchiser provide continuing assistance for franchisees through supervisors who visit regularly?

❏ Yes ❏ No   Does the franchising firm have an experienced manager with in-depth training?

❏ Yes ❏ No   Will the franchiser assist you in finding a good location for your business?

❏ Yes ❏ No   Has the franchising company investigated you carefully enough to assure itself that you can successfully operate one of its franchises at a profit both to it and to you?

❏ Yes ❏ No   Have you determined exactly what the franchiser can do for you that you cannot do yourself?

❏ Yes ❏ No   Does the franchise comply with all applicable laws?

❏ Yes ❏ No   If a product must be purchased exclusively from the franchiser or a designated supplier, are the prices to you, as the franchisee, competitive?

❏ Yes ❏ No   Does the franchise fee seem reasonable?

❏ Yes ❏ No   Do continuing royalty or percent-of-gross-sales payment requirements appear reasonable?

❏ Yes ❏ No   Are the total cash investment required and the terms for financing the balance satisfactory?

❏ Yes ❏ No   Does the cash investment include payment for fixtures and equipment?

❏ Yes ❏ No   If you will be required to participate in company-sponsored promotions and publicity by contributing to an "advertising fund," will you have the right to veto an increase in contributions required?

❏ Yes ❏ No   Will you be free to buy the amount of merchandise you believe you need rather than a required amount?

❏ Yes ❏ No   Can merchandise be returned for credit?

❏ Yes ❏ No   Would you be free to engage in other business activities?

❏ Yes ❏ No   If there is an annual sales quota, can you retain your franchise if it is not met?

❏ Yes ❏ No   Does the contract give you an exclusive territory for the length of the franchise?

❏ Yes ❏ No   Is your territory protected?

❏ Yes ❏ No   Is the franchise agreement renewable?

❏ Yes ❏ No   Can you terminate your agreement if you are not happy for some reason?

❏ Yes ❏ No   Is the franchiser prohibited from selling the franchise out from under you?

❏ Yes ❏ No   May you sell the business to whomever you please?

❏ Yes ❏ No   If you sell your franchise, will you be compensated for the goodwill you have built into the business?

☐ Yes ☐ No   Does the contract obligate the franchiser to give you continuing assistance while you are operating the business?

☐ Yes ☐ No   Are you permitted a choice in determining whether you will sell any new products introduced by the franchiser after you have opened your business?

☐ Yes ☐ No   Is there anything with respect to the franchise or its operation that would make you ineligible for special financial assistance and other benefits accorded to small business concerns by federal, state, or local governments?

☐ Yes ☐ No   Did your lawyer approve the franchise contract after he or she studied it, paragraph by paragraph?

☐ Yes ☐ No   Is the contract free and clear of requirements compelling you at any point to take steps that are, according to your lawyer, unwise or illegal in your state, county, or city?

☐ Yes ☐ No   Does the contract cover all aspects of your agreement with the franchiser?

☐ Yes ☐ No   Does the contract really benefit both you and the franchiser?

Questions to Ask About Your Market

☐ Yes ☐ No   Are the territorial boundaries of your market completely, accurately and understandably defined?

☐ Yes ☐ No   Have you done a study to determine whether the product you propose to sell has a market in your territory at the prices you will have to charge?

☐ Yes ☐ No   Does the territory provide adequate sales potential?

☐ Yes ☐ No   Will the population in the territory given you increase over the next five years?

☐ Yes ☐ No   Will the average per capita income in the territory remain the same or increase over the next five years?

☐ Yes ☐ No   Do you know that existing competition in your territory is not well-entrenched?

Questions to Ask About You, The Franchisee

❏ Yes ❏ No Do you know where you will go to get the equity capital you will need?

❏ Yes ❏ No Have you compared what it will take to start your own specialty beverage operation with the price you must pay for the franchise?

❏ Yes ❏ No Have you made a business plan? For example, have you worked out what income from sales or services you can reasonably expect in the first six months? The first year? The second year?

❏ Yes ❏ No Have you made a forecast of expenses, including a regular salary for yourself?

❏ Yes ❏ No Are you prepared to give up some independence of action to secure the advantages offered by the franchise?

❏ Yes ❏ No Are you capable of accepting supervision, even though you presumably will be your own boss?

❏ Yes ❏ No Are you prepared to accept rules and regulations with which you may not agree?

❏ Yes ❏ No Can you afford the period of training involved?

❏ Yes ❏ No Are you ready to spend much or all of the remainder of your business life with this franchiser, offering their product or service to the public?

To find coffee shop franchises online, visit Entrepreneur® (**www.entrepreneur.com**) and Franchise Solutions™ (**www.franchisesolutions.com**).

Conclusion

In conclusion, franchising creates distinct opportunities for the prospective small-business owner. Without franchising, it is doubtful that thousands of small-business investors could ever have started. As a new owner, you can draw from the experience and resources — promotional, managerial, structural, and material — of a large, established parent company. Unfortunately, not even the help of a good franchiser can guarantee success. You will still be primarily responsible for the success or failure of your venture. As in any other type of business, your return will be related directly to the amount and effectiveness of your investment in time and money.

Basic Cost Control for Beverage and Food Service Operations – An Overview

Currently, throughout the entire food and beverage service industry, operating expenses are up and income is down. After taxes and expenses, outlets that make money have bottom lines as low as 0.5–3.0 percent of sales. This tiny percentage, however, is the difference between being profitable and going under, and it drives home the importance of controlling your costs.

Cost Controls Are Crucial

To supplement income, most specialty coffee and tea shops carry a variety of "add-on" food items such as desserts, pastries, muffins, and savory snacks. Current trends also indicate the increasing popularity of the "healthy" sandwich. Many specialty beverage outlets try to even out their sales throughout the day. Sidelines include cold coffee products and ice cream-based confections during the warm months, and seasonal "warming" snacks in cold weather. Other shops try to increase their bottom line with merchandise bearing their shop's logo.

The Bottom Line

Understanding the implications of your bottom line only comes with constant review and the resulting familiarity with the relationships between the numbers and the workings of the business. This may seem like drudgery, but these numbers are the key to understanding labor productivity, portion control, purchase prices, marketing promotions, new menu items, and competitive strategy. This knowledge will free you to run the best, most profitable coffee and tea shop you can.

Cost-Control Program

It is vital that you integrate an ongoing cost-control program into your business, from day one. Too many businesspeople become cost-control converts only after suffering losses. The primary purpose of cost controls is to maximize profits, not minimize losses. Controlling costs works because it focuses on getting the most value from the least cost in every aspect of your operation.

Cost control is not accounting or bookkeeping; these are the information-gathering tools of cost control. Cost control can be defined by explaining its purposes:

- To provide management with information needed for making day-to-day operational decisions
- To monitor department and individual efficiency
- To inform management of expenses being incurred and income received, and whether they fall within standards and budgets
- To prevent fraud and theft
- To provide the ground for the business's goals (not for discovering where it has been)
- To emphasize prevention, not correction

This idea of prevention versus correction is fundamental. Prevention occurs through advanced planning. Your primary job is not to put out fires; it is to prevent them — and to maximize profits in the process. Cost controls are about knowing where you are going. Furthermore, most waste and inefficiencies cannot be seen; they need to be understood through the numbers.

Understanding those numbers means interpreting them. To do this effectively, you need to understand the difference between control and reduction. Control is achieved through the assembly and interpretation of data and ratios on your revenue and expenses. Reduction is the actual action taken to bring costs within your predetermined standards.

Effective cost control starts at the top of an organization. Cost control is an ongoing process that must be part of the basic moment-to-moment breathing of your business. Management must establish, support, and enforce its standards and procedures.

Ten primary areas are central to the cost-control recordkeeping procedures of any beverage operation:

1. **Purchasing.** Your inventory system is the critical component of purchasing. You will need to keep records of suppliers, prices, units of purchase, product specifications, etc.

2. **Receiving.** Check for correct brands, grades, varieties, quantities, weights, correct prices, etc. Incorrect receivables need to be noted and either returned or credited to your account.

3. **Storage.** Coffees, teas, and food ingredients should be stored at the correct temperature in a ventilated storage area that is free from contamination. Expensive items need to be guarded from theft.

4. **Issuing.** Procedures for removing inventory from storage are part of the cost-control process. This is a much more important aspect of cost control than it seems, because in order to know your beverage and food costs, you need to know a) your beginning inventory, b) how much was sold, and c) your ending inventory.

5. **Rough preparation.** How your staff minimizes waste during the preliminary processing of inventory is critical.

6. **Preparation for service.** The quality and care of beverage and food preparation determines the amount of waste generated in the preparation of standard recipes.

7. **Portioning/Transfer.** Introduce measures to avoid over-portioning. Final beverage and food preparation should be monitored regularly to ensure quality and quantity standards are being adhered to. This is a crucial element to cost control.

8. **Order taking/guest check.** Every item sold or issued needs to be recorded. This can be done by paper check or computer. Basically, it needs to be impossible for anyone to get food or drinks without having them entered into the system.

9. **Cash receipts.** Monitoring sales is crucial to cost controls. Under/overcharging, falsification of tips, and lost checks must be investigated after every shift. This record helps you to forecast the future.

10. **Bank deposits/accounts payable.** Proper auditing of bank deposits and charge slips must be conducted.

Cost Ratios

Owners and managers need to be on the same page in terms of the meaning and calculation of the many ratios used to analyze beverage, food and labor costs. It is important to understand how your ratios are being calculated so you can get a true indication of the cost or profit activity in your coffee, espresso, and tea shop. Numerous cost-control software programs with built-in formulas for calculating ratios and percentages are available.

Controlling Beverage and Food Costs

In order to control beverage and food costs effectively, there are four things you need to do:

- Forecast how much and what you are going to sell.
- Purchase and prepare according to these forecasts.
- Portion effectively.
- Control waste and theft.

Inventory and Product Management

The overriding objective for the manager of a specialty coffee and tea shop is to purchase the best quality inventory that can be resold for a maximum profit, with minimum waste. Sounds simple? On the surface, this seems like a straightforward formula but, in reality, product management requires considerable skill and attention to detail.

From ordering the freshest coffee beans, blends, loose teas, and other raw materials, to receiving, storage, and preparation, as well as the maintenance of essential equipment, you will constantly need to track and adjust your approach to product management in order to maximize return on your investment.

Accurate ordering and monitoring of products on a first-in, first-out basis is key to maintaining efficient inventory levels. Several inventory-control software packages specifically designed for the retail coffee and tea industry are available that can be tailored to your specific requirements. Computerized inventory control offers numerous advantages over a manual system, including greater accuracy, better stock control, forecasting potential, and timesaving.

The aim, of course, is to ensure consistent standards of quality and quantity while tying up the minimum amount of cash possible. And, in the retail coffee and tea business, where turnover can fluctuate from day to day and the quality of the raw ingredients is notoriously unstable, effective inventory management is often difficult to achieve, particularly when you first open for business. Once your coffee, espresso, and tea shop has been trading for a while, you will be able to estimate your required inventory levels, with a greater degree of accuracy.

Menu Sales Mix

The net profit potential of your specialty coffee and tea retail operation will depend on the dollar amount (unit value) of each product you sell and the item's profit margin; this is what is known as sales mix. It is important, therefore, that your equipment, the layout of your coffee and tea brewing area, and the necessary food preparation facilities should be designed around the recipes of your chosen beverage and food menus. During the early design stages of your beverage outlet, try to visualize delivery, processing, preparation, presentation, and washing requirements. Additionally, build flexibility into your plans to accommodate any future changes to your menus. When shopping for equipment, choose items based on the best equipment for your needs, not price.

The Menu Itself

Your beverage and food menus should communicate the concept and personality of your coffee, espresso, and tea shop. An effective menu does five key things:

1. Emphasizes what customers want and what you do best
2. Is an effective communication, merchandising and cost-control tool
3. Obtains the necessary check average for sales and profits
4. Uses staff and equipment efficiently
5. Makes forecasting sales more consistent and accurate for purchasing, preparation, and scheduling

The design of your menu will directly affect whether it achieves these goals. Do not leave this to chance. Plan to have menus that work for you. Certain practices can influence the choices your guests make. Instead of randomly placing items on the menus, single out and emphasize the items you want to sell. These generally will be items with low base ingredient costs and high profits that are easy to prepare.

Once you have chosen the contents of your menus, use design — print style, paper color, and graphic design — to direct the reader's attention to these items. In general, a customer's eye will fall to the middle of the page first. This is an important factor. However, design elements used to draw a reader's eye to another part of the menu can be effective as well.

Also, customers remember the first and last things they read more than anything else, so when you draw their eyes to specific items is also important.

Once you have an effective menu design, analyzing your sales mix to determine the impact each item has on sales, costs, and profits is an important practice. If you have costs and waste under control, looking at your menu sales mix can help you further reduce costs and boost profits. You will find that some items need to be promoted more aggressively, while others need to be dropped altogether.

Pricing

Pricing is an important aspect of your revenues and customer counts. Prices that are too high will drive customers away, and prices that are too low will kill your profits. But pricing is not the simple matter of an appropriate markup over cost; it combines other factors as well.

Price can either be market-driven or demand-driven. Market-driven prices must be responsive to your competitors' prices. This is also true when you are introducing new items for which a demand has not yet been developed. Opposite to these are demand-driven items, which customers ask for and where demand exceeds your supply. You have a short-term monopoly on these items and, therefore, price is driven up until demand slows or competitors begin to sell similar items.

The two basic theories of pricing are: 1) charge as much as you can, and 2) charge as little as you can. Each has its pluses and minuses. Prices generally are determined by competition and demand. Ultimately, you want your customers to know your image, and your prices to fit into that picture.

Here are four ways to determine prices:

1. **Competitive pricing.** Based on meeting or beating your competitions' prices, this is an ineffective method since it assumes customers are making their choice on price alone and not on quality, ambience, service, etc.
2. **Intuitive pricing.** If your sense of the value of your product is good, then it works; otherwise, it can be problematic.
3. **Psychological pricing.** If you change your initial prices, customers will perceive the items differently. If an item was initially more expensive, it will be viewed as a bargain and vice versa.
4. **Trial-and-error pricing.** This is based on customer reactions to prices and is not practical in terms of determining your overall prices, but can be effective with

individual items to bring them closer to the price a customer is willing to pay, or to distinguish them from similar menu items with a higher or lower food cost.

There are still other factors that help determine prices. Whether customers view you as a leader or a follower can make a big difference in how they view your prices. If people think of you as the best specialty coffee and tea shop in the area, they will be willing to pay a little more to frequent your establishment. Service also determines people's sense of value.

Financial Analysis

In order to make profits, you need to plan for profits. Many beverage outlets offering great products, great atmosphere, and great service still go out of business. The reason for this is they fail to manage the financial aspects of the business. This means that poor cost-control management will be fatal to your business. Furthermore, good financial management is about interpreting financial statements and reports, not simply preparing them.

A few distinctions need to be made in order to understand the language we are now using. Financial accounting is primarily for external groups to assess taxes, the status of your establishment, etc. Managerial accounting provides information to internal users that becomes the basis for managing day-to-day operations. This information is very specific and uses non-financial data like customer counts, menu sales mix, and labor hours. Daily and weekly reports must be made and analyzed in order to determine emerging trends.

Internal Controls

It is estimated that about 4 percent of annual gross sales in U.S. retail beverage and food industry are lost to employee theft. Clearly established and followed controls can lessen this percentage. Begin by separating duties and recording every transaction. If these basic systems are in place, then workers know that at each step of the way they will be held responsible for shrinkage. Management Information Systems (MIS) are common tools for accumulating, analyzing, and reporting data. In short, their goal is to prevent fraud on all levels. While no system is perfect, a good MIS will show where fraud or loss is occurring, allowing you to remedy the situation.

The key to statistical control, however, is entering transactions into the system. This can be done electronically or by hand; either way, if beverages or food or can be consumed without being entered into the system, your system is flawed and control is compromised.

Point-of-sale (POS) systems are also crucial for reducing loss. If your servers cannot obtain any food or beverage without a hard-copy check, or without entering the sale electronically, you have eliminated most of their opportunity to steal. Many electronic systems are available in the industry and once initial training and intimidation are overcome, they can seriously reduce the amount of theft and shrinkage in your shop.

Guest Tickets and the Cashier

There are various methods of controlling cash and guest tickets. Many of the cash registers and POS systems available on the market can eliminate a lot of the manual work and calculations. The systems described in this chapter are based on the simplest and least expensive cash register available. The register must have separate subtotal keys for beverages, food, (and liquor if you run a licensed operation) and a grand-total key for the total guest check. Sales tax is then computed on this amount. The register used also must calculate the beverages, food, and liquor totals (if applicable) for the shift. Most machines have these basic functions. Guest tickets must be the type that is divided into two parts. The first section is the heavy paper part listing the menu items. At the bottom is a space for the subtotals, grand total, tax, and a tear-away customer receipt. The second section is a carbon copy of the first. The carbon copy is given to the server, who then issues it to the prep staff who then start the preparation process. Some coffee and tea shops use handheld ordering computers and/or the tickets may be printed in the preparation area, at the time of entry into the POS system or register. Regardless, the waiter must receive a ticket in order to issue any item.

The tickets must have individual identification numbers printed in sequence on both parts and the tear-away receipt. They must also have a space for the server's name, date, table number, and the number of people at the table. Each member of the waitstaff is issued a certain number of tickets on each shift. These tickets are in numbered sequence.

For example, a server may be issued 25 tickets from 007575 to 007600. At the end of the shift, he or she must return the same total number of tickets to the cashier. No ticket should ever become lost; it is the responsibility of the waitstaff to ensure this. Should there be a mistake on a ticket, the cashier must void out all parts. This ticket must be turned in with the others after being approved and signed by the manager. The manager should issue tickets to each server.

In certain instances, the manager may approve giving away menu items at no charge. The manager must also approve of the discarding of beverages and food that cannot be served. A ticket must be written to record all of these transactions. Some examples are listed below:

- **Manager beverages and food.** All drinks and food that is issued free of charge to managers, owners, and officers of the company

- **Complimentary beverages and food.** All food issued to a customer compliments of the establishment. This includes all drinks and food given away as part of a promotional campaign.
- **Housed beverages and food.** All drinks and food that is not servable, such as spoiled, spilled, or incorrect orders.

All of these tickets should be filled out as usual, listing the items and the prices. The cashier should not ring up these tickets, but record them on a separate Cashier's Report Form and write the word "manager," "complimentary," or "housed" over the top of the ticket.

The manager issues cash drawers, or "banks," to the cashier. The drawers are prepared by the bookkeeper. Inside the cashier drawer is the Cashier's Report, itemizing the breakdown of the money it contains. The accuracy of the Cashier's Report is the responsibility of both the cashier and the manager. Upon receiving the cash drawer, the cashier must count the money in the cash drawer with the manager to verify its contents. After verification, the cashier will be responsible for the cash register. The cashier should be the only employee allowed to operate it.

Each member of the waitstaff will bring his or her guest ticket to the cashier for totaling. The cashier must examine the ticket to ensure:

- All items were charged for
- All items have the correct price
- All bar and wine tabs are included
- Subtotals and grand total are correct
- Sales tax is entered correctly

The cashier is responsible for filling out the credit card forms and ensuring their accuracy. The cashier will return the customer's credit card and receipt to the appropriate member of the waitstaff. At the end of each shift, the cashier must cash out with the manager. All the cash must be listed in the "Cash Out" columns on the credit card form and breakdown of sales entered into separate categories. Sales tax should not be included. All complimentary, housed, and manager amounts must be recorded. All checks must be itemized on the reverse of the form. Each ticket has to be itemized for total sales and total purchase count. Finally, a breakdown of all charged sales needs to be entered.

The total amount of cash taken in plus the charge sales must equal the total itemized ticket sales. All checks must be itemized on the back of the Cashier's Report and stamped "FOR DEPOSIT ONLY"; the stamp should include the shop's bank name and account number.

Should a customer charge a tip, you may give the server a "cash paid out" from the register. When the payment comes in, you can then deposit the whole amount into your account.

Miscellaneous paid-outs are for any items that may need to be purchased throughout the shift. List all of them on the back and staple the receipts to the page.

When everything is checked out and balanced, the cashier and manager must sign the sheet. The manager should then deposit all tickets, register tapes, cash, charges, and forms into the safe for the bookkeeper the next morning. The cash on hand must equal the register receipt readings.

Purchasing and Ordering

What exactly is the difference? Purchasing is setting the policy on which suppliers, brands, grades, and varieties of products will be ordered. Basically, purchasing is what you order and from whom. Ordering, then, is simply the act of contacting the suppliers and notifying them of the quantity you require. This is a simpler, lower-level task.

Buying also has its own distinctions. Open or informal buying is face-to-face or over-the-phone contact and uses largely oral negotiations and purchase specifics. In formal buying, terms are put in writing and payment invoices are stated as conditions for price quotes and customer service commitments. Customer service is possibly the most important aspect of the supplier you choose because good sales representatives know their products, have an understanding of your needs, and offer helpful suggestions.

Your purchasing program should do three things:

1. Allow you to purchase the needed amount of items at prices that meet your food cost goals
2. Maintain control over your existing inventory
3. Establish a set of procedures to be sure you receive quality product at the best price. These procedures should include creating written purchasing specifications for every product and selecting good, reliable purveyors.

The following steps will help you achieve these goals:

- You should do the purchasing yourself or assign a specific employee to do it. Make sure that this person keeps current with ever-changing food prices.
- Sometimes you may find that one vendor is less expensive than another for a while, and then this may shift. Keep current with competing vendors' prices.
- If you do not have a stock rotation program, you may be losing product due to spoilage.

- If you do not have a receiving policy in place for receiving orders from vendors, you may lose product in this part of your operation. Let's say, for example, you do not have any one person specifically assigned to check in orders. Normally one of your line cooks will do it. Let's also say that one day your order is late and arrives in the middle of lunch rush. No one can check the order for accuracy, so they just sign for it in a hurry. If this happens, you cannot immediately correct any mistakes there may be in the order. Furthermore, if your line cooks do not get to put the order away until several hours later, you will lose product because it has sat out too long and is now unsafe to serve.

- Only allow particular employees to retrieve or store items, or institute a sign-in/sign-out procedure. By keeping track of what comes in and goes out of your inventory, you can minimize losses attributed to theft, waste, and over-portioning.

- Purchasing specifications state the exact requirements for the amount and quality of items purchased. These specifications should include:
  - Product name
  - Quantity to be purchased (designated by unit such as pounds, can size, etc.)
  - Indication of grade, if applicable
  - Unit by which prices are quoted
  - What the product will be used to make

By creating purchasing specifications, you can control what items you purchase and maintain product consistency. This information is extremely important if you have more than one person that does ordering in your operation. If you have this written and readily available, all your employees can be sure they are ordering the correct items in the correct amounts.

You are also more likely to attain your desired food cost by keeping these records and maintaining purchasing controls. Keeping your food cost down will help you to maximize profits from your menu prices.

Purchasing and Inventory Software

Many food service operators use inventory-control software that saves a significant amount of time and money.

You can check the National Restaurant Association's website (**www.restaurant.org**) for vendors of this software (as well as many other products). Or, take a trip to their annual National Restaurant Association Exhibit each year in Chicago to see all the latest products available in the restaurant industry.

Culinary Software Services (**www.culinarysoftware.com**) has a software program called ChefTec, for inventory control, recipe, menu costing, and nutritional analysis.

Another website of interest is **www.foodprofile.com**. This site was established for the collection and distribution of product information for the food industry and is part of an initiative called Efficient Foodservice Response (EFR). Distributors pay to list their products on this site. It provides more than 65,000 items and has the most up-to-date product information available, including serving suggestions, nutritional information, cooking instructions, and ingredient statements. EFR is an industry-wide effort to improve efficiency in the purchasing process. To find out more about EFR, visit **www.ifdaonline.org**.

Production Controls

Physical production should also be considered when looking at controlling costs. Here are some control methods you should have in place for production:

- Be sure you schedule the appropriate amount of labor for shifts and pre-prep work.
- Be sure staff members are using the standardized recipe.
- Have inventory controls in place.
- Buy laborsaving equipment. You will be able to pay for the equipment in no time with the money you will save on labor.

Ordering Coffee and Tea Supplies

Most coffee and tea shops order their raw materials from a variety of different sources and wholesalers. However, it would help you streamline your ordering procedures (and save time!) if you could choose one company that carries the bulk of the items that you use on a regular basis. As a general guideline, you will need to order fresh coffee and tea from your suppliers once a week. Around 90 percent of wholesalers still sell coffee and tea in bulk, but increasingly, suppliers are now developing their own gourmet label blends.

Inventory, Storage and Accounts Payable

Ordering effectively is impossible unless you know your inventory. Before an order is placed, counts of stock should be made. Many software programs are able to determine order quantities directly from sales reports. Whether your inventory system is by computer or by hand, its purpose is to accomplish the following:

- Provide records of what you need
- Provide records of product specifications
- Provide records of suppliers
- Provide records of prices and unit of purchase
- Provide a record of product use levels
- Facilitate efficient ordering
- Increase the accuracy of inventory
- Facilitate the inventory process
- Make it easy to detect variance levels in inventory

Labor Productivity

Labor costs and turnover are serious concerns in today's retail beverage and food market. Increasing labor costs cannot be offset by continuously higher prices without customers turning away. Maximizing worker productivity, consequently, has become a key challenge, especially in view of the fact that the beverage and food service industry continues to be an entry-level arena for the unskilled and uneducated. A few of the causes of high labor costs and low productivity are poor layout and design of an operation, lack of labor-saving equipment, poor scheduling, and no regular, detailed system to collect and analyze payroll data.

Alcoholic Beverages Control

Ordering alcoholic beverages, such as cognac or Irish whiskey to accompany postprandial coffees and desserts, is becoming an increasingly popular choice in some of the newly established European-style coffee houses in certain parts of the United States. Additionally, the age-old European practice of moving on from a restaurant to a different venue for after-dinner coffee and liqueurs is also gaining in popularity. If your coffee, espresso, and tea shop is stepping onto the bandwagon with a license to sell liquor, you will need to understand the complexities of pricing such alcoholic beverages. It is not just a cost-markup exercise, but rather your prices will have to reflect the uniqueness of your operation and its overhead operating costs. The markup of alcohol in specialty coffee shops tends to be higher than in mainstream bars where liquor makes up the majority of sales.

In order to monitor your liquor costs accurately, you need to record the sales of each type of beverage separately. Separate keys for different alcoholic beverages on your register or a POS system need to be used. Unless an electronic system is used, however, a detailed sales mix is difficult to obtain. Purchasing and ordering alcohol, however, is in many ways, much simpler than purchasing and ordering other beverages and food, but the need to inventory correctly is no less crucial. In fact, alcohol needs to be guarded and inventoried more rigorously because of its cost, ease of theft, and possible abuses.

Etc.

All coffee is grown in an equatorial band between the Tropics of Cancer and Capricorn. Hawaii is the only U.S. state that produces coffee. The most famous Hawaiian coffee is Kona, from the big island of Hawaii. Some fine coffee also is grown on Maui. —**www.quartermaine.com**

6

Choosing the Best Equipment, Coffees, Teas and Food Products

Serving the best coffee, espresso or tea is the heart of your business. Customers that seek out specialty coffee expect a quality product. They also expect the business they frequent to have a love for and vast knowledge of the product. Therefore, you simply cannot afford to leave things to chance. Make sure you become extremely knowledgeable about the coffee and tea you serve and the equipment you use to prepare and serve it.

Because so many different specialty coffees and teas are available from wholesalers and other sources, we have dedicated an entire chapter to choosing the best beverage equipment and products available on the market today. Specialty coffees (and increasingly, teas) are an extremely important part of our modern lifestyle, but for owners of coffee, espresso, and tea shops, they are their lifeline.

Choosing the Right Equipment

Most items of equipment needed for the preparation of specialty coffees and teas are either purchased or leased, with all major specialty coffee and tea distributors offering similar basic contracts. Typically, the supplier will provide all the equipment necessary for coffee service including: brewing machines, filters, pots, and maintenance and installation of all equipment. All that is required from you is to sign a contract stating that you will buy their coffee exclusively. The price of all the equipment and maintenance is included in the price of the contract.

Alternatively, you could buy all your own equipment separately and pay to have someone install and maintain it. This would enable you to purchase coffee and tea from any company, possibly at reduced prices. However, a large capital outlay would be necessary to purchase equipment up front. It is important that you weigh the pros and cons of the coffee distributor contract method as opposed to purchasing your equipment and prime ingredients from a variety of sources. One of the major benefits of purchasing outright is that you can then depreciate the equipment against your income tax. If, however, you do not have the necessary capital to purchase your equipment, or if you are looking to establish a credit rating, you may prefer to lease. You also could consider renting before committing to either a purchase or lease; that way you could try out different types of equipment for minimal capital outlay.

Coffee- and Tea-Making Equipment

Since you will require a range of specialized pieces of equipment for grinding, brewing and beverage preparation, it is important that you first identify your specific needs before contacting various suppliers and obtaining several quotations. We also recommend that when comparing potential grinding and brewing systems, you contact the suppliers' existing customers; ask them how satisfied they are with the equipment and whether they have encountered any problems.

Which brewing equipment you choose is largely a matter of personal choice and suitability for the requirements of your establishment. But as a general guideline, there are two main brewing systems available on the market today: "in-line" and "pour-over." In-line systems are plumbed directly into the water supply, whereas pour-over models involve measuring the water and pouring it, by hand, through the top of the machine. Although pour-over models offer more freedom of control over the brewing process, they are not ideal for large coffee and tea shops with fast customer turnover.

- **Automatic drip.** This is probably the most popular coffeemaker used today. These come in many styles. You can find one that will automatically start the coffee for the time you set it. Some of these pour the coffee into a glass container; others use insulated carafes. Once the water runs through the system, the coffeemaker keeps the coffee warm. These are good because of their convenience, but you want to be careful about how long you serve the coffee after it has been brewed. If you have the type of automatic drip machine that has a "hot plate" for the carafe to sit on, the coffee can become undrinkable rather quickly. When possible, you should make a full pot of coffee rather than one or two cups at a time with these makers; they make better coffee when you use them at capacity.

- **Cones.** You can put these ceramic or plastic cones on top of a mug or pitcher, put in a filter, add grounds, then pour hot water over the grounds. One of the nice aspects to this type of coffeemaker is that you can stir the water and grounds as they steep; a step that many coffee nuts say you simply cannot skip. Of course, the down side of these makers is the inconvenience and the fact that you usually cannot brew more than a few cups at a time. You can find ceramic cones and pots at the Melitta® website at **www.melitta.com**. Another popular single cup brewing system is Keurig® (**www.keurig.com**).

- **French press.** The French press, or plunger pot, has been growing in popularity in the United States. You can find these in plastic, glass, or stainless steel. Essentially, they are a tall coffee pot with a plunger apparatus attached to a lid. The lid is attached to a post that has a fine mesh screen on the other end. You put the medium-ground grounds in the pot, add hot water, stir, and let steep for four minutes. Once the coffee has steeped, you push the plunger down and pour the coffee. This type of coffee maker is very elegant-looking and not messy.

When negotiating with the coffee salesperson, inform him or her that you want brand-new equipment. They are competing for your business, but once you sign the contract, you will be locked in to it. Use this leverage now while you have it. Various specialty teas may be purchased from these distributors. Sugar packets and sugar substitute packages also may be purchased from these companies. For an additional charge, your store's name and logo can be imprinted on the outside of each packet.

The Espresso Machine

A quality espresso machine is the backbone of any specialty coffee shop; a well-constructed, high-spec machine can make all the difference between serving an average, run-of-the-mill cup of coffee and the type of espresso experience that will "wow" your patrons and turn them into repeat customers. Standards and quality of espresso models available on the market today vary considerably, and with more than 50 different brands (the majority of them Italian) currently sold in the United States, choosing the machine that is right for your establishment can prove quite a headache!

Most espresso machines are similar in concept and design. All machines have certain components in common, differing only in the number and size of boilers and exterior design. The majority of machines have a single boiler, with size of boiler varying according to required output. Essentially, espresso machines have two basic functions: 1) to brew espresso "shots" by infusing hot water under high pressure, through ready-ground coffee, and 2) to draw steam from the boiler to whip and heat milk for lattés, cappuccinos, hot chocolate, etc.

Espresso machines also can be used to dispense hot water for brewing tea. We recommend, therefore, that as a backup to traditional methods of brewing tea in individual tea pots, you also explore the possibilities of dual-purpose equipment that can combine your brewing needs for both coffee and tea.

When choosing an espresso machine for your coffee, espresso, and tea shop, bear in mind the fact that the bulk of espresso consumed in the United States is served with steamed milk. While Europeans tend to consume less than 20 percent of their espressos with milk, a huge 95 percent of the U.S. population currently prefers espresso coffee served with steamed milk. The wear and tear on the steaming components used to draw steam for whipping milk is considerable. Additionally, the volume of steam generated to heat and foam milk has a significant effect on the machine's average brewing temperature. When brewing temperatures become unstable (a common occurrence when excessive steaming burdens the machine), the quality of the coffee is likely to suffer. Consequently, the steam wands, boiler pressure gauges and steam valves on machines used in the United States need to be highly durable.

Grinders

After your grinding and brewing equipment has been installed, and before you can use it, each appliance must be inspected by fire insurance underwriters to determine its safety and fitness for use. Additionally, make sure that all staff are thoroughly trained to use the equipment properly and that they know the simple basics of where the machine is plugged in and which water supply it is plumbed into. All staff should be familiarized with cleaning procedures according to the operational manual.

The importance of investing in a quality, in-house coffee grinder should not be underestimated. Not only is it part of the visual coffee experience, but beans ground to the perfect consistency are also absolutely essential to the extraction process and final flavor.

Essentially, integral espresso grinders perform two basic functions: 1) they grind roasted coffee beans to the required fineness for brewing, and 2) they dose and dispense the ground coffee into the coffee filter unit. Most commercial espresso grinders are constructed according to a similar basic model where measured, whole roasted beans are channeled from the "hopper" into the grinding component. The grinder comprises two plate or conical-shaped burrs that grind the beans to the desired consistency.

Although, on the surface, the grinding process seems straightforward, a skilled barista can have a big influence on the quality of the product. The trained eye of a skilled operator will monitor the coffee-grinding process to ensure that the beans are being ground evenly, that the "pour" is controlled to improve extraction rate and that any necessary adjustments are being performed during the grinding process. When choosing a grinder for your establishment, it is important that the equipment is constructed to the highest standards and offers control options that can maximize the quality and flavor of your beverages.

Milk Steamers

Correct milk steaming plays a vital part in the preparation of the perfect cup of coffee. And, as with the coffee grinder, making sure that you have the best steaming equipment can make or break your reputation for the best coffee in town!

Milk steaming involves drawing steam off the top part of the boiler. The typical espresso machine works by opening a valve during the milk steaming process, thus allowing the pressurized steam to flow through pipes by way of a steam wand into the milk. Most models have built-in temperature sensors that automatically cut out at a predetermined temperature. Add-on features to look for when choosing a milk steamer include milk-frothing devices that can be attached to the steam wand to dispense piping-hot, frothy milk directly into the cup.

Equipment Maintenance and Repair

Aim to eliminate downtime, or at least have procedures in place that minimize disruption when equipment breaks down or is out of action for maintenance. Whether your chosen supplier or suppliers carry out repairs themselves or subcontract to a service technician, you should always check out the qualifications of service providers and whether they carry a full range of parts with them. Since downtime can be disastrous for your business, we advise you to take out comprehensive maintenance coverage that offers a 24-hour emergency repair service.

There are things you can do to keep your espresso equipment in good working order. A regular cleaning schedule will go a long way in keeping your all your coffee equipment in good order. Here is a list of regular maintenance items for espresso machines:

- Keep all surfaces of your coffee machine(s) clean.
- Clear steam wands after each use and soak in hot water every night.
- Rinse filters on an ongoing basis.
- Backflush the groups of your espresso machine regularly.
- Remove and clean all brewing parts each day.

- Brush clean the dosing chamber of your espresso grinder each day.
- Pour a pitcher of very hot water down the drain box to keep the drainage system of your machine clear at the end of each day.

Just like a car, you should also keep up a regular maintenance schedule with your espresso and coffee equipment.

Choosing Gourmet Coffee and Tea Supplies

Your goal must be to find sources for the finest and most popular coffees and teas available. To do this, you must know what is available and what makes a fine coffee or tea. Once you know the basics, you can look at your options and decide what products to offer your customers. You will want to consider their likes and dislikes, as well as your own, in this selection process. For example, you might not like flavored coffees, but many of your potential customers could find them pleasing. A good way to give yourself a feel for what other people's tastes may be is to hold a tasting with your employees; they will give you a good sample to base your decisions on. And remember, your decisions on what varieties to offer is not written in stone. The first few months you are open you should keep track of what you customers are buying, and what they are asking for that you do not carry. After these initial months, you can solidify your menu.

Understanding Coffee Beans and Blends

Coffee is derived from the seeds of the coffee plant, which grows from sea level to approximately 6,000 feet above sea level. When the beans ripen, they usually have to be picked by hand because the cherries ripen at different times on a plant. The average coffee plant will yield about 1 to 2 pounds of roasted coffee per year and it is usually four to five years before a plant will begin producing seeds.

Once the beans are harvested, they must be processed. The cherry of a coffee plant is much like a nut; it has a hard outer skin, the sticky fruit pulp layer, a parchment casing and a thin silver skin. The four layers lay between the coffee harvester and what they call the green coffee bean. The cherries are processed by two methods: wet or dry processing. The wet method is predominately used in Latin American countries and usually produce a cleaner, brighter coffee (critics of the method, however, argue that the vast amounts of water used for the process are wasteful). Dry-processed coffees are usually more variable in flavor and often have a heavier body than wet-processed beans.

After the outer layers are removed from the green beans, the beans are milled and sorted. This is an important step because roasting time will vary for different sizes of beans. The beans are then processed and roasted according to complex coffee-producing specifications. Most beans are light or medium roasted at 400°F for 5 to 15 minutes, to produce a light or medium brown color and relatively mild taste. Other beans are dark roasted to produce an almost smoky, burnt flavor. The darkest roast coffees, such as French or Italian, are almost black in color and have a "charcoaly" flavor that enhances the taste of great espresso blends.

Coffee Beans with "Customer Appeal"

In general, there are two kinds of coffee: specialty and commercial. Most commercial types of coffee (the kind you buy in a can in the grocery store) come from the Coffea robusta species of plant. The specialty coffees come from Coffea arabica plants. Robusta plants tend to be those grown at lower elevations and are mainly cultivated in Africa. They have a higher yield than arabica plants and are more disease-resistant. The beans from these plants also contain twice the amount of caffeine as that in the arabica plants.

One of the most obvious differences between the two varieties we see as consumers is packaging: commercial coffee is ground and comes in tins or a plastic-encased brick, and specialty coffees are sold by the bean in bags. The main difference, however, is the superior flavor and aroma of specialty coffee. Most specialty coffees are purchased in one of three formats: 1) according to the country of origin, e.g., Colombia; 2) as a blend of two types of beans, e.g., Mocha Java (with these coffees, you will always see the word "blend" in the name); or 3) as a special type of roast.

The distinctive flavor of individual coffees depends largely upon their region of origin. For example, Java coffee has an earthy, full-bodied taste; Kenyan coffee has an almost fruity, full-bodied taste; whereas Costa Rican coffee tends to be lighter and more delicate-flavored. Columbian and Brazilian coffees have broad appeal and are often used to create the blends used for making espresso.

On the following page is a list of coffee areas and the predominant flavor of coffees from these regions. Use this list with caution, however. Just because more coffees produced by a region may be robusta does not mean you cannot find a good specialty coffee from the area.

The three main coffee-growing regions in the world are Africa/Arabia, Indonesia and Latin America. While the individual coffees grown in these regions can vary greatly, in general, African/Arabian coffees are bright and citrus-like; Indonesian coffees are earthy and have a lot of body; and Latin American coffees have a bright, clean acidity with a medium body. The following table gives a few more specifics of the coffees found in various parts of each region in very general terms.

| COFFEE GROWING REGIONS & FLAVORS ||
REGION	TASTE & FLAVOR CHARACTERISTICS
Latin America	
Brazil	Nutty, low acid
Colombia	Simple, heavy-bodied
Guatemala	Smoky, spicy
Costa Rica	Tangy, sweet
Mexico	Light, nutty
Jamaica	Neutral
Africa/Arabia	
Ethiopia	Winey or lemony
Yemen	Earthy, spicy
Kenya	Bright, hearty
Indonesia	
Java	Spicy, hearty
Sumatra	Earthy
Sulawesi	Sweet, buttery
India	Spicy

Source: Adapted from Kevin Knox and Julie Sheldon Huffaker Coffee Basics, John Wiley & Sons, Inc. New York: 1997, p. 48.

Coffees also can be blends of beans from different origins.

While coffees from various locals have different "flavors," the most important characteristic of coffee beans is probably the roast. Coffee beans can have hundreds, if not thousands, of flavors depending on how the beans are roasted. The longer the beans are roasted, the darker the bean and the more intense the flavor.

Roasting beans generally takes a short amount of time — only about 10 or 15 minutes. During roasting, the sugars within the bean become caramelized and this creates a substance known as coffee oil. That gives the coffee its flavor and aroma. Specialty coffees are usually roasted in small batches with the drum-roasting or hot-air roasting method. With the first method, beans are tumbled in a rotating drum as they are heated. With the second method, the beans are roasted by being circulated over hot air currents.

So, which is the right roast for your specialty coffee store? There is no one right answer. First and foremost, you must keep your customers in mind. You probably will want to offer a number of varieties because your customers' tastes will vary. As long as you are selling good quality coffee, you will be okay.

In general, there are three levels of roasting:

- **Light roast.** These are often referred to by various names including cinnamon roast, half city roast, and New England roast. These roasts are light-bodied and the flavor can be somewhat sour and grassy. These coffees are most often used for commercial-grade (canned) coffee.
- **Medium roast.** These also are referred to as full city roasts, American, regular and breakfast roasts. They have more body than light roasts, and they are a little sweeter. They are aromatic and have a higher acidity than light roasts.
- **Dark roast.** These roasts are referred to as Viennese, French, continental, and high roast. They are darker than light and medium roasts and the beans often have an oily sheen to them. They are a little spicy and have a full-bodied taste.

Tasting

With all these flavor choices, you will have to make some decisions about what coffees to offer. A good way to make these decisions is to have a tasting for you and your staff (including your staff will give you a range of tastes and opinions that will help mimic the tastes and opinions of your customers and potential customers).

Tasting, or cupping as it is referred to in the coffee industry, is similar to wine tasting. The proper cupping method is as follows:

Two tablespoons of coffee are finely ground and placed in each tasting cup, and then the cups are filled with filtered water that has not quite reached a boil. Let the coffee sit a few minutes, then use a spoon to stir the grounds that have risen to the top of the cup. While doing this, lean in close so you can inhale the aroma you are releasing. Let the coffee cool a little before tasting. As it cools, the grounds will sink back to the bottom of the cup. Use a spoon to taste and slurp — that will aerate the coffee as you taste it.

While you may not want to take your tasting experience quite to this level, you should be aware of the terms tasters use to describe coffees. These terms will help you and your staff describe, rate and choose the coffees you will sell.

Acidity

While acidity may sound like something you would not want in a cup of coffee, it is actually a desirable characteristic. As it pertains to coffee, acidity results in a pleasant sharpness. Without sufficient acidity, the coffee will taste flat.

Aroma

Aroma is difficult to distinguish from flavor. It contributes to the flavors we taste.

Body

Body is the feeling coffee has in your mouth. Body is often described as the weight of the coffee on your tongue. It is the thickness or richness of food or beverage on the tongue. Coffee body is often variable by region. Indonesian coffees, for example, generally have a heavier body than Latin American coffees. Brewing method also plays a role in the body of coffee. French presses and espresso machines produce a brew with a much heavier body than a brew from a drip machine.

Flavor

Flavor is the overall perception of the coffee. Flavor includes acidity, aroma, and body. It is the balance and homogenization of these senses that create your overall perception of flavor.

COFFEE FLAVOR CHARACTERISTICS	
Term	Description
Richness	Refers to full-bodied flavor
Complexity	Multiple flavors
Balance	No one flavor or characteristic takes over another
Caramelly	Candy-like
Chocolaty	A taste similar to unsweetened chocolate
Mellow	Typically lacking acid, a smooth taste
Nutty	An aftertaste of roasted nuts
Spicy	A flavor of spices (i.e., nutmeg, cloves, etc.)
Sweet	Not harsh
Bitter	Usually a result of over-roasting
Bland	Neutral
Flat	Lacks acidity
Grassy	Reminiscent of freshly cut lawn
Muddy	Thick and bland
Sour	Tart flavors similar to unripe fruit
Thin	Lacking acidity
Watery	A lack of body

Coffee Suppliers/Roasters

Before you start tasting coffees, you'll need to decided where to buy your beans. Fresh roasted coffee is best the day it comes out of the roaster. So, if you want to go all out and roast your own coffee, go for it. It will be fresh and delicious. If you decided to use a supplier rather than roast your own, you will need to find a reputable supplier.

Roasted beans that are exposed to air begin to stale quickly. In general, they have a shelf life of 7 to 10 days. It stays freshest if you keep whole beans in an airtight container (a solid glass jar with a rubber gasket to seal the lid). You can make it last longer by putting the whole beans in the freezer. If you are going to freeze it, seal the coffee bag in a freezer bag and put it in the back of the freezer where it will remain at a more constant temperature. Remove only the beans you intend to use that day and thaw them before grinding. Coffee beans lose their freshness because roasted beans slowly emit carbon dioxide, which helps keep their freshness. As the beans slowly release this gas, oxygen begins to permeate them and they begin to stale. Also, remember that once you grind the coffee, it goes stale in a few hours. Coffee aficionados do not recommend storing coffee in the refrigerator because coffee tends to absorb flavors.

Unlike mass-produced commercial coffees, "gourmet" coffees are usually roasted in small stores or specialist factories, using traditional roasting methods. As a retail operator, if you are not roasting your own coffee, in the interests of freshness and flavor, we recommend that you buy your coffee from the supplier who is closest to the roasting process. Specialty coffee suppliers typically fall into one of five categories:

1. Roast their own coffee in-house.
2. Part of a chain of specialty coffee purveyors who roast their coffee beans at a central location.
3. Buy their coffee from another specialty roaster.
4. Purchase their gourmet coffee from several roasters.
5. Buy their coffee green and have it roasted for them.

The Internet is also a good coffee resource. If you search on **Google.com** for "coffee roasters," you will be able to find a vendor that will ship beans to you.

Tips for Brewing Coffee

You can do several things to ensure a better cup of coffee:

- Grind the coffee appropriately for your coffeemaker. In general, grind it as fine as you can unless you are using a French press (for a French press, coffee beans should be a medium grind).
- The time of contact between the grounds and water is very important. It takes time for the water to extract the coffee flavor from the particles. In general, your coffee-brewing time should correspond to your grind: coarser-ground beans should be brewed for longer periods than finely ground beans.
- Do not be afraid to use enough coffee. For every 8 oz. (most coffee mugs are 8 oz. rather than 6 oz.), use 2-½ to 3 level tablespoons for every mug of water.
- Keep your coffeemaker clean, and rinse it with hot water before brewing.
- Use fresh water free of impurities. If your water does not taste good, your coffee is not going to either. If your water has a bad taste, consider using a filter or bottled water. If you have hard water in your area or water treated with a softener, you might want to consider this as well since these two conditions will create bad cups of coffee, too.
- Brew with hot water, not boiling water (a temperature of 200°F is ideal).

Espresso

Espresso purists would argue, however, that Coffea robusta should not be used in the making of espresso, whereas other experts contend that a small proportion of robusta can do no harm to the fullness, body, and flavor of any blend used for making great espresso. But, this is a matter for your customers to decide; ultimately, they will dictate the blend of coffee you use for making "perfect" espresso.

Standard Espresso Recipes

Most espresso-based beverages in the United States are made from a blend of dark-roasted coffee beans from different countries of origin. Generally, beans with greater acidity, such as Guatemalan or Kenyan coffee beans, are roasted especially dark in order to reduce their high acidity.

Typically, espresso drinks are served in three sizes: short (8 oz.), tall (12 oz.) and grande (16 oz.). Short and tall drinks will make up the bulk of your orders.

Use the following espresso recipes as guidelines only. Listen to what your customers say, and adapt your recipes accordingly. There is nothing like acquainting yourself with the preferences and favorite recipes of your regular customers for building repeat trade.

An easy way to add value to each check is to offer extra "shots" of your standard recipes. You could, for instance, promote "doubles" or "triples," based on the total number of shots in the standard recipe, where a double shot of espresso measures 2 ounces; a triple, 3 ounces; etc.

ESPRESSO RECIPES	
Name	Procedure
Espresso solo	"Solo" refers to a single shot of espresso; doppio is a double shot. Served in a 4- or 8-ounce demitasse cup and made up of 1 ounce straight espresso.
Espresso Americano	An American version of espresso made from hot water, diluted to the strength of drip coffee.
Espresso Romano	A demitasse of espresso served with a twist of lemon on the side.
Cappuccino	A basic cappuccino is made from 1 ounce of espresso in a cup and topped with equal parts of steamed and frothed milk, which should have a creamy, silky texture.
Café latte	Café latte consists of a larger proportion of milk than cappuccino and is made up of 1 ounce of espresso and steamed milk, filled to the brim of the cup, finished with a ¼-inch "topping" of steamed milk foam.
Café Mocha	Made from 1 ounce of espresso poured into a cup containing 1 ounce of chocolate syrup, filled with steamed milk and topped with a swirl of cream.
Ristretto	Sometimes referred to as a "short shot," Ristretto is made from between ¾ of an ounce and 1 ounce of espresso and is a sweet and aromatic version of Espresso Solo.
Café au lait	Traditionally made from equal proportions of scalded milk and regular brewed coffee, the term café au lait is used increasingly nowadays to describe a drink made from half regularly brewed coffee and half steamed milk, with very little foam. Usually, the steamed milk is poured into the cup or mug first, followed by the coffee.

ESPRESSO RECIPES	
Espresso macchiato	Solo espresso, but served with a teaspoon of steamed milk foam.
Latte macchiato	An 8- or 10-ounce glass of half hot, foamed milk into which a demitasse of espresso is slowly dribbled into the glass, creating a layered effect, with darker swirls towards the top, then topped with white foam.
Espresso con pana	Made with the required shot of espresso and topped with whipped cream.

Tips for Making Great Espresso

The two most important factors to keep in mind when preparing espresso are: 1) 1 ounce (which refers to the standard shot volume), and 2) 25 seconds or less (the ideal brewing time for the water to remain in contact with the coffee).

There is an art to brewing espresso that is dependent not least upon the skills of the trained barista. The fineness of the grind is crucial; so, too, is the temperature of the brewing water and the length of time that the water stays in contact with the ground coffee. The ideal extraction rate is approximately 19 percent of the ground coffee's dry weight. Over- or under-extraction can ruin your final product, as can less than perfectly fresh coffee blends and water containing too many impurities.

Other golden rules include: 1) always use freshly ground coffee, 2) measure the coffee shots carefully, and 3) make sure that you pack the portafilter correctly.

Essentially, espresso is brewed at speed (15 to 25 seconds), and under pressure (around nine atmospheres, or approximately 132 pounds per square inch). Espresso, as its name suggests, is meant to be drunk quickly, while still hot, in order to best appreciate its flavorsome aftertaste. Exceptional espresso should leave a refreshing aftertaste that lingers for up to 30 minutes.

Once you press the button to start the brewing process, it takes a few seconds for the coffee to appear in the spout of the portafilter. From around 5 to 15 seconds into the brewing cycle the espresso seems to drip rather than flow, at which stage the coffee should appear dark reddish-brown in color. From 15 to 25 seconds, the "crema" (the fine, foamy amalgamation of water and coffee oil that forms over the top of a properly brewed espresso) should continue to develop and thicken. At 25 seconds, the espresso will look as if it is flowing more rapidly, and it is at this point that you should concentrate on the color of the crema. At the precise moment when the crema turns light or golden brown in color, the brewing cycle must be stopped. If you extend the brewing process, the resulting espresso will start to thin out and become watery in texture and bitter in taste.

The proper handling of milk for espresso drinks, such as cappuccino or lattes, is also important. To properly steam milk, you must balance the steam wand on the surface of the milk. This will simultaneously heat and aerate the milk. The basic steps for steaming and frothing milk are as follows:

- Using a steaming pitcher half full of cold milk, insert the steam wand just below the milk's surface.
- Open the steam valve fully and lower the pitcher so the tip of the wand is on the milk's surface.
- When the milk is frothed enough, put the wand deep into the milk and wait until the milk reaches 150°F.
- Shut off the steam and remove the pitcher

Specialty Teas

To a large extent, the expansion of the retail gourmet coffee industry also has generated a consumer penchant for specialty teas, particularly organic and gourmet herbal teas. Other possible contributory factors that may account for the increasing popularity of specialty teas are increasing health awareness among customers and maybe simply a desire to return to the more leisurely and sociable lifestyle associated with the British tradition of pausing to "take tea." Specialty tea consumption is growing, with tea now representing 5 to 8 percent of specialty coffee shop sales in the United States, according to Specialty Coffee Retailer. Consumption, however, varies from region to region, so you will need to undertake some local research to establish your market potential.

Most gourmet coffee suppliers also stock a range of quality, specialty loose teas, packaged in airtight containers. Up-market teas generally are sold as blends derived from a number of tea-growing plantations within the same geographic region, or from several different countries.

Types of Tea

There are three basic types of tea: 1) black, 2) oolong, and 3) green. The main difference between prepared and finished teas is the way in which they are processed. The three different types of tea are the result of three different methods of processing, which are determined by whether the tea has been fermented during production and by the degree of fermentation.

- **Black tea.** Refers to leaves that have been completely fermented. By far the most common tea consumed worldwide (black teas are known as red teas in China), Black tea leaves are graded according to size, age, and leaf style.
- **Green tea.** Refers to under-fermented tea, where the leaves have been steamed straight after picking. Green tea leaves are graded according to leaf age and style.
- **Oolong tea.** Refers to leaves that have undergone partial fermentation to produce their distinctive fragrant flavors. Oolong tea leaves are graded according to quality.

Specialty teas, with customer appeal include:

Indian

- **Assam** tea is grayish-black in color. High-grade Assam may also have a hint of golden color. Assam tea tends to be strong, bright-colored, and rich, with honey-flavored aromas.
- **Darjeeling.** A high-quality tea harvested in the foothills of the Himalayas; produces distinctive, intensely aromatic black tea with a hint of Muscat flavor.

Ceylon (Sri Lanka)

- **Ceylon** is the third largest producer of teas worldwide, and the biggest exporter. Ceylon teas are nearly all black teas that range in quality from acceptable to truly superb. Essentially, you get what you pay for, so beware of compromising on quality in the interests of trimming your inventory budget.

China

- **Oolong.** The oolong tea, Ti Kuan Yin, for example has a slightly astringent, yet well-rounded, sweet flavor, whereas the more famous Lapsang Souchong has a more distinctly smoky flavor, which is the result of being processed over pine root fires.
- **Keemum,** from the Anhui province of China, is hugely popular in the United States. But, as with Ceylon teas, it varies in quality from fair to exquisite. Lower-grade teas from the Anhui region are often quite adequate for using in blends for making iced tea.
- **Fujan** province produces a wide variety of specialty teas including scented Jasmine teas, the best of which are made from Pouchong tea leaves. As a rule, the less overwhelming the scent of jasmine, the better the quality of the brewed cup of tea.
- **Puerh.** One of China's most ancient tea styles, Puerh is produced exclusively from the broad-leafed tea indigenous to the Yunnan region of China. Puerh tea has an intense, earthy flavor and is believed to possess medicinal properties.

Japan

- **Gyokuro.** Almost all tea grown in Japan is green tea, which is graded according to quality. The best is Gyokuro from the Honshu region of Japan.

Taiwan (Formosa)

Taiwan is reputed to produce the best oolong teas in the world, such as the elegant, naturally flavored Jade Oolong tea.

Tips for Preparing/"Steeping" Tea

Is it not somewhat ironic, that despite the availability of high-tech brewing equipment and the widespread use of preprepared tea bags, the best cup of tea is still prepared according to traditional methods? The only equipment you need is a water boiler, a vessel in which to steep the tea (the china teapot wins hands down!), the finest and freshest loose tea leaves you can purchase, a handheld tea strainer, a tea cozy to cover the teapot and maintain the tea at ambient temperature, and aesthetically pleasing china tea cups or mugs in which to serve your wonderful brew of distinctive colors, flavors, and aromas.

There is no great mystique to brewing top-notch tea. The secret lies in not rushing the process; time and patience are of the essence, for truly great tea cannot be hurried. Here are some tips for preparing the perfect cup of tea:

- **Liquid capacity.** The standard cup of tea is 5.5 liquid ounces; you will need to know the liquid capacity of the various teapots you use in your shop. As a general guideline, use 2 grams of tea leaves to each 5.5 liquid ounce cup. As tea leaves vary considerably in size and weight, you are advised to use an accurate gram scale. For example, an 11-ounce teapot will require 4 grams of tea leaves. Keep a record on hand of the capacity of your different teapots; new serving staff will appreciate these guidelines.

- **To boil or not to boil?** A consensus of experts conclude that the water used for steeping tea should be brought to a "rolling boil." Then, there are those who argue that the water should not be brought to boiling point. The fact is, each of the three distinct styles (black, oolong, and green) require different water temperatures for steeping. Black tea, for example should definitely be brought to a rolling boil of 212°F, oolong teas should be brewed at the slightly cooler temperatures of 195°F to 210°F, whereas green teas are best at around 180°F.

- **Type of water used for brewing tea.** The jury is out on this one, with certain tea cognoscenti insisting on the use of spring water; others will settle only for Seattle water. In general, however, the purer the water, the better. Additionally, water should always be poured freshly each time to ensure that the water is highly oxygenated, thus avoiding what experts refer to as a "flat" cup of brew.

- **The secrets of steeping.** Steeping, unfortunately, is an imprecise art and very much a matter of individual taste; but one thing that all tea lovers agree on is that nothing tastes worse than the bitter flavor of over-steeped tea. As a general rule, full, large-leafed tea leaves, such as quality oolongs, may take a little over 5 minutes, and smaller-leafed peak at under 4 minutes; delicate white teas, for instance may be ready after only 2 minutes. Herbal teas, on the other hand, are often best left for between 5 and 7 minutes. Be guided by the preferences of your regular customers who will be happy to advise you about what constitutes the perfect cup of tea!

Popularity of Iced Tea

Research has revealed that 85 to 90 percent of Americans prefer their tea iced. This trend shows no signs of abating, with the iced tea sector of the beverage market at around $3 billion. And, in response to customer demand, many coffee shops are introducing a range of iced teas as an alternative to the other beverages served in their establishment. Demand is certainly growing, and coffee and tea shop owners are happy to oblige. Consequently, many coffee shops have updated their beverage menu to carry a range of popular teas, iced teas in particular.

From a retail perspective, iced tea is easier to prepare and less time-consuming. Equipment suppliers are constantly vying with each other to develop new models of iced tea brewers that even an inexperienced employee can operate with minimal training. The emphasis is on push-button automatic features that remove the trial-and-error element of preparing the perfect cup of iced tea. It is simply a matter of pulling out the brew basket, placing the sealed filter bag of tea inside, pushing the basket back in and pressing a button.

Herbal Teas

Many teas contain almost as much caffeine as coffee, whereas herbal teas are caffeine-free. Additionally, herbal teas, particularly organically grown plants, are believed to possess health-boosting antioxidants and other medicinal properties. Health benefits aside, the delicate flavors of herbal teas are hugely appealing to the modern tea drinker's palate.

Other Beverages

Popular among espresso fans is a beverage known as Italian soda; a fizzy, sweet blend of flavored syrup (typically chocolate, ginger, root beer, peach or peanut butter flavors), soda water and ice with, occasionally, a dash of cream. Often customers will order an Italian soda at the same time as an espresso, in a similar way to Europeans ordering a glass of still water to accompany their "solo" espressos.

Other fast-moving lines in non-coffee items include bottled still and carbonated waters, seltzers, and fresh juices. If your available storage space and refrigeration capacity is limited, fresh juices could cause a problem. For that reason, we suggest that you stick to a couple of popular flavors, with perhaps one exotic fruit juice, on a rotating basis, and one Italian-style granita, a frozen "slush" drink made from a blend of different granita coffee flavors, fresh fruits and syrups.

Flavored, steamed milk drinks, as well as hot cocoa, made from chocolate syrup and steamed milk topped with whipped cream never seems to fall out of favor — a safe all-year-round bet. You may also wish to consider serving seasonal favorites, such as hot-spiced cider, mulled wine, and steamed eggnog during cold weather.

Food Products

Offering separate food menus can dramatically increase your profit margins, as well as providing a "come-on" for customers to linger longer in your establishment and spend more money on extra " little indulgences." Of course, the style and scope of your coffee, espresso, and tea shop will determine which food items to offer for minimal effort and maximum return. If your shop is a franchise, you probably will be obliged to purchase and sell only the range of "add-ons" stipulated by the franchiser.

Independent retailers, however, have greater scope and flexibility. In which case, depending on your location, you may wish to provide:

- **Dessert menu.** The ever-popular dessert menu is guaranteed to please, whatever the location of your establishment. Opt for an inspiring dessert menu that oozes exclusivity. You do not have to offer a huge selection of desserts and pastries; a limited choice of in-house "homemade" creations and recipes is much more likely to win the approval of your loyal clientele. Something chocolate always should be included. Also, think about pies, cakes, custards, and bread puddings. Also, consider offering items that are made with coffee — your coffee — such as espresso brownies, tiramisu, and espresso crème brulee. Make sure you advertise that these desserts are made with your fresh-brewed, fresh-ground coffee.

You may want to make suggestions on particular beverages that would go well with particular menu items, or offer specials such as a free coffee with the purchase of dessert.

- **Breakfast.** You may wish to serve an all-day breakfast, especially if you are near a university campus, near a highway, shopping mall, or service station. If you have the kitchen facilities, you may want to offer a full breakfast menu featuring the usual items of eggs, breakfast meats, pancakes, waffles, and French toast. You also may want to offer fresh muffins and scones. Make sure to offer some alternatives for the health-conscious as well, including fresh juices and maybe an egg white omelet or vegetarian breakfast links.
- **European café "come-on."** Serve mouth-watering, European-style baguettes, cram-packed with French cheeses and pickles or cranberry, if you are close to an art gallery or theater. This type of menu can be as extensive or limited as you want.
- **Liquor.** An alcoholic drinks menu could prove popular with customers. Do not stop with the usual fare of wine, martinis, and whiskey sours, however. Many alcoholic drinks are made with coffee. Create a coffee drink menu and feature it prominently to your after-dinner guests. Some options to include are Coffee Alexandra (made with coffee brandy, white crème de cacao, and cream), Irish coffee (coffee and Irish whiskey, topped with whipped cream), Kahlúa® and coffee, and Bailey's® and coffee. A variety of coffee and alcohol drinks also are made with ice cream.
- **Healthy snacks.** Healthy sandwiches made from organic breads and lighter fillings might go down well if you are located near a gym or fitness center or if your clientele are health-conscious.

If you do not currently offer healthy menu alternatives and would like to do so, there are many resources available to help you develop a healthy menu. Search the Web. Many sites provide healthy recipes, such as the American Institute of Cancer Research at **www.aicr.org**, the American Heart Association at **www.heart.org**, and the American Diabetes Association at **www.diabetes.org**.

There are also many good healthy cookbooks in print nowadays. To follow are just a few:

- *Vegetarian Cooking for Everyone* by Deborah Madison
- *The French Culinary Institute's Salute to Healthy Cooking* by Alain Sailhac, Jacques Pepin, Andre Soltner, Jacques Torresn, and the Faculty at the French Culinary Institute
- *Healthy Latin Cooking* by Steve Raichlen

- *Good Food Gourmet* by Jane Brody
- *Moosewood Restaurant Low-Fat Favorites* by the Moosewood Collective
- *Canyon Ranch Cooking* by Jeanne Jones

If you do not want to spend the time developing new recipes to include healthy alternatives, you can probably change some of your existing recipes. Try incorporating the following suggestions into your current menu program:

- Offer at least one vegetarian entrée.
- Offer at least one entrée without a butter or cream sauce. Try substituting a chutney or salsa for a high-calorie sauce.
- Replace the cream or whole milk in a recipe with skim milk or soy milk.
- Replace butter on vegetables with lemon and herb.
- Replace sour cream with yogurt.
- Make your own stock or pick a canned stock that is low in sodium.
- Try serving oven-baked fries rather than French fries.
- Offer more salads and fat/reduced-calorie salad dressings.
- Substitute chicken broth for milk in mashed potatoes.
- Use olive or canola oil instead of butter or shortening.
- Offer whole grain breads as part of a bread basket.
- Offer low-fat mayonnaise as a sandwich condiment.
- Offer sorbet as a dessert option.
- Offer a simple fruit dessert, such as baked pears, that is low in sugar and fat.
- Offer smaller portion sizes on some of your entreés.
- Use local produce, meats, and other products, and let your customers know you are using them.

Customize

Creating and offering signature items, or items no one else offers, is a good way to attract business. "Handmade" individually-wrapped Belgian chocolates or local sweet or savory specialty food products provided by a local supplier could also add to the "community" feel of your coffee, espresso, and tea shop. Some things to try to include:

- Chocolate spoons — serve with your more elaborate coffee drinks.
- Offer muffins and scones from the local bakery up the street.
- Use (and advertise that you use) organic products.
- Local produce — offer fresh strawberries, raspberries, and blueberries when in season, using these for your dessert menu.

Whether you decide to start with only tried-and-tested food items, or to experiment with new lines or a combination of the two, it is important that you seek customer feedback and refine your "add-on" menus on a regular basis.

- **Prix fixe menus.** If you are concerned with labor and food cost and want to serve full meals, you might consider a prix fixe menu. Prix fixe menus offer a complete meal at a set price. This may include an appetizer, entrée, and dessert, or it can be a five-course meal.

A lunch menu might look like this:

Gazpacho or chicken tortilla soup
Green salad
Black bean or chicken enchiladas
Espresso flan..$9.75

A menu like this offers your customers some choice, but it allows you to prepare a limited amount of food, saving on labor and food costs.

Etc.

Recipe for Classic Irish Coffee

Ingredients

6 ounces of hot, fresh brewed coffee
1 teaspoon of brown sugar
1 ½ ounces of your favorite Irish whiskey
heavy cream

Preparation

Combine fresh brewed coffee with the whiskey and sugar. Mix well until sugar dissolves. Float whipped cream on top taking care not to break the surface of the coffee.

—**irishcoffeerecipe.com**

7

Profitable Menu Planning – For Maximum Results

The prosperity of any specialty beverage business is often directly attributable to its menus, atmosphere, and service. Many establishments can thrive without a fanciful atmosphere or quality service, but none can survive without exceptional menus. The manager must examine the shop's atmosphere and clientele carefully. Based upon these observations, he or she can then design a menu, or several separate menus, which will be effective.

The objective of this chapter is to present the coffee, espresso, and tea shop manager with complete guidelines for planning successful and profitable menus. It would be impractical in these pages to list specific examples of potential menu items. There are many excellent beverage books dedicated to the topic of specialty coffees and teas that describe menu and recipe ideas in detail. The following sections will illustrate a basic outline from which you can plan your own exclusive menu. Each of the procedures described plays an integral part in developing your cost-control system.

Menu Style

Most specialty coffee and tea shops have a main beverage menu with detailed descriptions of the various gourmet coffees and teas offered, as well as a brief overview of their production methods. "Add-on" items, such as sandwiches, savory snacks, desserts, or alcoholic beverages, can be listed either on separate menus or included in your main beverage menu; much depends on the scope and range of the leading products you wish to sell. There are certain advantages to offering separate menus, particularly a dessert menu, including exclusivity, quality, and "special treat" appeal. Customers will be hard-pressed to resist the temptation of a beautifully illustrated dessert menu or an enticing separate sandwich menu; they are more likely to indulge if they think they are ordering that little extra treat.

Menu style describes how much or how little variety the menu offers. Do you serve a limited or expansive menu? The things that may influence whether you offer a limited menu include the available preparation area, the overall size of your operation, and labor costs. Menus with more options, however, do have a broader appeal. The key to making the most of a limited menu is to prepare and combine the same ingredients in different ways, thus offering many choices that are more imaginative but still controlling inventory and costs.

There are advantages to both the limited and extensive menu styles:

Limited

- You need less equipment and less beverage and food preparation space.
- Beverage and food prep is simplified and can be speedy.
- You need fewer, less-skilled prep employees.
- Purchasing your inventory is easier and less time-consuming.
- Space needed for inventory is lessened.
- Cost and quality controls are simpler.
- Operating costs are lower.
- Customer turnover can be increased because transaction time is quicker.

Extensive

- You can appeal to a broader customer base.
- New customers will be intrigued.
- The menu can be more responsive to customer taste.
- The menu is more flexible.
- You can charge higher prices for specialty items.
- Regulars will return more often because they have a greater number of options.

So, how many menu items should you offer? You want to provide the customer with variety, but not at the expense of your ability to control inventory and cost, nor by overtaxing your production or serving staffs. Research has shown that 60 to 75 percent of menu items sold are the same 8 to 12 items, regardless of the number of choices offered.

Developing the Menu Selections

All menu items selected must fit into the physical workings of your coffee, espresso, and tea shop. Thus, the menu should be finalized before designing, selecting equipment for, and laying out the available beverage and food preparation area. This is necessary for maximum efficiency of time, labor, and equipment. The design and layout of your establishment's work areas must meet the needs of your menus. If it does not, the entire operation will become slow, disorganized, and inefficient. Inefficiency can only result in a drop in employee morale and in the shop's profit margin.

Just as the work space must meet the demands of the menu, the personnel employed to prepare the menu items must be selected to fit into the design of your shop. Careful consideration must be given to the number and type of employees needed. For example, are your menus simple enough for inexperienced workers to prepare? Will the food items be prepared ahead of time or upon receipt of the order? When will these employees be needed and for how long? Will there be enough room in the prep area for everyone to work at the same time? Who will supervise them?

Once the menus are finalized, it will be necessary for management to become thoroughly familiar with every aspect of each menu item. Extensive experimentation with preparation methods is essential, and all employees will need to take the time to find out everything there is to know about the menu items.

Portion Control

The rule for developing a portion size is to use the largest portion feasible but charge accordingly. It is far better to serve too much than too little. The crucial element, which must be constantly reinforced, is that every menu item must be a specific weight, volume, or size. Portion control is the basis for the business's entire cost-control program. Its importance cannot be overstated. Portion controlling is an effective way to control costs, but it also serves another important function: it maintains consistency in the final product.

Truth and Accuracy in the Menu

Care must be taken when compiling the final menu to ensure its complete accuracy. Few coffee and tea shop managers would deceive their customers on purpose, as their establishment would only suffer in the end. However, you must become aware of the unintentional inaccuracies you may have in the menu and the governmental regulations regarding this area. All states have one or more laws that requires that any organization selling a product must not misrepresent the product in any manner with intent to deceive. Many states have specific "truth in menu" legislation.

Every statement made, whether it is oral by the waitstaff or written in the menu description, must be completely accurate. For example, "Real maple syrup" must be 100 percent real maple syrup. Words and descriptions to watch are: fresh, real, homemade, and 100 percent. The description printed on the menu must be exactly the product you are serving.

Nutritional Claims on Menus

If you want to include menu items that are marketed as healthy (i.e., heart-healthy, low-fat, reduced-fat, cholesterol-free, etc.), make sure you have the nutritional information for these items readily accessible. Items described as "fresh" are included in this category. Some establishments are beginning to list ingredients and "Nutritional Facts" labels on the menu for the convenience of their customers. Such a label indicates the item's value in calories, total fat, cholesterol, sodium, carbohydrates, protein, etc. Since 1997, retail beverage and food outlets restaurants have been included in the FDA's nutritional labeling laws. FDA regulations state that if you make health/nutritional claims on your menu, you must be able to demonstrate there is a reasonable basis for making them and that they are consistent with the claims established under the Nutrition Labeling and Education Act. Some states now require food purchased for take-out to be labeled in this manner. Several software programs available will perform these calculations for you and print labels.

Menu Size and Cover

The menu cover should reflect your establishment's image as well as its identity. It can include graphics (the shop's logo) and copy. If your outlet is in a historic building, for instance, you may want to include a drawing or photo of the building on your cover. If you are operating a family business that has been in existence for generations, you may want to put a paragraph or two of copy about the family's history or service philosophy. Remember, the cover is the first step in the menu's role as a communication tool, and it is the first place on paper you can communicate your identity to the customer. The ideal menu dimensions are 9 inches wide by 12 inches tall. Of course, other sizes can work as well, and the number of items on the menu will partially determine the menu size. Keep in mind that the menu size should be manageable for the customer.

The cover should be of some durable material; part of its function is to protect interior pages. It can be leather, vinyl, laminated paper, or plastic. Your establishment's identity will help you choose the appropriate cover material. The cover's color also should be chosen with care. The color should tie into the theme and décor of your coffee, espresso, and tea shop; but remember, color does have a psychological impact, so you will want colors that will evoke pleasant images and feelings. Bear in mind that the more colors you use for your menu, the more expensive the printing process becomes.

You also may want to include general information on the cover, such as your hours of operation, address, telephone number, the forms of payment you accept, and any special services you provide. While your regular customers may not need this information, new customers will appreciate it, and it will make it easier for them to return if they know when you are open and how to find you again.

Menu-Design Software

With the advent of the personal computer, a number of menu-design software programs have been developed in recent years. The software is generally very easy to use, having built-in templates, artwork, etc. Your finalized menu can be printed on a laser printer. Color, artwork, and graphics may be added.

Table tents and other promotional devices can also be used. The initial cost of the software will be recouped easily as you save in design and printing costs. In addition, you will have complete control over the design process. Changes can be made instantly. Daily menus can be made, which is a great way to accommodate special purchases that might have been made. The ability to generate new menus easily allows instant price changes to reflect market conditions. One such software program is Menu Pro™. Visit **www.softcafe.com** for more information.

Copyrighting the Menu

Before printing the menu, you would be wise to obtain a copyright. Copyrighting the menu protects it from being reproduced in any form without your written permission. This would be extremely important if you prepared original artwork or wrote the menu in an interesting and novel way. Obtaining a copyright is a very simple procedure.

One of the pages of the menu, preferably the first or second, must contain the copyright registration. This notice must include the following three elements: the name of the copyright owner, the year of publication and the symbol © and/or the word "Copyright" (e.g., COPYRIGHT 2014 ABC Coffee, Espresso & Tea Shop Corporation).

The copyright application Form TX may be found at the at this website: **www.copyright.gov**. The registration process normally takes about four weeks and currently costs $35 for online filing.

Printing the Menu

As indicated in the previous section, creatively printing the menu will have a marked effect upon the marketing of your offerings. Menus can be handwritten on single pieces of plain 8-½" by 11" paper or card; printed on boards, tables, or walls; or spoken verbally; the possibilities are limitless. The menu easily can be turned into a promotional vehicle for your establishment and can be used as a crucial internal marketing tool. It is the way you communicate to your customer your objectives and identity. Your menu design will directly impact guest-check averages, so it can help you achieve your profit goals. A well-designed menu can attract a customer's attention to specific items and increase the chances that the customer will purchase those items. For instance, if you put an item in a box on the menu, the customer's eye will be drawn to this area of the menu.

Regardless of how creatively the menu is used, it should be typeset and either printed by a professional or with the professional menu software previously described. Simply using an unusual type style will dress up any menu. Discuss the possibilities with your local printer or graphic artist, or contact a company specializing in menu production.

Artwork should be used if at all possible; use the shop's logo if nothing else. Your local printer may have an artist on staff or know of some freelancers in the area who can help, but why reinvent the wheel? Atlantic Publishing has several books dedicated to restaurant operations that will give you some great ideas. You can find these resources at **www.atlantic-pub.com**.

Projecting Menu Costs

Recipes and Procedures Manual

Your Recipes and Procedures Manual will contain all the restaurant's recipes, preparation procedures, handling instructions, and ordering specifications. This manual, if properly used, will ensure perfection and consistency every time a menu item is prepared.

Pricing Individual Menu Items

In order to assess the price that you must charge for a menu item accurately, you must know the exact cost of that item. Projecting menu costs is simply a matter of mathematics.

You will need the completed Recipes and Procedures Manual and the current price lists from your suppliers. From your sales representative, obtain projections on the average yearly prices for the major items you order, such as coffee beans and loose tea blends. Then, using the Recipes and Procedures Manual and the current price lists and price projections, compute the cost of each beverage or food recipe item and place the amount in the column under Current Cost. Round all the amounts off to the nearest cent. Should estimates need to be given, it is better to figure a little high in order to cover yourself.

Projecting the Actual Average Cost per Customer

It will be relatively easy to compute the actual average cost per customer once your shop is set up and operating. The actual average cost per customer should be projected once every month. This ensures that the estimates used in computing the menu costs are accurate. To project the actual average cost per customer, keep a list of all the food items you do not charge for during a specific test period and their prices. You can develop this list from the invoices that detail daily purchases. Add into this figure the dollar amount of ingredients you have on hand at the beginning of the test period. At the end of the test period, subtract the amount in hand from the total. Divide the total cost by the number of customers served during that period. This figure is the average actual cost per customer. Use it in projecting menu costs instead of any estimates you have made with this figure.

Menu Prices

Projecting menu prices is a complex procedure because of the number of factors that must be considered. In order to operate profitably, most retail beverage and food operations must achieve and maintain their cost of sales at 35 to 45 percent. The cost percentage is the total beverage and food cost divided by the total sales for a given period.

Computing what you must charge for each item on the menu is relatively easy. The total portion cost (the cost of the ingredients) divided by the menu price (the selling price) must equal an ingredient cost percentage of between .35 (35 percent) and .40 (40 percent).

Portion Costs ÷ Menu Price x 100 = 35% – 45%

Simply plug different menu prices into the formula until you reach the desired beverage and food cost percentages.

While pricing may seem like simply a mathematical exercise or a lucky guess, it is neither of these. Pricing is based on a mark-up of cost, which is figured by determining food cost, sales history, and profit margin, but pricing strategy does not end there.

Indirect Factors

Pricing decisions will be influenced by indirect factors as well:

- Human psychology
- Market conditions
- Location
- Atmosphere
- Service style
- Competition
- Customers' willingness to pay

Market conditions affect every industry. When the economy is bad, stores are likely to see fewer profits because people may be eating out and traveling less. Prices are demand or market driven. The market will ultimately be a large determinant of your prices. Your prices need to not only reflect the cost of the item but also what the competition is charging and what the customer is willing to spend on an item.

Market-driven prices are more responsive to competition. Prices that are demand-driven, however, will be higher. These may be signature items or simply items that are hot, new trends.

Location and atmosphere are also important in determining menu prices. If you go to a nice sit-down café, you will be willing to pay a higher price for a cup of coffee than if you take a to-go cup away from a coffee cart or drive-thru location.

What the competition is charging also must be taken into consideration. If you are serving the exact same item as the shop down the street for $3 more, you invariably will lose customers to the other store, all other things being equal.

The final item on the list, customers' willingness to pay, is very important. All the other factors make no difference if your customers think your prices are too high for what they are receiving. Remember, your customers are not concerned with your costs; they are concerned with getting their money's worth when they dine out.

Ask yourself these questions about indirect factors when pricing your menu:

- What is the atmosphere and décor of your store? Can you make it enhance your customers' experience?

It may be time to consider remodeling your shop if it has not been updated for a number of years. Or, perhaps just a fresh coat of paint could spruce up your dining room and make it an attractive, comfortable place for a cup of tea.

Along with décor, think about your store's cleanliness. Customers do not want to spend time in a store that is dirty, nor do they want to eat with utensils that have not been properly cleaned. Keep a regular cleaning schedule (and pest-control schedule) so your specialty coffee store is an attractive venue.

- What type of service do you offer?

While your customers definitely want quality beverages, good service is just as important.

- Where are you located?

This is an important factor in determining what you will be able to charge. If you are in a middle-class neighborhood, you will not want your prices to be on the cutting edge, even if your coffee is. If you are in a more urban environment, you can probably do both.

- What is your customer base?

If your customers are college students, you know they have limited spending budgets so you do not want to price yourself out of the market.

Psychology

Customer psychology is an indirect pricing factor that must be kept in mind as well.

We have all seen the WalMart® ads with the smiley face cutting the price signs. Prices go from $5.99 to $4.88, or $2.95 to $2.45. Notice the prices end in odd amounts (in restaurants, these amounts are usually fives and nines). Psychologically, these prices are perceived as lower than a price that ends in zero. So, $12.95 is lower than $13.00 in the customer's mind. When the difference involves three or four digits, the difference in perception is increased: $9.95 is much less than $10.00.

Think about the last time you made a major purchase, such as an appliance or a car. More than likely when you saw the $995 sticker, your mind perceived that as $900, or less than $1,000, rather than $1,000.

Another psychological factor that comes into play is the mental budget people keep for monthly expenditures. Mental accounting plays a role in how much a customer is willing to pay. We all keep mental tabs on how much money we have, what we need for bills that month, and how much we can spend on entertainment. Most people include their grocery money as part of their bills' budget and their entertainment money as a separate budget. Some people even go so far as to have separate banking accounts for each category of expense (i.e., they have separate checking accounts for monthly bills, house repairs, car expenses, etc.).

These days, people generally eat out as a convenience and a substitute for making a meal at home, or they eat out as a social activity — as entertainment on the weekend or for special occasions such as birthdays and anniversaries.

Value

A customer determines value by looking at three things:

- Quality
- Quantity
- Price

Value is subjective; it is not the same for all customers at all times. In general, a lower-priced item has value; however, if the customer feels that the drink, food, or service is poor, the lower price itself will become less valuable, and the customer will be willing to pay a higher price to receive a higher-quality product.

In addition, if you are using high-quality ingredients, you can charge more than other establishments that use inferior ingredients. Your food cost will be higher if you are using higher-quality ingredients, but this will be offset by the higher price you are able to charge for the product. And while this change may balance itself out, you can increase revenues by attracting customers that are willing to pay for quality ingredients. This will help to increase your profits.

The complications arise when you have determined the price you must charge in order to make the desired profit. Some of the prices you would need to charge would be simply too high. No one would ever purchase the item at that price. What you must do in these cases is balance out the menu with high and low food-cost items. Find out what other shops in the area are charging for similar beverages and food items. Your clientele will dictate what the market will bear. The manager must set the menu prices based on what customers will spend and what must be charged in order to make the desired profit margin.

Etc.

The United States is the world's largest consumer of coffee, importing 16 to 20 million bags annually (2.5 million pounds), representing one-third of all coffee exported. More than half of the U.S. population drinks coffee. The typical coffee drinker has 3.4 cups of coffee per day, which translates into more than 450,000,000 cups of coffee daily. —**www.discountcoffee.com/coffee-trivia**

8

Inventory Control – For Maximum Profits

Effective inventory control is the anchor of your business. It is critical, therefore, that you incorporate good inventory-control procedures into your regular, daily, management routines. Basically, you will need to know how much of an item you have in stock, minimum reorder levels, and how long it will take for delivery.

The cash you have tied up in inventory (which can range from anywhere between 15 and 25 percent or more of your total operating capital), should be made to work for you; look at it as an investment that needs to be monitored, analyzed, and adjusted to yield maximum profits.

Establishing an Inventory-Control System

Keep it simple, but above all, take time to think about the specific inventory-control requirements that may affect your coffee, espresso, and tea shop. Too often, small start-up businesses fall into the trap of over-complicating the business of establishing an inventory-control system; they end up spending hours of their valuable time on unnecessary documentation and duplication of records. Bear in mind that time, too, is money and this precious commodity needs to be costed into the equation.

The key to getting it right is to implement a straightforward, workable system from the start, before you are up and running. Your inventory-control system must be in place before you start ordering and receiving inventory. So many activities require your attention as opening day draws ever closer, that you may be tempted to let inventory control take care of itself and hope that all will be fine in the end. It will not.

A simple inventory-control system will give you an important handle on your business, from the start. For example, it will tell you whether you are carrying too much (or too little) stock and whether you are realizing maximum profits regarding investment per unit, as well as optimum return on your storage, display, and handling costs. Aim to maintain inventory at its lowest level to ensure seamless service, while at the same time not running out of any items or, conversely, carrying excess stock.

Choosing an Inventory-Control System for Your Establishment

You could introduce several, straightforward methods of inventory control, depending on your particular operation. What all methods have in common is that they tell you how many items or products you have in stock and how many you need to order to meet customer and production demands.

A number of software packages on the market today are specifically designed to streamline the process of inventory control in the beverage and food industry. Not only do such packages offer one of the best ways for making the most of your inventory, they also free up valuable time needed for developing your start-up business. All systems will also help you reduce:

- Inventory shrinkage (which is usually due to employee theft)
- Reduce customer theft
- Incorrect inventory storage
- Inaccurate or false recordkeeping of all items ordered, received and used

Physical Inventory Count

A physical count should be carried out at the very least once a year for tax purposes. Far better (and more efficient) is to keep an ongoing record. Ideally, you should combine both systems of periodical physical counts and a perpetual inventory record.

Perpetual Inventory

The perpetual inventory is a checklist of the items used daily in your shop. In order to set up a perpetual inventory system, all you need to do is to keep a large ring binder containing a file card or inventory record sheet for each item of your inventory. List the following column headings at the top of each card or sheet:

- Item name
- Supplier code (if applicable)
- Item description
- Supplier contact details including phone number or email
- Unit price
- Your selling price for retail items (or percentage of gross price of prepared product)
- Order date
- Number of items
- Date received
- On-hand stock level
- Build-to amount (reorder level based on minimum requirements)

Purchasing

The goal of purchasing is to supply your specialty beverage business with the best goods at the lowest possible cost. There are many ways to achieve this aim. The buyer must have favorable working relations with all suppliers and vendors. A large amount of time must be spent meeting with prospective sales representatives and companies. The buyer's responsibility is to evaluate and decide how best to make each of the purchases for the business. Purchasing is a complex area that must be managed by someone who is completely familiar with all of the shop's needs. The most critical element to grasp when purchasing is the overall picture. Price is not the top priority and is only one of the considerations in deciding how and where to place an order.

Cooperative Purchasing

Many beverage operators have formed cooperative purchasing groups to increase their purchasing power, since they all have a large number of items in common. By cooperatively joining together to place large orders, they usually can get substantial price reductions. Franchise organizations and chain shops generally have a centralized purchasing department and, often, large self-distribution centers.

Inventory Levels

The first step in computing which items and how much of them to order is to determine the inventory level or the amount needed on hand at all times. To determine the amount you need to order, you must first know what you have in inventory. Walk through the storage areas and mark in the "On Hand" column the amounts of each item in stock. To determine the "Build-To Amount," you will need to know when regularly scheduled deliveries arrive for that item and the amount used in the period between deliveries. Add on about 25 percent to the average amount used; this will cover unexpected usage, a late delivery, or a back order. The amount you need to order is the difference between the "Build-To Amount" and the amount "On Hand." Experience and customer demand will reveal the amount an average order should contain. By purchasing too little, the shop may run out of supplies. Ordering too much will result in tying up money. Buying up items in large amounts can save money, but you must consider the cash-flow costs.

Beginning Inventory — The Math

The beginning inventory is the total dollar value of supplies on hand when the shop opens. This figure represents the starting point from which you can then compute individual costs. Each category — beverage, raw ingredients, food, liquor, and operational supplies — has its own beginning inventory figure.

To determine the cost for each category, simply add the beginning inventory value to the total purchases of that category for the month. Inventory the amount left at the end of the month and subtract it from total of the beginning inventory and purchases. The percentage of cost is the total cost divided by the total sales. The important thing here is to compute an accurate beginning inventory figure for your starting point. A buying schedule should be set up and adhered to. This would consist of a calendar showing:

- On which days orders need to be placed
- When deliveries will be arriving
- What items will be arriving from which supplier
- The price the sales representative quoted
- Phone numbers of sales representatives to contact for each company

Post the buying schedule on the office wall. When a delivery does not arrive as scheduled, the buyer should place a phone call to the salesperson or company immediately.

A "Want Sheet" may be placed on a clipboard in the beverage and food preparation area. This sheet should be made available for employees to write in any items they may need to do their jobs more efficiently. This is a very effective form of communication; employees should be encouraged to use it. The buyer should consult this sheet every day.

Determining Reorder Levels

Every time you sell or use an item, write it down and deduct it from the ongoing balance. Reorder levels are determined by the following factors:

- Minimum cost per unit in which the supplier will provide the item
- Supplier quantity discount rates
- Seasonal discount rates
- Special offers
- Discount available for cash or quick payment
- Delivery lead time
- Shifting trends and popularity of certain items

Another factor that may influence your reordering pattern is the economy in general; a depressed economy means that people are less likely to pay for "small indulgences" such as a gourmet cup of coffee. If you have a constantly tight rein on your perpetual inventory, you are less likely to end up with items that have passed their sell-by date. Likewise, you will be able to identify at a glance which items are fast movers and which items should be discontinued because they are not moving fast enough and are occupying too much storage space. Soon, you will reach the point when you can determine your reordering requirements with a high degree of accuracy.

Receiving and Storing Inventory

Deliveries only should be received during the prescribed times, outside busy periods. The preparation crew is normally responsible for receiving and storing all items (excluding liquor). The buyer also should be present to ensure that each item is of the specification ordered.

Receiving and storing each product is a critical responsibility. Costly mistakes can come about from a staff member who was not properly trained in the correct procedures. Listed below are some policies and procedures for receiving and storing all deliveries. A slight inaccuracy on an invoice or improper storing of a perishable item could cost the business hundreds of dollars.

Additionally, watch for a common area of internal theft. Collusion could develop between the delivery person and the employee receiving the products. Items checked as being received and accounted for may not have been delivered at all; the driver simply keeps the items. All products delivered to the shop must:

- Be checked against the actual order sheet
- Be the exact specification ordered (weight, size, quantity)
- Be checked against the invoice
- Be accompanied by an invoice containing: current price, totals, date, company name, and receiver's signature
- Have their individual weights verified on the pound scale

- Be dated, rotated, and put in the proper storage area immediately (for label resources, visit **www.daymarksafety.com**, or call 866.517.0490)
- Be locked in their storage areas securely

Credit slips must be issued or prices subtracted from the invoice when an error occurs. The delivery person must sign over the correction.

Keep an invoice box (a small mailbox) to store all invoices and packing slips received during the day. Mount the box on the wall, away from work areas. Before leaving for the day, the receiver must bring the invoices to the manager's office and place them in a designated spot. Extreme care must be taken to ensure that all invoices are handled correctly. A missing invoice will throw off the bookkeeping and financial records and statements.

Rotation Procedures

Your profits can be seriously affected if you do not rotate your stock on a first-in, first-out basis. Establish written guidelines for stock rotation and make sure that all employees follow the four basic steps for reducing wastage to a minimum:

- New items go to the back and on the bottom
- Older items move to the front and to the left
- In any part of the organization, the first item used always should be the oldest.
- Date and label everything.

Issuing

All raw materials from which portionable beverage or food items are prepared, must be issued on a daily basis. Whenever one of these bulk items is removed from a freezer or walk-in, it must be signed out. When a part of a case or box is removed, the weight of the portion removed must be recorded in an "Amount" column on the Sign-out Sheet, which should be on a clipboard affixed to the walk-in or freezer. Once the item is signed out, the weight must be placed in the "Amount Used or Defrosted" column on a separate Preparation Form. At any one of these stages, pilferage can occur. The signing-out procedure will eliminate pilferage. Products such as dry goods or cleaning supplies may be issued in a similar manner.

9

Successful Management of Operational Costs and Supplies

Chapter 7: Profitable Menu Planning — For Maximum Results described, in detail, only the costs that pertain directly to each item or product sold from the menu. Obviously, many other costs are involved in presenting beverages, food, and liquor products to the public. These additional costs are called operational costs. Operational costs cover all of the non-beverage, non-food, and non-liquor supplies used in preparing these items.

Labor and the cost of equipment are not considered direct operational expenses under this scenario. Labor is computed as a separate cost. Equipment is a capital expenditure and may be depreciated over several years. The operational supplies and costs considered here are only those products that must be continuously renewed each month as they are used up, lost, or broken.

Operational supplies and cost are divided into separate categories so that each may be broken down and analyzed. As with beverages, food, and liquor, a cost for each operational category will be projected at the end of each month. Setting up each category accurately is crucial, as this information will be used later on in projecting budgets and profit and loss statements.

Operational Categories

The following pages list each operational category and some examples of the type of supplies that belong to each. Based on the examples given, list on the Operational Ordering Form and the Operational Inventory Form all of the operational supplies the shop will need. Separate each page by category, and clearly label each category on the form. Always keep the order and inventory forms up to date. Whenever a new product is ordered, enter the new item on both forms. When it comes time to do the weekly order and monthly inventory, you will not miss or forget anything, as all the items will be listed. Certain items may fit into two categories because they are used in several areas of the shop. Place the item in the category where it is used the most. This will not affect the cost projection as long as the item is listed in only one category.

China and Utensils
Specialty coffee cups, saucers, plates, serving bowls, dishes, silverware, etc.

Glassware
All glasses, water glasses, liquor glasses, carafes, decanters, etc.

Beverage and Food Preparation Supplies
All of the non-food materials used in preparing beverages and food items, such as utensils, spatulas, ladles, scales, trays, knock-boxes, shakers, dispensers, thermometers, pourers, pitchers, chargers, measuring cups, measuring spoons, prep knives, scoops, graters, foil, cling wrap, filter paper, etc.

Liquor Preparation Supplies
Miscellaneous supplies, such as mixing spoons, straws, swords, napkins, pour spouts, corkscrews, etc.

Table Service Supplies
All of the miscellaneous supplies used in the front-of-shop, such as candles, matches, menus, salt and pepper shakers, sugar bowls, tent-card holders, coffeepots, teapots, tea cozies, creamers, flower vases, etc.

Cleaning Supplies
All of the miscellaneous cleaning supplies used by both the staff and the maintenance company, such as soap, paper towels, chemicals, vacuum bags, garbage bags, etc.

Office Supplies
All of the supplies used in the offices, such as stationery, paper, tape, rubber bands, etc.

Uniforms

Encompasses the cost of purchasing employee uniforms, such as aprons, smocks, hats, pants, dresses, etc.

Laundry and Linen

Covers all napkins, tablecloths, kitchen towels, bar towels, and soap purchased by the business from a laundry service or for an in-house system. Does not include the cost of the off-site services of a laundry company, as this normally is computed separately.

Ordering Operational Supplies

All of the procedures for storing, ordering, and receiving beverages, food, and liquor also apply to operational supplies. Ordering operational supplies must be carefully thought out. Too large an inventory (back stock) will tie up capital at expensive interest rates. However, one careless server who drops a tray of glasses can destroy what little reserve you have, so there must be a large enough inventory to cover the unexpected. One to two cases of each item in the storeroom should suffice. Portion-control items, such as scales, scoops, and ladles, are often difficult to obtain; when you find a supplier that has the size and type you desire, order several, and keep them in reserve. A common, but poor, excuse for not portion-controlling products is that the employee does not have access to the right type of utensil. Management's responsibility is to provide the employees with proper tools so that they can do their jobs efficiently.

Allow a lead time of several weeks when ordering specialty coffee cups and other items of china. Your distributor probably does not stock all the different types of chinaware and must purchase specially from the manufacturer.

Additionally, insufficient quantities of place settings will result in extra work, slow service, and, hence, a slow turnover of customers. Always maintain an adequate supply of stock in and out of the storeroom. The storeroom should be a separate room or closet and the manager must be the only person who has the key. Do not create a situation where it is easier for an employee to run to the storeroom for a new case of coffee cups than to help the dishwasher catch up.

Beginning Inventory

Computing this figure is similar to computing the beginning inventory amount for beverages, food, and liquor; however, there is one difference. The beginning inventory amount for each operational category is the dollar amount that is in storage when the operation is totally set up. This means that all the tables are set and there is plenty of stock in the beverage and food preparation areas. The reason for this is that operational supplies are projected for each month.

When you first open, the cost of setting up the shop is considered a one-time start-up cost. Operational costs are, thus, a measure of how well you controlled these costs following start-up. Separating this start-up cost may have some additional tax advantages. Your accountant will be able to advise you on this possibility.

Etc.

Most Expensive Coffee in the World

Indonesia's Kopi Luwak is made from coffee beans that are eaten, partly digested, and then excreted by the Asian palm civit, a weasel-like animal. It sells for more than $600 per pounds or $50 per cup. —**www.livescience.com/16297-coffee-facts-national-coffee-day-infographic.html**

10

The Essentials of Beverage and Food Safety, HACCP, and Sanitation Practices

Improper handling of perishable items or disregarding sanitation procedures will undoubtedly lead to hazardous health conditions and the spread of severe sickness and infectious diseases. In extreme circumstances, this could lead to death. It also would result in the closure of your business. There is no excuse for neglecting any health or sanitation procedure. It is the responsibility of the shop manager to guarantee the wholesomeness of the shop's products.

This chapter describes the fundamental methods and procedures that must be practiced in order to control beverage and food contamination, the necessary personal safety practices, and how to avoid the spread of infectious diseases. Management must provide employees with the training, knowledge, and tools that will enable them to establish and practice the proper handling of raw materials, as well as essential sanitation procedures. Using this chapter and under the guidance of your local department of health, you and your staff can obtain training and knowledge. First, however, the shop must be equipped with the proper tools, training, and working conditions. Employees never will establish good sanitation procedures if they do not first have the proper environment in which to practice them.

Aside from what is required by law, the management should provide training materials, proper training sessions or clinics, hand sinks in every prep area, hand and nailbrushes, labels for dating and rotation procedures, disposable towels, gloves, first-aid kits, germicidal hand soaps, employee bathrooms and lockers, scrub brushes, uniforms, hairnets, thermometers, test kits, and quality, color-coded utensils.

Beverage and food service establishments may harbor all types of bacteria, bugs, and animal pests. Any environment that provides food, water, and warmth for an extended time, will become host to these intruders. In order to eliminate contamination, all that is necessary is to make the living conditions unfavorable for these unwanted intruders.

What Is HACCP?

Hazard Analysis of Critical Control Points (HACCP) is a system for monitoring the food service process to reduce the risk of food-borne illness. HACCP focuses on how food flows through the process — from purchasing to serving. At each step in the food-preparation process, there are a variety of potential hazards. HACCP provides managers with a framework for implementing control procedures for each hazard. It does this through identifying critical control points (CCPs). These are points in the process where bacteria or other harmful organisms may grow or food may become contaminated.

Why Use HACCP in Your Facility?

As a beverage and food service manager, you are responsible for protecting your customers by serving safe and wholesome beverages and food. To accomplish this, you have to educate your employees and motivate them to put into practice at every step what they have learned about beverage and food safety. To do this, you need a systematic process for identifying potential hazards, for putting safety procedures in place and for monitoring the success of your safety system on an ongoing basis.

HACCP is based on this principle: If the raw ingredients are safe, and the process is safe, then the finished product is safe. Implementing HACCP involves seven key steps. As you proceed through these steps, you will:

1. Assess the hazards at each stage of the preparation process

2. Identify "critical control points" in the process where hazards can be controlled or prevented

3. Establish "critical limits" using standards that are observable and measurable

4. Monitor the "critical control points" using flow-charts to follow potentially hazardous products through the preparation process

5. Take corrective action as needed

6. Develop a recordkeeping system to document the HACCP process

7. Verify your system's effectiveness and monitor your results

Verifying your system's effectiveness involves examining your records to ensure that employees are entering actual, valid data. Additionally, an inspection by the Board of Health can provide a good assessment of whether your process is working.

HACCP's Eight Key Steps for the Beverage and Food Service Process

There are multiple hazards at, and specific preventative measures for, each of the following eight key HACCP steps.

HACCP Step 1: Purchasing

The goal of purchasing is to obtain wholesome, safe, perishable raw materials to meet your menu requirements. Safety at this step is primarily the responsibility of your vendors. Suppliers must meet federal and state health standards. They should use the HACCP system in their operations and train their employees in sanitation. Let vendors know up front what you expect from them. List your required safety standards in your purchase specification agreements. Ask to see their most recent board of health sanitation reports, and tell them you will be inspecting trucks on a quarterly basis. Good vendors will cooperate with your inspections and should adjust their delivery schedules to avoid your busy periods so that received items can be received and inspected properly.

HACCP Step 2: Receiving

The goals of receiving are: 1) to make sure products are fresh and safe when they enter your facility, and 2) to transfer the items to proper storage as quickly as possible.

HACCP Step 3: Storing

In general, there are four possible ways to store perishable items: 1) in dry storage, for longer holding of less perishable items; 2) in refrigeration, for short-term storage of perishable items; 3) in specially designed deep-chilling units for short periods; and 4) in a freezer, for longer-term storage of perishable foods. Each type of storage has its own sanitation and safety requirements.

HACCP Step 4: Preparing

Freezing perishable items keeps most bacteria from multiplying, but it does not kill them. Bacteria present when the food item is removed from the freezer may multiply rapidly if thawed at room temperature. Beware of cross-contamination. Never thaw foods on a counter or in any other non-refrigerated area.

HACCP Step 5: Beverage Brewing and Food Cooking

All items must be accurately weighed, measured, and then processed at the correct temperatures. Monitor the accuracy of heating equipment with each use by using thermometers.

HACCP Step 6: Serving and Holding

Food that has been cooked is not necessarily safe. In fact, many outbreaks occur because improper procedures were used following cooking. Although it may be tempting to hold food at temperatures just hot enough to serve, it is essential to keep prepared foods in hot-holding equipment above 140°F, and cold foods in a refrigeration unit or surrounded by ice below 40°F.

HACCP Step 7: Cooling

Here, as at other critical points, every move you make can mean the difference between the safe and the unsafe. It is often necessary to prepare foods in advance or use leftover foods. Unfortunately, this can easily lead to problems unless proper precautions are taken. In fact, problems at this stage are the number one cause of food-borne illness. The two key precautions for preventing food-borne illness at this point in the process are rapid cooling and protection from contamination.

HACCP Step 8: Reheating

In reheating and serving leftovers, just as in all phases of the beverage- and food-preparation processes, you must be careful to avoid contamination.

Some key points:

- Always wash hands with soap and warm water for at least 20 seconds before serving customers.

- Use cleaned and sanitized long-handled ladles and spoons so bare hands do not touch food.

- Never touch the parts of glasses, cups, plates, or tableware that will come into contact with food.

- Never touch the parts of dishes that will come into contact with the customer's mouth.

- Wear gloves if serving items by hand.

- Cover cuts or infections with bandages, and if on hands, cover with gloves.

- Discard gloves whenever they touch an unsanitary surface.
- Use tongs or wear gloves to dispense muffins, rolls, sandwiches, or desserts.
- Clean and sanitize equipment and utensils thoroughly after each use.
- Use lids and sneeze guards to protect prepared food from contamination.

Sanitary Self-Service

Like workers, customers also can act as a source of contamination. Unlike workers, customers — especially children — are generally not educated about food sanitation and may do the following unsanitary things: using the same plate twice; touching food with their hands; touching the edges of serving dishes; sneezing or coughing into food; picking up items such as muffins, pastries, rolls, etc., with their fingers; consuming beverages or eating while in line; dipping their fingers into foods or drinks to taste them; returning food items to avoid waste; and putting their heads under sneeze guards to reach items in the back.

Be sure to observe customer behavior; remove any beverages or foods that may have been contaminated. Also, as a precautionary measure, serve sealed packages of crackers, breadsticks and condiments, and prewrap, date, and label sandwiches, if possible.

A First-Rate Facility

Safe and sanitary beverage and food service begins with a facility that is clean and in good repair. The entire facility, work areas as well as equipment, should be designed for easy cleaning and maintenance. It is important to eliminate hard-to-clean work areas, as well as faulty or overloaded refrigerators or other equipment. Also, eliminate dirty surroundings and any conditions that will attract pests. Remember, the easier the workplace is to clean, the more likely it will stay clean.

The Difference Between Clean and Sanitary

Heat or chemicals can be used to reduce the number of bacteria to acceptable levels. They also can be used for certain other harmful microorganisms.

Heat sanitizing involves exposing equipment to high heat for an adequate length of time. This may be done manually by immersing equipment in water maintained at a temperature of 170°–195°F for at least 30 seconds or in a dishwashing machine that washes at 150°F and rinses at 180°F. For either method, it is important to check water temperature frequently. Thermometers and heat-sensitive tapes and labels are available for determining whether adequate sanitation temperatures have been achieved. To sanitize an object with chemicals, immerse it in or wipe it down with bleach or sanitizing solution.

For bleaching, 1 tablespoon of 5 percent bleach per gallon of water. For using commercial products, follow the manufacturers' instructions. The EPA regulates chemical sanitizers, and manufacturers must follow strict labeling requirements regarding what concentrations to use, data on minimum effectiveness, and warnings of possible health hazards. Chemical test strips are available for testing the strength of the sanitizing solution. Because sanitizing agents become less effective as they kill bacteria and are exposed to air, it is important to test the sanitizing solution frequently.

Sanitizing Portable Equipment

To clean and sanitize portable equipment properly, you must have a sink with three separate compartments: for cleaning, rinsing, and sanitizing. There should be a separate area for scraping and rinsing food and debris into a garbage container or disposer before washing, and separate drain boards for clean and soiled items.

Sanitizing In-Place Equipment

Larger and immobile equipment also should be washed, rinsed, and sanitized, taking care to unplug all electrically powered equipment first.

Floors, Walls, and Ceilings

Floors, walls, and ceilings should be free of dirt, litter, and moisture. Clean walls regularly by swabbing with a cleaning solution or by spraying with a pressure nozzle. Sweep floors, then clean them using a spray method or by mopping. Swab ceilings, instead of spraying them, to avoid soaking lights and ceiling fans. And do not forget corners and hard-to-reach places.

Ventilation

Good ventilation is a critical factor in maintaining a clean beverage and food service environment. Ventilation removes steam, smoke, grease, and heat from the prep areas and equipment. This helps maintain indoor air quality and eliminate condensation and airborne contaminants.

Storerooms

Like all areas of the facility, storerooms must be kept clean and litter-free. To accomplish this, be sure to sweep and scrub walls, ceilings, floors, shelves, light fixtures, and racks on a routine basis. Check all storage areas frequently — this includes your refrigerator and freezer as well as your dry-storage room. To avoid chemical contamination, store cleaning supplies and chemicals in a separate area away from the prep areas.

Restrooms

Restrooms should be convenient, sanitary, and adequately stocked with the following: toilet paper, liquid soap, disposable paper towels and/or air blowers, and covered trash receptacles (the trash receptacle lid should open with a foot pedal). Scrub restrooms daily and keep the doors closed. You also may want to provide brushes to wash fingernails and sanitizing solution for soaking the brushes.

Bacteria

Most bacteria are microscopic and of no harm to people. Many forms of bacteria are actually beneficial, aiding in the production of such things as cheese, bread, butter, alcoholic beverages, etc. Only a small percentage of bacteria will cause food to spoil and can generate a form of food poisoning when consumed. Bacteria need food, water, and warmth in order to survive. Their growth rate depends upon how favorable these conditions are. Bacteria will grow most rapidly when the temperature is between 85°F and 100°F. In most cases, the growth rate will slow down drastically if the temperature is hotter or colder than this. Thus, it is vitally important that perishable food items are refrigerated before bacteria have a chance to establish themselves and multiply.

The greatest problem in controlling bacteria is their rapid reproduction cycle. Approximately every 15 minutes, the bacteria count will double under optimal living conditions. An important consideration when handling food products is that bacteria need several hours to adjust to a new environment before they are able to begin multiplying rapidly. Thus, if you had removed a perishable product from the walk-in refrigerator and had inadvertently introduced bacteria to it, advanced growth would not begin for several hours.

Bacterial forms do not have a means of transportation; they must be introduced to an area by some other vehicle. People are primarily responsible for transporting bacteria to new areas. The body temperature of 98.6°F is perfect for bacterial existence and proliferation. A person coughing, sneezing, or wiping their hands on a counter can introduce bacteria to an area. Air, water, insects, and articles onto which they have attached themselves, such as boxes, blades, knives, and cutting boards, may transmit bacteria.

Dangerous Forms of Bacteria

The following section describes a number of harmful bacteria that may be found in a beverage or food service operation:

Clostridium Perfringens

One of a group of bacterial infectious diseases that will cause a poisoning effect. These bacteria are extremely dangerous because they are tasteless, odorless, and colorless and, therefore, nearly impossible to detect. In order to survive, the bacterium will form a spore and surround itself. Clostridium Perfringens typically thrive within a temperature range of 65°–120°F, but may survive through long periods of extreme temperature and then multiply when the conditions are more favorable. Keeping cooked food consistently above 148°F or below 40°F eliminates Clostridium Perfringens bacteria.

Clostridium Botulism

Botulism is a rare infectious disease, but it is far more lethal than the other types. Botulism exists only in an air-free environment like that of canned goods; however, several national food packers have reported outbreaks in their operations. Examine all canned goods closely before using. Look for dented, leaking cans, and swollen cans or jar tops.

Staphylococci Poisoning

Staphylococci bacteria (staph) are perhaps the most common cause of food poisoning. Staph bacteria can be found everywhere, particularly in the human nose. The bacteria by themselves are harmless. The problem arises when they are left uncontrolled to grow in food items. Food that has been left out, unrefrigerated, for just a few hours can produce the poisonous toxins of staph bacteria. To prevent staph poisoning, follow refrigeration procedures precisely. Only remove the refrigerated food items that you will be using right away.

Salmonella Infection

Salmonella bacteria are found in some packaged foods, including eggs, poultry, seafood, and meat. Thorough cooking and following refrigeration procedures is essential in order to protect against salmonella.

Controlling Bacteria

The first step in controlling bacteria is to limit their access to your coffee, espresso, and tea shop. Make certain that all products entering the shop are clean. Keep all perishable food products stored and refrigerated as prescribed. Clean up any spills as you go along, making the environment unsuitable for bacteria to live.

Routinely remind employees that one of the most common causes of food-borne illness is cross-contamination: the transfer of bacteria from food to food, hand to food or equipment to food. Coverings, such as plastic wrap and holding and serving containers, also can harbor bacteria that can spread to food. A can opener, a plastic-wrap box or a food slicer can also become a source of cross-contamination if not properly sanitized between uses.

Personal hygiene is the best way to stop bacteria from contaminating and spreading into new areas. Hands are the greatest source of contamination. Hands must be washed constantly throughout the day. Every time people scratch their heads or sneeze, they are exposing their hands to bacteria and will spread it to anything they touch, such as food, equipment, and clothes. Hand and nail brushes, antibacterial soaps, and disposable gloves should be provided, even if not required by law. Proper training and management follow-up is also critical.

An employee who has the symptoms of the common cold or any open cuts or infections should not go to work. By simply breathing, he or she may be inadvertently exposing the environment to bacteria. Every employee must practice good basic hygiene:

- Short hair, and/or hair contained in a net
- Clean shaven, or facial hair contained in a net
- Clean clothes/uniforms
- Clean hands and short nails
- No unnecessary jewelry
- A daily shower or bath
- No smoking in or near prep areas
- Hand washing before starting work, periodically, and after handling any foreign object: head, face, ears, money, food, boxes, or trash.

Are Your Hands Really Clean?

Hand washing is perhaps the most critical aspect of good personal hygiene in retail beverage and food service. Workers should wash their hands with soap and warm water for 20 seconds. When working with food, they should wash gloved hands as often as bare hands. Hand washing is such a simple, yet very effective method for eliminating cross-contamination. Try the following exercise:

First, you will need a fluorescent substance and a black light. (One possible source for these is the Glo Germ™ Training Kit. Visit **glogerm.com** for more information. Using these materials, you can show trainees the "invisible dirt" that may be hiding on their hands:

- Have employees dip their hands in the fluorescent substance.
- Tell employees to wash their hands.
- Have employees hold their hands under the black light to see how much "dirt" is still there.
- Explain proper hand-washing technique.
- Have employees wash their hands again, this time using the proper hand-washing technique.
- Have employees once again hold their hands under the black light.

AIDS

AIDS is not an airborne, waterborne, or food-borne disease; it cannot be transmitted through air, water, or food. The only medically documented manner in which HIV, the virus that causes AIDS, can be contracted is by sexual contact, shared needles (usually associated with drug addiction), infusion of contaminated blood, or through the placenta from mother to fetus.

- You cannot contract AIDS through casual, social contact.
- You cannot contract AIDS by touching people.
- You cannot contract AIDS through shared bathroom facilities.
- You cannot contract AIDS by breathing air in which people have sneezed or coughed.
- You cannot contract AIDS by sharing food, beverages, or eating utensils.

This means that, with regard to AIDS, beverage, and food service operations are safe places to work, eat, and drink.

Bugs, Insects, and Animal Pests

Bug and insect infestation in a retail beverage and food operation is the result of poor sanitation practices. Aside from being a nuisance, they are a threat to food safety. Flies, cockroaches, and other insects all carry bacteria and many, because of where they get their food, carry disease. Bugs, insects, and animals require the same three basic necessities of life as bacteria do: food, water, and warmth. When healthful, thriving bugs and insects are visible, this indicates that proper sanitation procedures have not been carried out. Eliminate the environment that these pests need to live, and you will be eliminating their existence. Combining proper sanitation practices with periodic extermination spraying will stop any problems before they start.

To prevent the spread of flies in your establishment, keep doors, windows, and screens closed at all times. Ensure that garbage is sealed in airtight containers and is picked up regularly. All trash must be cleaned off the ground: flies can deposit their eggs on the thinnest scrap of food. Dumpsters must be steam cleaned and deodorized periodically. They never should contain any decaying food scraps.

All doorjambs and building cracks, even the thinnest ones, must be sealed. Be cautious when receiving deliveries. Bugs may be in the boxes or crates. The greatest protection against cockroaches is your exterminator. Chemicals sprayed in the shop must be of the non-residual type. These are safe and approved for use in beverage and food service establishments. Rodents are prolific breeders, producing as many as 50 offspring in a lifespan of one year. They tend to hide during the day, but they can be discovered by their telltale signs: droppings, holes, nesting materials, gnawing, and tracks on dusty surfaces.

Animal pests, such as rats and mice, may be very serious problems for any retail beverage or food operator. These rodents can eat through a cement wall to gain access to your building. Rats will eat any sort of garbage or decaying food available and are infested with bacteria and, often, disease. They have been known to bite people, as have their fleas, which also spread their bacteria and disease. Once they have become settled in an area, they are very difficult to eliminate. Ensure that your building's foundation is airtight. Keep all food products at least six inches off the floor; this enables the exterminator to get under the shelving to spray. Rat bait, a poisoning capsule resembling food, is particularly effective when spread around the building and dumpsters. As with any poison or chemical you use, make certain that it is labeled clearly and stored away from food-storage areas.

Safety in the Beverage and Food Preparation Areas

By its nature, the beverage and food service environment is full of potential hazards to employees' safety. Brewing equipment, grinders, knives, slicers, glass, hot surfaces, and wet or greasy floors are only a few of the hazards workers may face every day. Fortunately, most accidents also involve human error and, therefore, can be prevented.

Heat and Burns

Burns can result from contact with brewing and steaming equipment, water boilers, hot surfaces, such as grills, and other types of heating equipment. Burns, in particular can be caused by escaping steam encountered during the preparation or serving of hot drinks.

Cuts

It is not just knives that can cause trouble. Workers can hurt themselves or their coworkers with the sharp edges of equipment and supplies or with broken glass. Nails and staples used in food packaging also can be dangerous. To prevent cuts, take the following precautions. Use a pusher to feed coffee beans into a grinder; use appropriate tools (not bare hands) to pick up and dispose of broken glass; immediately place broken glass into a separate, clearly marked garbage container; take care when cutting rolls of kitchen wrap with the cutter; be careful with can openers and the edges of open cans; never use a knife to open cans or to pry items loose; turn off and unplug grinders and when removing the contents and for cleaning purposes; use guards on grinders and slicers; replace equipment blades as soon as they are cleaned; and be aware that left-handed people need to take extra care when working with equipment designed for right-handed operators.

Electrical Shock

Because of the variety of electrical equipment used in your shop, electrical shock is a common concern. To prevent electrical shock:

- Properly ground all electrical equipment.

- Ensure that employees can reach switches without touching or leaning against metal tables or counters.

- Replace all worn or frayed electrical cords.

- Use electrical equipment only when hands are dry.

- Unplug equipment before cleaning.

- Locate electrical switches and breakers to permit rapid shutdown in the event of an emergency.

Strains

Carrying equipment or any other items that are too heavy can result in strains to the arms, legs or back. To prevent strains:

- Store heavy items on lower shelves.

- Use dollies or carts when moving objects that are too heavy to carry.

- To move objects from one area to another, use carts with firm shelves and properly operating wheels or casters.

- Do not carry too many objects at one time; instead, use a cart.

- Do not try to lift large or heavy objects by yourself.

- Use proper lifting techniques. Remember to bend from your knees, not your back.

Slipping and Falling

Anyone who slips and falls onto the floor can be badly hurt. Be sure your facility does not have hazards that put workers at risk. To prevent slips and falls:

- Clean up wet spots and spills immediately.

- Let people know when floors are wet; use signs that signal caution and prominently display them.

- Wear shoes that have nonslip soles.

- Do not stack boxes or other objects too high; they can fall and cause people to trip.

- Keep items, such as boxes, ladders, step stools, and carts, out of the paths of foot traffic.

Fires

Fire extinguishers should be available in all areas where fires are likely. But be careful — do not keep extinguishers so close to the equipment that they will be inaccessible in the event of a fire. All employees should be trained in avoiding fires as well as in the use of fire extinguishers and in evacuation procedures. Remember; always call the fire department first, before using a fire extinguisher.

Choking

Anyone can choke on food if they are not careful. That is why an important part of food service safety is being alert to your customers. Here is what to look for, and what to do:

- If a person has both hands to the throat and cannot speak or cough, it is likely he or she is choking.

- If this person can talk, cough, or breathe, do not pat him or her on the back or interfere in any way.

- If this person cannot talk, cough, or breathe, you will need to take action; use the Heimlich maneuver, and call for help immediately.

- All food service employees should be trained in the use of the Heimlich Maneuver and posters with instructions on how to perform it should be posted near the employee dining area.

Exposure to Hazardous Chemicals

Improper exposure to cleaning agents, chemical pesticides, and chemical sanitizers may cause injury to the skin or poisoning. To protect workers from exposure to hazardous materials, special precautions need to be taken, including certain steps that are required by law.

For example, the U.S. Department of Labor's Occupational Safety and Health Administration (OSHA) requires beverage and food service establishments to keep a current inventory of all hazardous materials.

Manufacturers are required to make sure hazardous chemicals are properly labeled and must supply a Material Safety Data Sheet (MSDS) to be kept on file at the facility. The MSDS provides the chemical name of the product and physical hazards, health hazards, and emergency procedures in case of exposure.

Information about each chemical — including its common name, when it is used, who is authorized to use it, and information from the MSDS — also must be provided to workers. To prevent improper exposure to hazardous materials, make sure:

- Only properly trained workers handle hazardous chemicals

- Employees have safety equipment to use when working with hazardous chemicals

- Employees wear nonporous gloves and eye goggles when working with sanitizing agents and other cleaners

Improper handling of food products or neglecting sanitation and safety procedures certainly will lead to health problems and/or personal injury. A successful beverage and food service operation must develop a reputation for serving quality products in a safe environment. Should there ever be a question in your customers' minds as to the wholesomeness or quality of a product, your shop would quickly lose its hard-earned reputation.

Sanitation Information Resources

There are many food safety information resources on the Web. Log on to the following sites for more information.

- The USDA has training materials available on their website (as well as HACCP materials) at **http://fsrio.nal.usda.gov/nal_web/fsrio/fseddb/fseddbsearch.php**.

- The Food Safety and Inspection Service of the U.S. Department of Agriculture, at **www.fsis.usda.gov/Food_Safety_Education/index.asp**, has information and training resources.

- The American Food Safety's website, **www.americanfoodsafety.com**, offers courses in food safety and Food Protection Manager Certification.

- The National Restaurant Association's Educational Foundation at **www.nraef.org** offers ServSafe certification.

- Food Safety First, **www.foodsafetyfirst.org** offers videos to use for training.

Other sites include:

- Gateway to U.S. Government Food Safety Information — **www.foodsafety.gov**

- Bad Bug Book — **www.fda.gov/Food/FoodSafety/FoodborneIllness**

- Safety Alerts — **www.fda.gov/safety/recalls**

- Safe Food Consumer — **www.safe-food.org**

- Food Safe Program — **http://foodsafe.ucdavis.edu**

- International Food Information Council Foundation — **www.foodinsight.org**

Etc.

September 29 is National Coffee Day. September is National Food Safety Month.

11

Computers and Your Beverage and Food Service Operation

This chapter will introduce you to the value of computer systems and information management to the beverage and food service industry. It will also explore the emerging e-business opportunities available to the hospitality industries through the Internet and other new technologies.

Computer Systems for the Beverage and Food Service Industry

Computers are here and integrated into every facet of the food service industry. The main use of computers in the beverage and food service industry can be summarized as a key system that will help operations, track sales and purchases, keep track of inventory, compare prices, maintain ledger and payroll, develop menus, and minimize wastage.

According to a study commissioned by 13 United States and Canadian beverage and food-related associations, the implementation of an efficient computer-based food service response program could trim an estimated $14.3 billion in costs annually from the food service industry in the two countries alone.

A computerized system creates a paperless beverage and food preparation area, linking buyers to distributors via the Internet. Beverage and food supplies are ordered online and paid for by electronic transfer. Participating vendors tag goods with bar codes that are read by laser scanner. At the beverage and food service operation, information is stored immediately in an in-house computer, and the computer's inventory database is instantly updated.

Benefits accrue across the board: precise inventory management, timely deliveries, reduced warehouse levels, and increased work space.

Front-of-the-House Computer Systems

Point-of-Sale Systems

The most widely used technology in the beverage and food service industry is the touch-screen, or point-of-sale (POS) system. The POS system is an offshoot of the electronic cash register. Touch-screen POS systems were introduced to the beverage and food service industry in the mid-1980s and have penetrated around 90 percent of the hospitality industry nationwide. From fine dining establishments to fast food, the touch screen is effortless. In fact, a child could be trained to use it in a few minutes. Such systems will pay for themselves.

Understanding the numbers collected by a POS system will give the operator more control over inventory, labor scheduling, overtime, customer traffic, and service. Understanding the POS system ultimately clarifies the bottom line, knocking guesswork out of the equation.

A POS system comprises two parts: the hardware (or equipment) and the software (the computer program that runs the system). This system allows waitstaff to key in their orders as soon as the customers give them. Additional keys are available for particular options and specifications, such as "Solo," "Americano" and "Ristretto." (See section on standard Espresso Recipes, Chapter 6: Choosing the Best Equipment, Coffees, Teas, and Food Products). Some systems prompt the waitstaff to ask additional questions when the item is ordered, such as, "Would you like extra cream topping or chocolate shavings with the espresso?" Some will even suggest a side dish or dessert.

The order is sent through a cable to printers located throughout the establishment, including the office. All orders must be printed before they are prepared, thus ensuring good control. When a server has completed the ordering, a guest check can be printed, and later presented. Most POS systems allow certain discounts and require manager control over others. Credit cards, cash, and checks can be processed separately, and then reports can be generated by payment type.

Some benefits of using a POS system:

- Increases sales and accounting information
- Custom tracking
- Reports waitstaff's sales and performance
- Reports menu item performance
- Reports inventory usage
- Processes credit card purchases
- Accurate addition on guest checks
- Prevents incorrect items from being ordered
- Prevents confusion in the prep area
- Reports possible theft of money and inventory
- Records employee timekeeping
- Reports menu-sales breakdown for preparation and menu forecasting
- Reduces time spent walking from work area to serving area

As the labor market continues to diminish, touch screens with POS systems will become even more necessary. During peak seasonal periods, ordering beverages and food may be like pumping your own gas; customers will key in their own selections, and then slide their credit cards through to pay.

Many POS systems have been enhanced to include comprehensive home delivery, frequent guest modules, and fully integrated systems with real-time inventory, integrated caller ID, accounting, labor scheduling, payroll, menu analysis, purchasing and receiving, cash management, and reports. Up-and-coming enhancements and add-ons include improved functionality across the Internet, centralized functionality enabling "alerts" to be issued to managers and voice-recognition POS technology.

Stand-Alone Software Applications

While there are literally dozens of software packages available to assist the restaurant manager, this discussion will concentrate on what we consider to be the current market leaders. It will provide some insight as to how they work, what they can do for your coffee, espresso, and tea shop, and what benefits you will realize if you include them in your operation-management practices. These systems are what we refer to as "stand-alone," as they are not part of a POS system:

ChefTec

ChefTec (**www.cheftec.com**) is an integrated software program with recipe and menu costing, nutritional, and inventory-control analysis:

- **Recipe and menu costing.** Store, scale, and size an unlimited number of recipes. Write recipe procedures with beverage and culinary spell-checker. Instantly analyze recipe and menu costs by portion or yield. Update prices and change ingredients in every recipe with the touch of a button. Cost out bids for catering functions. Attach photos, diagrams, and videos to bids, or add pictures of plate layout to recipes for consistency.

- **Nutritional analysis.** Preloaded with USDA information. Add your own items. Calculate nutritional value for recipes and menus. Provide accurate, legal information on "low fat," "decaffeinated," etc. Print out "nutrition facts" labels. Allows you to add your own specialty items. Calculate nutritional values for your recipes and menu items. See at a glance which menu items are low fat, low calorie, etc.

- **Inventory control.** Preloaded inventory list of 1,900 commonly used ingredients with unlimited capacity for adding additional ingredients. Import purchases from online vendors' ordering systems. Track fluctuating food costs. Compare vendor pricing. See impact of price increases on recipes. Automate ordering with par values. Use handheld devices for inventory. Generate custom reports. Track rising product costs automatically. Compare vendor pricing at the touch of a button, from purchases or bids. Enter invoices quickly using the "auto-populate" feature. Generate customized reports on purchases, price variances, bids, and credits. Lists ingredients in different languages, including Spanish, French, and German.

NutraCoster

NutraCoster (**www.sweetware.com**) calculates the product cost (including labor, packaging, and overhead) and nutritional content for any size batch of food. Include unlimited number of ingredients and process stats. Print camera-ready "nutrition facts" labels that comply with the requirements of the Nutrition Labeling and Education Act (NLEA). The "overhead calculator" allows you to factor overhead costs into your item cost. No more "rules of thumb" or "fudge factors." Nutritional analysis now accounts for nutrient changes during processing, such as water gained during boiling or brewing or other changes in nutritional value. Print multiple "nutrition facts" labels per page. Include ingredient listings with nutrition facts. Supports unlimited simultaneous users.

NutraCoster also offers additional libraries with nutritional information for specific brand-name ingredients.

MenuPro

MenuPro (**www.softcafe.com**) allows you quickly to create your own professional menus at a fraction of the cost of printshop menus. Whether you need "daily specials" or an elaborate dining room menu, MenuPro gives you quick, top-quality designs and artwork without the expense or hassle of using a graphic artist or desktop publisher.

Employee Schedule Partner

Employee Schedule Partner (**www.espsoftware.com**) is a complete software package for employee scheduling. Point-and-click: Make a schedule without touching the keyboard. Click a button and the software will fill your schedule with employees automatically. Click a button to replace absent employees and a list of available employees with phone numbers will appear. The online coach will give helpful hints to new users. Accommodates an unlimited number of employees and positions. You can manually override selections at any time and track employees' availability restrictions. Schedule employees to work multiple shifts per day. Track payroll and hourly schedule totals for easy budget management. Schedules can begin on any day of the week. Track stations as well as positions. Specify maximum hours per day, days per week, and shifts per day for each employee. Lock any employee into a scheduled shift so the program will not move them when juggling the schedule. Save old schedules for reference when needed. The software is even password-protected to prevent unauthorized use.

Employee Time Clock Partner

Our hands-down favorite time clock software is Employee Time Clock Partner. This is a complete employee time clock software package. It is very powerful, yet simple to use. Automatically clock in and out (just enter your employee number and you are clocked in or out). Employees can view their time cards to verify information. Password-protected so only management may edit time card information. Even calculates overtime, both daily and weekly. Management can assign Employee ID number or PIN (personal identification number).

QuickBooks

Our favorite accounting package, without a doubt, is QuickBooks by Intuit. The QuickBooks's 2013 Premiere version is rich in features including the QuickBooks Inventory Center, which allows you to access inventory items from one place. QuickBooks is available at **www.quickbooks.com**. Another popular account package is Sage 50 (formerly Sage Peachtree) (**http://na.sage.com**).

Desktop Publishing Applications and Ideas

There are hundreds of reasons to own and use a computer in your work as a beverage and food service manager. The computer, if used effectively, will save you an enormous amount of time and money.

Here are just a few ideas for desktop publishing: print your own customer and/or employee newsletters, table tents, menus, business cards, employee-of-the-month certificates, customer gift certificates, advertising posters, employee manuals, beverage lists, special menus, and office stationery.

Here is a list of the most popular desktop publishing software programs for the PC. You can find out more about these programs at **http://desktoppub.about.com/cs/win/index.htm**.

- Adobe InDesign
- Greenstreet Publisher
- Microsoft Publisher
- QuarkXPress
- Ragtime Solo

Ragtime Solo and Greenstreet are good options for a small-business owner because these programs cost less than some of the others.

What Is the Future of Computers in Beverage and Food Service?

The beverage and food service operation of the future will most likely resemble what it does today — with integrated software and hardware solutions to increase productivity, eliminate waste, and increase profits.

The POS computer that will allow operators to monitor inventory and costs more closely, website reservations, marketing and e-commerce will increase the return on investment in a Web presence, bringing in more guests than ever imaginable. Customers may enter their own menu selections into laptop POS systems right from their tables. Patrons will be able to pull up a screen showing all menu items, then select dishes with a push of a button. Consumers also will be able to customize beverage and food recipes, thus creating a paperless operation.

Effective Use of Email

Careful consideration should be given to your choice of domain names and email addresses, as these represent your company. Purchasing a domain name that directly represents your coffee, espresso, and tea shop is an outstanding opportunity to gain the use of the corresponding email addresses. Seek out a domain name that clearly states to the casual observer that any email sent to this address will be directed to the manager. We will discuss websites and why a website is critical to every beverage and food operation later in this chapter.

Why Use Email?

There are several reasons, including:

- **Convenience.** One advantage of using email is that you send your message when it is convenient for you, even if it is four o'clock in the morning. Your recipient responds at his or her convenience as well.

- **Cost.** No more toll telephone calls. No more "telephone tag." You can send dozens of emails throughout the world simultaneously; they will be delivered in mere seconds, and it costs nothing. Communicate with all your purveyors or employees with one written message, free.

- **Keeping everyone "in the loop."** Email can be sent to many people at the same time.

To receive e-mail, you must have an address (sales@atlantic-pub.com, for example). Additionally, we highly recommend utilizing a virus-scanning program for all incoming and outgoing email.

Do I Need a Website?

In a word, "YES"! If your coffee, espresso, and tea shop already has a website, you are already reaping the benefits of being online. Each day, the Internet reaches millions of people who use it for work, play and research. The Web is the best marketing tool in the world; it allows your establishment to be visible anywhere in the world. New services, such as digital cities, online city guides, and other beverage and food service sites, will increase your website and shop's visibility to levels unheard of. The Internet is a powerful tool that should be put to work for your business.

Do you need a website? Use the checklist of potential advantages below and see for yourself. Place a check mark next to each benefit that would serve your business:

- ❏ Reduce costs of goods sold through reduced personnel
- ❏ Additional global sales and marketing tool
- ❏ Gather marketing information
- ❏ Analyze and evaluate marketing information
- ❏ Generate additional sales
- ❏ Lower your phone expenses

- ❏ Improve communication
- ❏ Establish more frequent communications with customers
- ❏ Establish more meaningful communications with customers
- ❏ Reduce fax costs
- ❏ Reduce courier costs
- ❏ Deliver electronically encoded resources around the world
- ❏ Supplement employee training through electronic updates and bulletins
- ❏ Broadcast press releases
- ❏ Communicate to people who are not available right now
- ❏ Submit invoices and expenses more quickly
- ❏ Reduce international communications costs and improve response time
- ❏ Ease of collaboration with colleagues
- ❏ Establish contact with potential "strategic partners" worldwide
- ❏ Identify and solicit prospective employees
- ❏ Provide immediate access to your menu
- ❏ Permit customers to place orders electronically
- ❏ Reduce costs of goods sold through reduced personnel

Websites are promoted in the mass media, on commercials, on billboards, and in magazines. You even hear them on the radio. The Web is the most economical way to communicate with a worldwide audience. Can you think of any other tool that lets you advertise or sell products to a worldwide market, 24 hours a day, for a minimal monetary investment? Technology provides incredible ways to convey information about your business, products, and services. The possibilities for visual marketing are endless — the return on investment, enormous.

What to Put on Your Website

Consider using a professional website designer. He or she can help you take your establishment rapidly from no Web presence to a lively, active website. What kind of information could your coffee, espresso, and tea shop put on the Web? Here is a brief list of a information that you could add to your website:

- **Photos.** A picture is truly worth a thousand words. Carefully select high-quality images and photos to "sell" the beauty of your establishment.

- **News, events, and specials.** The opportunities are endless. Consider developing a Web-based distribution list from your long list of loyal customers, and use email to promote your monthly and weekly events.

- **Menus.** These are not just basic menus, but menus with full color photographs!

- **Directions.** Introduce a link to **Mapquest.com** or **Google Maps (maps.google.com)** on your site. Customers can enter their address and get door-to-door directions from their home to your coffee, espresso, and tea shop.

- **Products for sale.** You could operate an online store that sells unique products from your establishment. For a minimal investment, you gain access to many more potential customers who visit the store "virtually" through the Internet.

- **History.** Every establishment has a history. Sometimes a history is truly unique — a story worth telling. Your website can do this for you.

- **Area attractions.** Sell your coffee, espresso, and tea shop and your local community to the website visitor.

The opportunities are endless. Be imaginative!

How Do You Get an Effective Website?

The choice is entirely yours. There are thousands of Web development companies. Consider companies specializing in the beverage and food service industry. We recommend Gizmo Graphics Web Design of Land O' Lakes, Florida (www.gizWebs.com). They have put together a solid, high-quality, low-cost package that offers a comprehensive cradle-to-grave cost approach, which includes all annual hosting fees, domain registrations, and annual support.

Some other popular Web development companies include:

Wix (**www.Wix.com**): Free Flash website creation. Can choose pro Wix designers to make your site. Flash photo galleries and professional designs available

Web (**www.web.com**): Provides site design, search engine optimization, and website hosting. Enables users to attract customers and sell products online

Homestead (**www.homestead.com**): Choose your design, customize, and publish your own site. $4.99/month after a 30-day free trial

Some words of caution:

- Do not overlook the little details.

- A website can be a significant investment, but it is critical that you hire a professional if you want professional results.

- Keep in mind the "hidden costs." Many developers do not include website hosting, domain name registration and renewal, support, and continued development services after site completion.

- Make sure you promote your site. A site is worthless if no one knows it exists. Search engine registration is a critical part of a successful website.

A website is an investment, not an expense. In the current marketplace, if you do not have a Web presence, you are missing the boat! The Internet is the wave of the future; jump aboard now and ride the potential wave of success!

Etc.

Coffee is the second largest traded commodity in the world, oil is the largest. Dorothy Jones of Boston was the first American coffee trader. She was granted a license to sell coffee in 1670. —**www.essentialwonders.com**

12

Successful Employee Recruitment

Depending on the size of your operation, you will need to hire key staff to run your coffee, espresso, and tea shop. It is extremely important to hire the right people. Not only should they have a passion for specialty gourmet coffees and teas, but they also must be reliable and honest individuals who are great team players.

The Labor Problem in the Beverage and Food Service Industry

The food service industry in the United States has nearly the highest employee turnover rate (exceeding 100 percent in one year in many units) and one of the lowest average dollar sales per employee of any industry. The reasons for these statistics are many and varied. However, they can be boiled down to the fact that the industry, in general, has done little in the past 15 years to alleviate its poor working environment. Unfortunately, low pay; few benefits; long hours that include night, weekend, and holiday shifts; hard physical work (mostly while standing); and little interest on management's part in addressing these issues are the rule rather than the exception. Because of the currently low unemployment rate, luring workers into the beverage and food service is not easy, nor is retaining them.

The Beverage and Food Service Labor Employment Predictions

According to a 2012 report by the National Restaurant Association, employment of 12.3 million workers were employed in the beverage and food service industry in the U.S., making it the second largest private sector employer. Growth above the national average is expected to continue in the industry with the largest area of growth is the entry-level food prep and service group, according to the U.S. Department of Labor Statistics. However, food service management jobs rank in the list of the 30 highest projected employment declines. Predictably, these jobs also have among the highest employment turnover.

The turnover of beverage and food service workers is not likely to slow any time soon. "Slower population growth and a decreasing overall labor force participation rate are expected to lead to slower civilian labor force growth from 2010 to 2020," notes a 2012 report by the Bureau of Labor Statistics. "The baby-boom generation moves entirely into the 55-years-and-older age group by 2020, increasing that age group's share of the labor force from 19.5 percent in 2010 to 25.2 percent in 2020. The 'prime-age' working group (ages 25 to 54) is projected to drop to 63.7 percent of the 2020 labor force. The 16- to 24-year-old age group is projected to account for 11.2 percent of the labor force in 2020."

The country's tight labor conditions are forcing beverage and food service companies to seek out new sources of labor including minority groups, welfare recipients, senior citizens, and the physically handicapped. As a result, the workforce is becoming more diverse. In addition, the industry is extending its recruiting efforts beyond traditional methods, such as newspaper ads or signs posted in the shop or restaurant, to high schools, college campuses, retirement communities, state agencies, and the Internet.

Recruiting Sources

So where do you find good employees? Running an advertisement in the local paper is always the first thing that comes to mind, but this may not be your best resource for employees. Consider the following alternatives as well:

- **Promoting from within.** Promoting from within is an excellent source for employees. Not only does this method motivate your current workers, but it also saves you money on training because these people already know a great deal about the establishment and position. It is much easier and cheaper to find bussers and hosts/hostesses from the outside and train them than to recruit and train a new server.

- **Employee referrals.** Ask your employees if they have friends or relatives who are looking for work. Often an employee will not recommend a friend unless they are sure this friend is not going to embarrass them by doing a poor job, so you are likely to get good new employees this way. Offer an incentive to employees for helping you recruit. You could offer an employee a $25 bonus for each referral; if the person works out and stays on for a year, give both the employee and the new hire a cash bonus at the end of that year.

- **Open house.** Hold an open house to find new employees, This strategy is particularly effective if you are looking to fill several positions at once. These take more work than a regular interview, but it may be worth it. Get your managers or other employees to help, and make sure to advertise the open house as well.

- **Off-site recruiting.** Planning on going to a restaurant trade show? It is an excellent place to recruit. Consider using other events for recruitment purposes, such as wine tastings, food festivals, and career fairs.

- **Customers.** Got a regular customer looking for employment? What a great source! You know they already like your store, so they will probably make a good salesperson for it.

- **Industry organizations and websites.** Many industry websites have pages for posting jobs and resumes. These resources are often better places to find skilled labor than blindly posting in a local newspaper. Check out a few of the following sites:
  - National Restaurant Association (**www.restaurant.org**)
  - Nation's Restaurant News (**www.nrn.com**)

- **Area colleges.** Many college students are looking for a source of income and a schedule that can work around their classes. Advertise in the school newspapers to attract these individuals. As many as 1,000 colleges also offer culinary arts or restaurant management programs. Look at the following websites for examples: Texas State Technical College™ at **www.waco.tstc.edu**, and Phoenix College at **www.phoenixcollege.edu**.

- **Culinary schools.** Check out local and national culinary schools. They usually have a spot on their Web pages for people to post resumes. Some examples include the Culinary Institute of America, **www.ciachef.edu**; Sullivan University in Louisville, Kentucky, at **www.sullivan.edu**; and New England Culinary Institute® at **www.neculinary.com**. The National Restaurant Association's website has a listing of culinary/hospitality schools across the country. For more information log on to **www.restaurant.org/careers/education/schools**.

Hiring Employees for Your Coffee, Espresso & Tea Shop

The key to hiring good, competent employees is to put aside personal prejudices and select one applicant over another only because you feel he or she will have a better chance of being successful at the job. What a potential employee is qualified for and capable of doing is often quite different from what he or she actually will do. The purpose of this section is to provide the interviewer with the information necessary to determine if the applicant has the qualities needed.

An Overview of What to Look for in Potential Employees

Following is a list of desirable characters to look for in potential employees:

- **Stability.** You do not want employees to leave in two months; look at past employment records. Stability also refers to the applicant's emotional makeup.

- **People-oriented.** An outgoing personality is also a must for any employee who works in a coffee and tea shop.

- **Achievers and doers.** You do not want individuals who have to be led around by the hand; look at past employment positions and growth rate.

- **Motivation.** Why is the applicant applying to your establishment? Why the specialty coffee and tea industry in general? Is the decision career-related or temporary? Does the applicant appear to receive his or her motivation from within?

- **Independence.** Is the applicant on his or her own? Does he or she appear to be financially secure? At what age did he or she leave home? And for what reasons?

- **Maturity.** Is the individual mentally mature enough to work in a stressful environment? Will he or she be able to relate and communicate with other employees and customers that may be much older?

- **Determination.** Does the applicant seem to always finish what he or she starts? Does he or she seem to look for or retreat from challenges? Examine time at school and at last job.

- **Work habits.** Is the applicant aware of the physical work involved? Has the applicant done similar work? Does he or she appear neat and organized? Look over the application; is it filled out per the instructions? Neatly? In ink? Examine past jobs for number and rate of promotions and raises.

Hiring the Best Barista

In many countries, particularly throughout Europe, the role of barista is considered an honorable profession and a very respectable way to earn a living. In Italy, for instance, the espresso bartender, or barista, is held in high esteem, as the job of creating perfect espresso is viewed as a career that requires considerable training. There are even schools to educate people on how to become "professional" baristas and servers. In the United States for the most part, this is not the case. In many instances, you will be interviewing a student, working parent, or someone else looking for part-time employment or even in-between employment.

With the recent advent of specialty coffee shops in the United States, attitudes are clearly beginning to change. Offering quality, gourmet products is no longer enough; specialty beverages today also need to be served with flair. Savvy coffee shop owners are wise to invest more time and money in hiring and training the right people for the job. They know that the future success of their business depends largely upon whom they hire as baristas and waitstaff. In today's highly competitive market, a highly skilled barista can add more than value to one's business; he or she can determine its future success (or failure).

Consequently, you will need to give serious thought to how you can hire and keep top-notch baristas that can produce the best cup of coffee in town, as well providing outstanding service to your customers. You will have to devise a strategy that makes them want to stay in the job, rather than move on to work for the competition.

Motivate, encourage, offer tangible incentives — whatever it takes to maintain a happy workforce. Part of making sure that your barista and his or her fellow workers want to "stay put" is to provide them with all the necessary tools and equipment that can make their job easier, thus allowing them to take pride in their work.

Specifics of What to Look for When Hiring a Barista

Bear in mind that people often frequent specialty espresso shops as much for the experience of watching the barista prepare the espresso, as for the actual drink itself. Because espresso preparation is such an intensely visual procedure, barista-customer interaction is central to the whole ordering process. Therefore, when interviewing potential baristas, look for a "performer" with personality, as well as a reliable and honest employee. Ask yourself, for example, whether you think they possess the following qualities:

- Do they have a passion for preparing and serving specialty, gourmet, up-market beverages?

- Do they reflect the image which you hope to project?

- Do they have a gregarious, fun personality that will attract repeat customers?

- Do they appear courteous and friendly?

- Do they demonstrate the ability to work well under pressure and present a calm "front" when things may be going wrong?

- Do they possess good physical coordination and manual dexterity?

- Are they detail-oriented, while working at speed?

- Do they show a willingness to learn how to stay ahead of the evolving retail beverage industry?

- Do they show a genuine product knowledge?

- Are they honest, reliable, and good timekeepers?

Specifics to Look for in Servers and Food Preparation Staff

Everyone you decide to employ in your coffee, espresso, and tea shop has an important role to play in the overall success of your business. As with the barista, the waitstaff and food preparation staff must possess that extra "oomph" that can set your shop apart from the competition. Their duties may not, on the surface, appear quite as glamorous or rewarding, but they are nonetheless a vital part of achieving customer satisfaction. You should, therefore, put as much care and attention into hiring the best employees available and subsequently creating a working environment that allows them to take pride in their job. Look for the following characteristics in potential servers and food preparation staff:

- Reliability
- Sense of responsibility
- Willingness to perform mundane, repetitive tasks
- Staying power
- Determination
- Enthusiasm
- Outgoing personality
- Attention to detail
- Willingness to listen

Hiring a Dishwasher

If your coffee, espresso, and tea shop is big enough to warrant a dedicated dishwasher, take care whom you assign to the task. The dishwasher position is, unfortunately, often thought of as an unimportant position that anyone can be trained to perform quickly and cheaply. However, a dishwasher is as important as any other employee. The dishwasher is responsible for supplying spotless, sanitized cups, mugs, and other chinaware to the serving area and clean utensils to the barista and other servers and food prep staff. A slowdown in the dishwashing process will send repercussions throughout the shop. Improperly cleaned china, glassware, or flatware can ruin an otherwise enjoyable experience. The dishwasher handles hundreds of dollars worth of china and glassware every day. Accidentally dropping a tray of specialty coffee cups and saucers can erase a day's profits.

Key Points for Conducting Employment Interviews

- Treat all applicants considerately and show a genuine interest in them, even if they have little or no chance of obtaining the job. Every applicant should be treated as a potential customer, because they are.

- Make certain that you are on time and ready to receive the applicant. Arriving late or changing appointment dates at the last minute will give the applicant the impression that you are unorganized and that the shop is run in the same manner.

- Know the job being offered thoroughly. You cannot possibly match someone's abilities with a job you do not know or understand completely.

- All interviews must be conducted in privacy, preferably in the interviewer's office. Interruptions must be kept to a minimum.

- Make the applicant feel at ease. Have comfortable chairs and possibly beverages available. Speak in a conversational, interested tone.

- Applicants will be full of questions about the job, its duties, the salary, etc. Newspaper advertisements tell only a little about the job and your company, so allow plenty of time for this important discussion.

- Whenever possible, let the applicants speak. You can learn a great deal about them by the way they talk about themselves, past jobs, former supervisors, and school experiences. Watch for contradictions, excuses and, especially, the applicant being on the defensive or speaking in a negative manner. Avoiding subjects is an indication that there was a problem there in the past; be persistent to get the whole story, but do not be overbearing. Come back to it later if necessary.

- Never reveal that you may disapprove of something an applicant has done or said; always appear open-minded. On the other hand, do not condone or approve of anything that is obviously in error.

- Always ask a few questions they do not expect and are not prepared for: What do they do to relax? What are their hobbies? What is the last book they read? Try to understand their attitudes, personalities, and energy levels.

- Perhaps one of the most useful things you can ask when interviewing prospective employees is: What were your favorite parts of your previous job? Look to see if the things they liked to do with previous employers fit with the things you will be asking them to do for you. This is vital; it is important to cross-train employees to do as many jobs as possible, and it helps to know which of those jobs will be a good fit. Often in interviewing prospective food service employees, you will get two types of applicants — those who say they prefer the "people part" of the job (talking to and serving customers) and those who like the "product part" of the job (preparing beverages and food).

- Be sure to ask at least one behavior-based question; this will be very useful in getting at how an applicant responds in real-life work situations and how well he or she is able to handle them. For example: "What would you do if a customer complained that the espresso does not taste right?" or, "What would you do if your seemingly happy patron did not leave any tip at all?"

Unlawful Pre-Employment Questions

This section is not intended to serve on behalf of, or as a substitute for, legal counsel, or even as an interpretation of the various federal and state laws regarding equal and fair employment practices. The purpose of this section is only to act as a guide to the type of questions that may and may not be legally asked of a potential employee.

A thorough discussion of this subject with both the state and federal labor offices and with your lawyer would be in order. Standard employment applications may be purchased at your local office supply store. Before you use these forms, let your lawyer examine one to make certain that it does not contain or insinuate any questions that might be considered illegal.

The Federal Civil Rights Act of 1964 and other state and federal laws ensure that a job applicant will be treated fairly and on an equal basis, regardless of race, color, religious creed, age, sex, or national origin.

In order to support these regulations, you cannot ask applicants certain questions in the aforementioned categories. There is a fine line between what may and may not be asked of applicants. Use basic common sense in regard to the type of questions you ask. Any illegal question would have no bearing on the outcome of the interview anyway, so avoid questions that are related to, or might evoke an answer that infringes upon, the applicant's civil rights.

Consider the following areas of sensitive pre-employment questioning:

- **Age/date of birth.** Age is a sensitive pre-employment question and an area of great concern for any establishments with a liquor license. For more information about the Age Discrimination in Employment Act, visit **www.eeoc.gov/policy/adea.html**. If you need the date of birth for internal reasons, e.g., computations with respect to a pension or profit-sharing plan, this information can be obtained after the person is hired.

- **Drugs, smoking.** It is permissible to ask an applicant if he or she uses drugs or smokes. The question also affords an employer the opportunity to obtain the applicant's agreement to be bound by the employer's drug and smoking policies and to obtain the applicant's agreement to submit to drug testing.

- **Other problem areas.** Questions concerning whether an applicant has friends or relatives working for the employer may be improper if the employer gives a preference to such applicants. Questions concerning credit rating or credit references have been ruled discriminatory against minorities and women. Questions concerning whether an applicant owns a home have been held to be discriminatory against minority members, since a greater number of minority members do not own their own homes. While questions about military experience or training are permissible, questions concerning the type of discharge received by an applicant have been held to be improper, because a high proportion of other-than-honorable discharges are given to minorities. The Americans with Disabilities Act prohibits general inquiries about disabilities, health problems, and medical conditions.

A list of prohibited questions, some of which are obvious but used to illustrate the point:

- How tall are you, anyway?
- What color are your eyes?
- Do you work out at the gym regularly?
- Do you or anyone you know have HIV?
- Did you get any workers' comp from your last employer?
- How old are you, anyway?
- Have you been in prison?

- Are you really a man?
- Do you rent or own your home?
- Have you ever declared bankruptcy?
- What part of the world are your parents from?
- Are you a minority?
- Is English your first language?
- I cannot tell if you are Japanese or Chinese. Which is it?
- So, which church do you go to?
- Who will take care of the kids if you get this job?
- Is this your second marriage, then?
- Just curious: Are you gay?
- Are you in a committed relationship right now?
- How does your boyfriend feel about you working here?

Screening Potential Employees

Screening job applicants will enable you to reject those candidates who are obviously unsuitable before they are referred to a lengthy interview. This saves both you and the applicants time and money. An assistant manager or someone knowledgeable about the shop's employment needs and practices can do the preliminary screening. Potential job candidates may then be referred to the manager for intensive interviews. All applicants should leave feeling they have been treated fairly and had an equal opportunity to present their case for getting the job. As previously stated, this is an important part of public relations. Who knows; the applicant that just left may be your next customer.

Base your preliminary screening on the following criteria:

- **Experience.** Is the applicant qualified to do the job? Examine past job experience. Check all references.

- **Appearance.** Is the applicant neatly dressed? Remember, he or she will be dealing with the public; the way the applicant is dressed now is probably better than the way he or she will come to work.

- **Personality.** Does the applicant have a personality that will complement the other employees' and impress customers? Is he or she outgoing but not overbearing?

- **Legality.** Does the applicant meet the legal requirements?

- **Availability.** Can the applicant work the hours needed? Commute easily?

- **Health and physical ability.** Is the applicant capable of doing the physical work required? All employees hired should be subject to approval only after a complete physical examination by a mutually approved doctor.

- **Make certain the application is signed and dated.**

All applicants at this point should be divided into one of the three following categories:

- **Refer applicant.** Refer applicant to the line manager for interview.

- **Reject.** Describe the reasons for rejection, and place the application on file for future reference.

- **Prospective file.** Any applicant that is not qualified for this position but may be considered for other areas of the operation should be placed in a prospective applicant file.

The Final Selection and Decision

Reaching the final selection as to whom you offer the position is often a difficult procedure. You may have many applicants who are qualified and would probably become excellent employees, but which one do you decide upon? Always base your choice on the total picture the applicants have painted of themselves through the interviews, resumes, and applications. Gather advice from those who interviewed or had contact with the individuals. Not only will this help you reach the correct decision, but it also will make the rest of your staff feel a part of the management decision-making team. Whomever you select, he or she must be someone you feel good about having around, someone you hopefully will enjoy working with, and whom you feel will have a very good chance of being successful at the job.

When you offer the job, make certain the applicant fully understands the following items before accepting it:

- Salary, including starting pay, salary range, expected growth rate, the day payroll is issued, company benefits, vacations, insurance, etc.

- Job description, including list of job duties, hours, expectations, etc.

- Time and start date, including to whom he or she should report on the first day of work.

Rejecting Applicants

Rejecting applicants is always an unpleasant and difficult task. The majority of the applications will be rejected almost immediately. Some applicants will ask the reason for rejection. Always be honest, but use tact in explaining the reasoning behind the decision. Avoid a confrontation, explaining only what is necessary to settle the applicant's questions. Usually it will be sufficient to say, "We accepted an applicant who was more experienced" or "…who is better qualified." As mentioned before, some applications may be transferred into a "prospective file" for later reference. Inform the applicant of this action, but do not give the impression that he or she has a good chance of being hired, nor state a specific date when you will be looking for new employees.

There are many federal regulations concerning hiring employees, so make sure you know the rules before you start. A great resource for federal laws is the U.S. Department of Labor's Employment Law Guide. To access this information, log on to **http://www.dol.gov/compliance/guide/index.htm**. You can also log onto **www.dol.gov/elaws**. The U.S. Department of Labor's elaws provides business owners with an interactive tool that provides information about federal employment laws. The Uniform Guidelines on Selection Procedures is another useful guide in making your hiring decisions. This can be viewed at **www.uniformguidelines.com/uniformguidelines.html#3**. Finally, the Council on Education in Management's website, **www.counciloned.com**, is a good human resources source for information and training.

Employee Handbook/Personnel Policy Manual

Federal law mandates that all employers, regardless of size, have written policy guidelines. Employee handbooks/policy manuals are used to familiarize new employees with company policies and procedures. They also serve as guides to management personnel. Formally writing down your policies could keep you out of court, prevent problems and misunderstandings, save time spent answering common questions, and look more professional to your employees. Explaining and documenting company policy to employees has been proven to increase productivity, compliance, and retention. Detailed in the following chart are some common areas to be covered.

Lack of communication, along with inadequate policies and guidelines, have been cited as major factors in workplace legal disputes. Failure to inform or notify employees of standard policies has resulted in the loss of millions of dollars in legal judgments. Simply not being aware that their actions violated company policy has been an effective defense for many terminated employees. Most important is to have the employee sign a document stating he or she has received, reviewed, understands, and intends to comply with all policies in the manual.

If you have ever written a policy document before, you know how time-consuming it can be. Even if you were a lawyer, it would likely take you 40 hours to research and write a comprehensive employee manual. To pay someone to draw one up for you can cost thousands of dollars. Atlantic Publishing has put together a standard employee handbook guide for the food service industry. All you have to do is edit the information. The template contains all of the most important company handbook sections, and it is written in Microsoft® Word so that customizing and printing your manual will be as easy as possible. (The program is available at www.atlantic-pub.com, or 800-814-1132.)

Topics to be covered in the employee handbook:

- Standards of Conduct
- Absenteeism
- Performance Reviews
- Benefits Program
- Benefits Eligibility
- Insurance
- Insurance Continuation
- Personal Appearance
- Conflicts of Interest
- Workplace Monitoring
- Suggestions
- Bereavement Leave
- Social Security
- Pre-Tax Deductions
- Military Leave
- Medical Leave of Absence
- Contributions
- Office Equipment
- Employment Classification
- Break Policy
- Overtime
- Salary and Wage Increases
- Job Abandonment
- Acts of Misconduct
- Affidavit of Receipt
- Unemployment Compensation
- Employee Conduct
- Punctuality
- Neatness of Work Area
- Personal Phone Calls
- Mandatory Meetings
- Employee Relations
- Company Vehicles
- Confidentiality
- Violence
- Holidays
- Vacation
- Harassment
- Personnel Files
- Outside Employment
- Rehiring Employees
- Substance Abuse
- Family Leave of Absence
- Employee Discounts
- Workers' Compensation
- Jury Duty
- Payroll
- Travel Expenses
- Voluntary Resignation
- Termination Procedures
- Equal Employment Opportunity
- Bonus Plan
- Work Performance
- Availability for Work
- Personal Mail
- Communications
- Problem Resolution
- Disciplinary Guidelines
- Safety
- Weapons Policy
- Severe Weather
- Orientation
- Criminal Convictions
- Employment References
- Employment of Relatives
- Searches
- Solicitations
- Company Property
- Tools and Equipment
- Hours of Work
- Recording Time
- Educational Assistance
- Reimbursable Expenses
- Performance-Based Release
- Other Forms of Separation

Personnel File

Once the applicant is hired, an individual personnel file should be set up immediately. It should contain the following information:

- Application
- Form W-4 and Social Security number
- Name, address, and phone number
- Emergency phone number
- Employment date
- Job title and pay rate
- Past performance evaluations
- Signed form indicating receipt and acceptance of Employee Handbook/Personnel Policy Manual
- Termination date, if applicable, and a detailed account of the reasons for termination

Job Descriptions

Many coffee shops have functioned for years without written job descriptions, but having job descriptions not only makes your life easier; they also can help protect you in wrongful termination suits.

- **Components of a job description.** A job description should include the job title, a summary of the job, tasks (an outline of the job's duties), experience and skills required (this includes number of years of previous experience, math skills, educational level, etc.), name of supervisor, and the working conditions (if there is heavy lifting, air-conditioned facility, long hours on feet, etc.). The next page has an example of a server's job description.

- **Reasons to have job descriptions.** One reason to write and use job descriptions is that it helps you select a qualified employee in the first place. Job descriptions also help new hires know what you expect from the position. They can be used as training checklists, and they are important documents in wrongful termination and discrimination in hiring lawsuits. Finally, job descriptions are good measuring sticks for performance review evaluations.

- **Resources for writing job descriptions.** Check out the National Restaurant Association's Model Position Description for the Restaurant Industry at **www.restaurant.org**, or by calling 800-482-9122. This book contains job descriptions for the various restaurant jobs. You also can get information on writing job descriptions and other staff management issues by attending one of the organization's restaurant staff management workshops.

SAMPLE JOB DESCRIPTION

JOB TITLE: Server

SUPERVISOR: Assistant Manager

JOB DUTIES:

The server's main job function is to take care of and serve the guest in a timely manner.

THE ESSENTIAL FUNCTIONS OF THIS POSITION INCLUDE:

- Takes food and drink orders
- Delivers orders to the guest in a timely fashion
- Serve food
- Refill beverages
- Process customers' payment
- Clear tables
- Sets up tables at beginning of shift (This includes refilling salt and pepper shakers and setting silverware and linen.)
- Side duties include preparing bread baskets, setting up salad bar, and assisting bartender.
- Restocking service area

REQUIRED SKILLS AND QUALIFICATIONS:

- Outgoing, pleasant personality
- Desire to please customer
- Math skills
- Previous restaurant experience
- Ability to lift 30 pounds and stand for eight hours
- Ability to work in a team environment

WORKING CONDITIONS:

The person in this position will work in an air-conditioned restaurant facility. The job requires long hours on feet, lifting, carrying, walking, and bending.

13

Successful Employee Motivation and Training

Employees are one of the greatest resources a retail beverage and food operation has, but this resource will be wasted if management does not first recognize it and then supply the proper incentive and motivation necessary to harvest it.

Employee Motivational Factors

Recent research on behalf of the hospitality industry revealed that different employees are motivated by different things. Money, although important, was not necessarily the main motivator. Recognition and respect for their work, as well as perks such as travel rewards, played a much larger part in determining the length of time a person stayed in the same job.

Management, therefore, must make every conceivable effort to relieve employees of toilsome work and make their jobs more rewarding; the results can only be positive.

How to Motivate Employees

Management must provide employees with: better training; higher salaries; insurance programs; flexible scheduling; shorter workweeks; childcare and transportation vouchers; incentive plans; safe, clean working conditions; proper training; tools; evaluations; financial security, if possible; adequate benefit packages; and the opportunity for advancement; as well as an amicable, structured and just working environment. The cost of providing these basic necessities, which have eluded the industry for so long, can be easily substantiated when compared to the ramifications of losing — and the cost of replacing — a discontented skilled employee.

Above all, management needs to facilitate employee pride in a job well done; a key to achieving job satisfaction is thorough training for all employees.

How to Create a Contented Workforce and Retain Employees

The reality is that employees, as well as management, directly control the quality and presentation of the beverages and food served in their establishment. It is also a fact that a disgruntled and unmotivated employee will not produce or perform as well as a satisfied one. Management, therefore, should always take the initiative to resolve problems, however apparently insignificant, because the fault lies with management. Even simple accommodations, such as separate employee lockers, restrooms, and break rooms, are a rarity; they are, nevertheless, useful motivational tools for employee retention. Air-conditioning in hot preparation areas may be virtually nonexistent. Light and noise levels are usually inadequate, causing fatigue, inefficiency, and accidents. All of these poor physical conditions have been resolved in the manufacturing industry, where the turnover rate is around 8 percent and employees remain for several years or, as in Japan, where employees are virtually guaranteed economic security for their entire lifetimes.

Operators must recognize the importance of employees to their success and take the necessary steps to ensure their economic security, physical comfort and, above all, their motivation to stay in the job. Employee relations are an area where corners cannot be cut; the long-term results will outweigh the initial cost. Competent, skilled labor is a finite resource that is in great demand. Skilled labor will work only for organizations that appreciate their skills and can provide them with the proper compensation for their efforts. The industry as a whole should bring its labor policies and procedures up to date before it loses its personnel to other industries or is forced to change by union organization.

First, consider the indirect cost to your business when an unmotivated and unhappy employee prepares a beverage or food item or provides poor service to a regular customer. Just as word-of-mouth advertising can be great publicity, it also can cause your venture to come crumbling to the ground from comments like, "The coffee was all right, but our server was slow and unconcerned." Discontented employees will not be concerned about looking out for your business's interests. Chinaware will get broken or carelessly thrown away. Coffee, tea, and food costs will rise, and work areas will be left unorganized and dirty. Why should employees care about the shop's profits when they barely make enough to survive?

Consider the direct cost of replacing an employee: recruiting expense, interviewer's salary and time, administrative costs, training expense, medical exams, the loss of sales and the cost of materials due to training mistakes, the labor cost paid before the employee's full productivity is reached, and the trainer's and supervisor's salaries. Consider the cost of termination: paperwork, exit interviewing, and, possibly, unemployment compensation. According to the American Management Association, the cost to replace an employee who leaves is, conservatively, 30 percent of his or her annual salary. For those with skills in high demand, such as the barista, the cost can rise to a frightening 1.5 times the annual salary. Your ability to retain the kind of workers you want and need has a direct impact on the profitability and effectiveness of your organization.

Training

The most serious problem facing labor relations in the beverage and food industry today is the lack of trained personnel and structured, industry-wide training programs. The manufacturing industry realized the importance of training programs and implemented them decades ago. New employees in the retail beverage and food industry, however, are often thrown into jobs, with little or no formal training. While on the job, they must gather whatever information and skills — whether correct or not — they can. Blame for this situation lies with management. Managers regard training as a problem that must be dealt with quickly and all at once, so that the new trainee can be brought up to full productivity as soon as possible. Yet, it is bewildering to note that few operators of retail beverage outlets in the United States strive to make the employee's job any easier or more enjoyable by using modern training procedures.

Investing time in training your employees is one of the best ways to reduce staff turnover and increase productivity. Unfortunately, most operators feel they cannot substantiate or rationalize any investment in an employee's training simply because they feel the employee will probably quit in a month or two; they think, "Why bother?" Of course, this starts the whole cycle of recruitment and training all over again.

Training Objectives: An Overview

Getting employees to do things right means taking the time to train them properly from the start so that they understand what needs to be done, how to do it, and why it should be done that way. Effective training, however, involves more than simply providing information. Training is not a problem, and it cannot be "solved" and then forgotten. Managers and supervisors at every level must soon realize that training is a continual process; as is learning, it must never stop. The most effective training technique is interactivity. Get people to stand up and do things. Show them how to operate the espresso machine, set a table, look for lipstick on a glass, wash their hands properly, use a thermometer, or wash the coffee cups. Let the employees participate.

Most managers and supervisors think of training as teaching new employees skills, such as operating equipment, serving beverages, or dishwashing. Training needs to be far more than that; management must look beyond its own interests and start to consider the employees' interests, goals, needs, and desires, if the business is to have long-term success.

Employees must know not only their jobs and how to perform them, but how their performance affects others in their jobs in other parts of the operation. Employees must visualize their positions as an integral part of an efficient machine, not as a separate, meaningless function.

Take, for example, the plight of the dishwasher. Dishwashers are vitality important to the success of your business and, yet, few managers, and virtually no other employees, are consciously aware of their importance. Rather than being treated with dignity and respect, they are generally considered insignificant, menial laborers. They are often paid minimum wage with little and usually no benefits, expected to do all the dirty work, cleaning up after others and working in poor conditions while all the other employees shout orders and instructions. The only time they are really communicated with is when they do something wrong or when someone needs something done or a mess needs to be cleaned up. Is there any wonder why an entirely new crew will have to be trained in two weeks? Many managers themselves do not fully realize the importance of this function or that it is far harder to find a good dishwasher than it is a good waitperson. We have always mandated that each new hire perform at least one shift in this position to fully understand its importance. Try giving the dishwashing staff an hour-long break during the busy lunch period and see the resulting chaos.

Tailoring Training to Meet Individual Requirements

Telling employees that their position and performance is crucial to the shop's success and showing them the reasons why are two entirely different things. The importance of performing the job in the manner in which they were trained must by physically demonstrated to employees, as well as the ramifications of varying from these procedures.

Using the earlier example of the frustrated dishwasher, let's apply this philosophy with some practical, hands-on management. Start the training program by having the dishwasher come into the shop and join you for coffee or a preshift snack. While the waitperson is performing his or her service, point out the importance of having clean, lipstick-free coffee cups, and explain why silverware and glasses must be checked for spots. Show them why the waitstaff needs their stock quickly and what happens if they do not get it. Type out a list describing the cost of each cup, saucer, plate, glass, and so forth in the shop. This is the most effective way to show why they must be so concerned and careful about breakage. List the cost of the other articles that pertain to their job, such as the coffee- and tea-brewing equipment, dishwashing machine, chemicals, soaps, utensils, etc.

Show them that you are concerned with both them and their performance. Pay more than the other coffee and tea shops in the area so that you will attract the best people. Set up some small benefits such as a free espresso per shift. A financial incentive is often an effective type of motivating force. Establish bonuses for the dishwasher, such as giving him or her 3 to 5 cents extra for each customer served that night. The small cost of these little extras will be substantiated with lower turnover rates and higher production.

Apply this principle of demonstrating rather than lecturing to illustrate your points, and you will have the basis for a good training program and good employee relations.

- **Computer training (CD or online).** The food service industry, like so many other industries, can offer many courses and training subjects to their employees either online or as a CD. The benefits of this type of training include being able to work at your own pace and being cost effective.

Here are some resources for this type of training:

- **www.ei-ahla.org** — The American Hotel and Lodging Association's Educational Institute offers distance-learning courses in food safety, food and beverage service, and management.

- **www.nraef.org** — The National Restaurant Association's Educational Foundation in conjunction with educator and state restaurant association partners, offers ProStart®, an industry-driven curriculum geared toward high school students providing real-life work experience, study of culinary techniques, nutrition, safety, customer service, and management skills. Students who complete the full program are eligible to earn the ProStart National Certificate of Achievement.

Orientation and Instruction for New Employees

A complete orientation of the trainee to his or her new job and the company is an intricate part of the training process. The entire orientation will take less than 30 minutes; unfortunately, however, it is rarely done. There is no excuse for not giving the new employee a good introduction before he or she starts the actual training.

Described below are some basic orientation practices:

- Introduce the new employee to yourself and the company.
- Introduce the new employee to all of the other employees.
- Introduce the new employee to his or her trainer and supervisor.
- Explain the company's employee and personnel policies. Present him or her with the Employee Handbook/Personnel Policy Manual.
- Outline the objectives and goals of the training program:
  - Describe the training, where and how it will take place.
  - Describe the information that will be learned.
  - Describe the skills and attitudes that will be developed.
- Set up a schedule for the employee. It should include:
  - The date, day, and time to report to work during training
  - Who will be doing the training and who is the supervisor
  - What should be learned and accomplished each day
  - The date when the training should be completed

At this point, the trainee may be presented to the trainer. The trainer must be a model employee who is thoroughly knowledgeable about and experienced in the job. He or she must be able to communicate clearly and have a great deal of patience and understanding.

Online Resources

A good online resource for information on developing an orientation program is Prometheus Training (**www.ptrain.com**).

Training for Food Preparation and Waitstaff

New and established food preparation and serving staff all should receive proper training in how to prepare food items to the highest of standards with minimum wastage. They also must be shown how to provide exceptional service and how to treat customers as individuals.

Training of new recruits may take several days or, in some cases, several weeks; a great deal depends on the employees' previous experience and aptitude. The initial training period, however, can be significantly reduced if you have a training plan in place rather than lurching from one crisis to another.

An effective training schedule should involve the following seven simple steps:

1. Get to know the new recruit as an individual; gain the employee's confidence by putting him or her at ease.

2. Take time to find out about their previous experience and how much they really know about the specialty coffee and tea business.

3. Always emphasize the importance of the various stages of a specific task; do not cut corners when explaining and demonstrating even the simplest of tasks.

4. Ask the new employee to perform each task under supervision; welcome questions.

5. Only let the recruit work unsupervised when you are entirely satisfied with his or her performance.

6. Keep criticism to a minimum.

7. Review performance periodically, and ask for feedback.

Once the employee has completed the training, the trainer or supervisor should prepare a final written report and evaluation. This report should describe the strengths and weaknesses of the trainee, his or her knowledge of the job, quality of work, attitude, and a general appraisal of the employee. Ask employees for their opinion on the training program; they may have some thoughts on improving it. This same question should be presented to the employee after two weeks of work. Find out if the training program adequately prepared the trainee for the actual job.

Atlantic Publishing (**www.atlantic-pub.com**) offers a 60-minute training video, *The Complete WaitStaff Training Course*. Both English and Spanish language versions are available.

Special Training for the Barista

Gone are the days when you can leave the training of a barista to chance. It is vitally important that new baristas are comprehensively trained to operate all the necessary equipment and to prepare top-notch beverages according to standard recipes. We strongly recommend that you provide ongoing training in addition to the basic, one-on-one training session offered by the salesperson who supplies your coffee-making equipment. Customer expectations are high in the specialty coffee and tea business. If you want to charge premium prices for your gourmet coffees and teas, your barista must be trained to deliver a polished performance as well as a superb product.

Equally important is the need to keep up to date with new trends, techniques, and ideas in this fast-growing area of the beverage market. The skills required of a barista are constantly evolving; state-of-the art training is crucial if you want to stay ahead of the competition. You may wish to explore the seminars offered by the growing number of consultants who specialize in the retail coffee industry. The Specialty Coffee Association of America (**www.scaa.org**) offers regional seminars in espresso training, for example. These seminars cover how to prepare espresso, proper packing and tamping methods, the science of espresso extraction, recipes, menu design, operations and marketing, and equipment maintenance. Other training programs are available from Visions Espresso Services, Inc. (**www.visionsespresso.com**) and the Bellissimo Coffee Advisors (**www.coffeebusiness.com**).

Outside Help in Training

When training sessions involve several people or even the entire staff, it is a good idea to bring in outside help for your meetings. These people are experts in their fields. Often just a phone call is enough inducement. Reward these people for their time and effort with a complimentary gift certificate.

There are great resources for outside training information available to assist in your training programs: videos, posters, books, software, etc. One great source for all these products is Atlantic Publishing. (**www.atlantic-pub.com** or 800-814-1132).

Training Management

Before you start to train your waitstaff, make sure your management and team leaders are properly trained. Many management employees are promoted through the ranks; many of these people have no management experience at all. Get them that training so they can effectively manage the rest of the staff, or you will start seeing problems such as turnover and sloppy work.

Hospitality Management Courses

Check with your area colleges and vocational schools. Many have hospitality management programs. It would be wise to enroll your new managers in one of these programs.

The number of online options available to the restaurant industry is growing. Check out the following websites for distance learning courses that could be useful to your managers:

- **www.ecornell.com** — Cornell University School of Hotel Administration's online courses include Managing People More Effectively and other courses in hospitality marketing, management of hospitality human resources and hospitality accounting. You can register over the phone at 866-ecornell (866-326-7635).

- **www.ahlei.org** — The American Hotel and Lodging Educational Institute also offers many hospitality and management courses online.

- **www.ciaprochef.com** — The Culinary Institute of America offers a variety of e-learning courses.

Role of Communication

Communication between you and your staff is just as important as the communication between your servers and your customers.

- **Engage in active listening.** How many times have you caught yourself daydreaming or planning when you were supposed to be listening to someone? It happens to us all at times. When communicating with your staff, however, you want to engage in active listening. Make sure they know you heard them. As you are listening nod, lean forward, and maintain eye contact. Using short verbalizations such as "I see" or "uh huh" lets the person know you are following them. Verify that you understand by repeating. You can say "I hear you saying …" or "You seem disturbed by …"

- **Eliminate negative speaking.** The words we choose have a major impact on how people hear what we are saying. Replace phrases such as "I can't," "I should have," and "What's wrong with" with phrases like "I haven't yet," "Starting now I will," and "How can we improve?"

- **Overcome cultural barriers and achieve diversity.** The restaurant industry has a very diverse employment base. Teach yourself and other employees tolerance and show respect for all race, gender, sexual preference, and religious differences. Teach each other about "where I'm from." If you have a bilingual staff, you also should provide language assistance, including English for foreign speakers and foreign words/phrases for English speakers.

There are many sources for bilingual training. Berlitz˚ Languages Centers can provide online and group training. For the center nearest you, log on to **www.berlitz.com**. The National Association for Bilingual Education tracks federal polices that can help employers. You can reach them at **www.nabe.org**. Worldwide Classroom (**www.worldwide.edu**) is another website to find language instruction. You also might check with area colleges. If there are language programs, you may be able to find a college graduate student willing to take on a freelance project. For cultural diversity training products, visit the National MultiCultural Institute website (**www.nmci.org**).

- Watch interactions among staff for ones being excluded. Ask those excluded what they need to be part of the team. A good way to include loners is to get mixed groups together for "games" and coach them, and involve all employees in decisions.

- Building trust. In order to get the best from your staff, you need to build trust. When working in a team environment, there are three levels of trust:

HIGH
"I'm not concerned because I'm certain that others will not take advantage of me."

LOW
Needs to see that "I get my fair share" and others don't take too much.

NONE
"I'll get them before they get me."

You can build trust many different ways. Try spending social time together. Make some jobs two-person ones (e.g., cleaning, napkin folding, etc). Encourage discussion of problems, issues, and let staff know that asking for help is okay. Improve communication and eliminate fear of ridicule or reprisal. Make room for the personal: "I feel," "I think," "What do you feel about…?" Provide positive reinforcement for helpful behavior, and allow time for trust to grow.

Banish untrusting behaviors. Make sure that no one on your staff or management team engages in the following behavior:

- Ignoring people
- Embarrassing someone in front of others

- Failing to keep confidence
- Avoiding eye contact
- Withholding credit where due
- Interrupting others
- Not helping when they can
- Taking over for someone who doesn't need help
- Breaking a promise

- **Lead by challenge and positive reinforcement.** Set goals just ahead of expectation and reward employees when the goal is reached. Try using scoreboards: 102 days since last accident, 2,453 meals served, 134 orders without mistakes, etc. Continually set new goals, but do not make goals too hard to reach. Be sure that people know you mean what you say and say what you mean. People feel secure in knowing what is expected.

- **Recognize, reinforce and compensate outstanding performance.** Recognition by itself is reinforcement and may not need compensation. A specific and timely "well done!" often holds as much weight as monetary compensation, but monetary rewards have their place as well. Have a ready supply of movie passes and other "goodies" to distribute to the deserving. Even keep some in your pocket for any meritorious action you just happen to see in passing. Match the size of the reward to the size of the performance accomplishment. Have an annual "Academy Awards'" ceremony with categories suited to your business (Biggest Helping Hand, Most Infectious Smile, Most Improved Performance, etc.). Make it a big deal, with invitations, a special menu, and let each employee bring a guest. Post the categories, explaining criteria, and solicit nominations for winning candidates. Set up a committee to select the winners and find an appropriate token to serve the function of the Oscar statuette.

- **Sales incentives.** Start with the result in mind and work backwards. Communicate specifically. For instance, tell your staff you are looking for a particular percentage increase in dollar sales of some item, such as desserts, break that down into how many desserts per day, per shift, per person need to be sold, and be sure that is a manageable goal for each team member. Remember, this is not a quota, but a goal for the team. It allows for more than one "winner" while the whole team wins. This also may be an opportunity to motivate the "slower" employees back into peak performance. Everyone should be in on both planning, carrying out incentives and the reward system for goals accomplished. Some rewards for good work include money, recognition, time off, getting favored assignments, promotion or advancement, freedom, personal growth, having fun, and prizes.

Evaluating Performance

Evaluating each employee's job performance is a crucial element in developing a structured work environment and sound employee relations. Every employee must be aware of his or her strengths and which areas of his or her job performance need improvement. Quarterly or periodic one-on-one evaluations help break down the communication barriers between management and employees. Many of an employee's work-related problems, thoughts, and ideas can be revealed in the evaluation session. However, remember to keep in mind that evaluations are only a part of the communication process and should not be considered as a substitute for daily communication. Management must always be available to listen. Communication is an ongoing and continual process.

Consider these points before filling out the evaluation forms:

- Know the employee's job description thoroughly; evaluate how well the employee meets the job requirements rather than comparing him or her with other employees.

- Always conduct the evaluation in private, with no interruptions.

- Do not let just one incident or trait — positive or negative — dominate the evaluation; look at the whole picture.

- Evaluations should balance positive and negative attributes; never be one-sided. A totally negative evaluation will almost never motivate a poor employee.

- Review past evaluations, but do not dwell on them. Look for areas where improvement or a decline in performance has taken place.

- Always back up your thoughts and appraisals with specific examples; allow plenty of time for the employee's comments. Remember, you could be wrong.

- Do not cover too much material or expect the employee to make a drastic change overnight.

- Begin the evaluation with the employee's positive points, and then direct the discussion to areas that need improvement.

- Certain personality traits and deficiencies may not always be changeable. Do not overemphasize them, but show how they might affect the employee's job performance and the performance of others.

- Finish the evaluation on a positive note.

- After the evaluation, make certain that you follow up on the thoughts, ideas, and recommendations that were brought out during the evaluation.

- Evaluations are confidential; file them in the employee's personnel file.

Ongoing Training

All employees should be reminded constantly of the importance of attention to those small details that affect customer perception of your coffee, espresso, and tea shop. Simple things like ensuring that tables are properly set before service and then promptly cleared after service can have a profound impact upon whether a customer returns to your shop or the next coffee and tea shop down the street. The best employees are always busy, even during "quiet" periods, routinely performing additional duties such as dusting and cleaning the service area, as well as cleaning all floors of spilled food and debris, and notifying the person responsible for ordering inventory before supplies run out.

Product knowledge is another important aspect of ongoing employee training. Take time to keep all employees in the loop about new lines in gourmet coffee and teas. Emphasize to your employees why you decided to introduce these new taste-bud tantalizing products. Encourage them to pass the information on to customers. Make sure that all servers can answer any detailed questions about ingredients and flavorings and that they have detailed knowledge of how the beverages are prepared.

Etc.

The first espresso machine was made in France in 1822. James Mason invented the coffee percolator on December 26, 1865. Melitta Bentz a housewife from Dresden, Germany, invented the first coffee filter. She was looking for a way to brew the perfect cup of coffee without the bitterness caused by overbrewing. The coffee filter and filter paper were patented on June 20, 1908. On December 15, 1908, Bentz and her husband Hugo started the Melitta Bentz Company. — **http://inventors.about.com**

14

Successful Labor Cost Control

So often in the beverage and food industry, the solution to a high labor cost is to lay off employees, to lower wages, or to cut back on hours and/or benefits. These shortsighted measures will cut the labor cost initially, but over time, they will result in lower overall productivity, a decrease in the quality and service, low morale, and a high turnover rate. Occasionally, some employees may have to be laid off due to a drastic decrease in sales or to initial over-hiring, but this should occur only rarely.

Controlling the labor cost of your coffee, espresso, and tea shop will require daily management involvement. It cannot be accomplished with one swift action at the end of each month. Described in the following sections are some practical suggestions that may be used to streamline your operation so that it may run more efficiently, effectively, and profitably.

Scheduling

The greatest tool management has in controlling labor cost is scheduling and, yet, scheduling is most often so poorly done that it becomes more a part of the problem than of the solution. In many cases, the employee's schedule is scribbled on a piece of paper or, worse, verbally communicated with little thought as to what is actually needed.

The overall objective in scheduling for your establishment is to place the most efficient employee at the job and shift where he or she will achieve maximum productivity at minimum expense. The general rule is to err on the side of caution and over-schedule rather than under-schedule, especially in the early stages of business.

Only after several months of operation will you be able to assess your precise labor needs with a degree of accuracy. During the first couple of months, be sure you have plenty of employees available should it become suddenly busy. Many customers will understand that you have just opened and do not have all the bugs quite worked out yet, but they are still paying full price for everything. Do not get caught short on trained personnel. The beverage and food service on opening day should be consistent with that of several months later.

Computer Software for Improved Labor Scheduling

In recent years, computer software has helped management enormously in scheduling employees. This software simplifies the time-consuming, labor-intensive, manual processes involved in scheduling employees, maximizing resources, controlling labor costs, and retaining a qualified staff. Most software systems enable the manager to quickly determine the right employee for each position and shift. Most of the software is easily integrated with time, attendance, and payroll systems. All of these systems will save money and enhance employee satisfaction and retention. The software will range in price from a few hundred dollars to several thousand dollars.

Scheduling

In order to make your store profitable and keep within your budgets, you must keep your labor costs under control. How you schedule labor will have a major impact on labor costs.

- **Determining labor cost for a shift.** Once you have written the schedule for a particular shift, multiply the hours each employee worked by their hourly wage. Now, project what your sales will be for that shift, and divide it by the number you came up with for the labor cost for the shift. This will give you a labor percentage. Is this figure acceptable from a profit standpoint? If not, you may want to make some adjustments in your scheduling.

- **Consider letting team leaders do their own scheduling.** Team interaction is good for team spirit. By having leaders schedule their team's hours, you can encourage this interaction, and have someone to help you with the headaches of scheduling. Make sure team leaders let shifts overlap by a few minutes so as to ease the turnover from one group to the next, and keep track of requested vacation time and other predictable time off so you can prepare your requirement listings ahead of time.

Whether you or team leaders do the scheduling, keep the following in mind:

- Try to schedule at least one day off each week, preferably two, for each employee.
- Watch for burnout from over-scheduling.
- Have alternates tagged in case of last-minute emergencies.
- Make sure to have at least one team leader on each shift.
- **Scheduling software.** Visit Asgard Systems, Inc. at **www.asgardsystems.com**, Staff Trak at **http://staftrak.com**, and Madrigal Soft Tools at **www.madrigalsoft.com** to view examples of some available scheduling software. Also, log on to **www.restaurantresults.com** for a listing of additional software.

Prepared Beverages and Foods

Prepared and portioned beverage and food ingredients that are ready to use can save a substantial number of preparation hours and, thus, a lot of labor costs. Before committing yourself to using any of these products, inspect a sample to ensure that the product will equal or exceed the desired quality level. Examine the additional cost of the item: Could you produce the same product with less overall cost? Remember to consider the additional cost of labor, equipment, utilities, and so forth in your projection. Most often, the manufactured product is considerably cheaper, as it was prepared in large quantities using commercial equipment and procedures. Prepared ingredients also will contribute to your overall consistency, as the processed product is always consistently produced.

Work Area Layout and Equipment Design

An efficiently designed preparation area, with labor-saving equipment is by far the most effective way to reduce labor costs. After several months of operation, examine your work space in action. Look at each employee: What are his or her motions and movements? How many steps must be taken to reach the various beverage and food items, as well as more stock? Look at the position and layout of the equipment: Is it set up the most efficient way possible? Ask the employees how they would like their work areas set up and how work areas could be made more efficient. They are the real experts — they work the same job every day. Look at the waitstaff's work areas: Could they be made more efficient? These investigations and their results will create faster and better service.

A specialty beverage business consultant or designer may be brought in to analyze your setup. In order to design the most efficient systems possible, this person will need to know everything about your equipment, staff, menus, preparation procedures, and sales. This is why it might be advantageous to contact one of these individuals after you have been operating for a while and have made all necessary changes. However, a designer certainly would be valuable in the initial planning stage. The savings derived from the increase in productivity and in employee morale created by your new setup will offset the cost of this consultant.

Every year new pieces of equipment, large and small, expensive and inexpensive, are introduced that will save time, labor, and energy. Gone forever are the days when cheap labor will replace the need for new modern equipment. Beverage and food service workers, using modernized machines, practical, efficient layout, and processed foods, will be producing more and more, in fewer numbers. Aside from saving additional labor costs, new mechanization will reduce product handling, eliminate work drudgery, and make each task, as well as the overall job, more enjoyable for the employee.

The large initial capital expenditure for new equipment usually can be financed over several years through either the manufacturer or distributor. The total cost may be depreciated over several years and written off as a business tax-deductible expense.

The Decision to Terminate an Employee

There comes a time when an unsatisfactorily performing employee, after being evaluated and given a fair opportunity to correct his or her deficiencies, must be terminated. Discharging an employee is always a difficult and unpleasant task, but it must be done for the good of your business. Although it may be an unpleasant experience, it is far worse to let the employee stay on. Before long, the entire staff's morale will drop, causing a decrease in productivity.

The decision as to whether an employee should be terminated or retrained is difficult and often prejudiced by your inability to examine the entire picture of the employee's performance. The final decision to discharge an employee should be reached after carefully weighing the pros and cons, never in anger or when tired or under stress. Ask the employee's supervisor for an evaluation of the situation and the employee. Examine the employee's training, supervision, and past evaluations. Make certain the employee has been given a fair opportunity to prove him or herself. Also, be certain that neither you nor any member of your management staff has in any way contributed to, caused, or perpetuated the problem.

Immediately after reaching your decision to terminate the employee, set up a meeting with him or her. Do not let more than 24 hours go by; you do not want this information to leak out.

The employee's supervisor should be present during the exit interview. He or she will be able to add support and witness the action. This is important, as the employee may use some legal means to gain a settlement. Conduct the exit interview in a private room with no interruptions. Should the employee disagree with your reasoning or points, give him or her the opportunity to discuss them, but make sure you back up everything you say with proven facts and statements. Remain seated and calm during the proceedings; do not get up quickly or move suddenly. Never touch the employee, except when shaking hands. These actions may be misinterpreted and lead to a confrontation.

Fill out a report on the termination proceedings, and file it in the employee's personnel file. This report will be important should the employee decide to challenge the action. Develop a plan to fill the vacancy as soon as possible. Keep in mind that it will take several months before a new employee can be brought up to full productivity and that, after training, he or she may not work out at all.

Although nothing can fully prevent a former employee from filing a lawsuit, there are ways to decrease the likelihood of litigation: Be honest with the employee about his or her performance and the reason for the termination, treat employees consistently and aggressively investigate claims of discrimination. Above all, document the chances you have given employees to improve before your decision to terminate them. If a termination is challenged, and there are no records of the problems cited as reasons for termination and indicating opportunities given to correct these problems, there could be a problem. Keep in mind your notes do not have to be very detailed, but a dated description of a problem or of the employee's progress that is slipped into a personnel file helps dramatically.

The other employees always perceive the termination of an employee as a threat to their security. You may even be looked upon as unfair or exceedingly harsh. Sometimes an explanation is needed to soothe the other employees; in most cases, though, the reasons will be obvious to them, and they will be on your side. Still, and again, document everything.

Etc.

More than 25 million people are employed in the coffee business world-wide. —**www.discountcoffee.com/coffee-trivia**

SAMPLE EMPLOYEE WORK SCHEDULE

Prepared By: _____ **Week Of:** _____

EMPLOYEE	SUN	MON	TUE	WED	THURS	FRI	SAT

15

Successful Public Relations: How to Get Customers in the Door

Without effective public relations, your coffee, espresso, and tea shop is likely to go to the wall. You may offer the best espresso in town, but if people do not know about it, they cannot buy it; it is as simple as that. Devising a sound marketing strategy is one of the most important aspects of your successful pre-opening activities and should be part of your business plan (see Chapter 1: Successful Pre-Opening Activities: Business Plan).

Seek out all the information you can about marketing before opening day. Hire an expert or, better still, indulge in a little "guerilla"-style marketing. Get out into the locality, size up the opposition, advertise your presence, and seek the opinion of the local community. You will need to look at the broader picture, which means monitoring how the big specialty beverage operators are marketing themselves. Above all, remain flexible, open-minded, and ready to adapt your marketing strategy at a whim; basically, do anything it takes to stay ahead of the crowd and win the fickle hearts of your potential customers.

What is Public Relations?

Public relations (PR) is the message a person, company, or organization sends to the public. It is a planned effort to build positive opinions about your business through actions and communications about those actions. In short, it is any contact your organization has with another human being and the resulting opinion. This opinion may or may not be accurate, but it comes from everything the public reads, sees, hears, and thinks about you. Effective PR has been described as becoming a positive member of your community and getting credit for it. Good PR sends a positive message to the public about your establishment.

PR should be part of your overall marketing communications program. This includes advertising, internal communications, and sales promotion. Speeches, contests, promotions, personal appearances, and publicity are parts of PR, but really, the results generated from all of these parts — including acquiring unpaid-for media space and time — are PR. It is who the public thinks you are and the nurturing of that opinion in a positive way.

What PR Does (and Doesn't Do) for You

If done well, PR distinguishes you from the pack in the eyes of your customers. It leaves them with a favorable impression of you and great tidbits of information to pass on to their friends about your establishment. It makes you newsworthy in a great way and can help save your reputation and standing in your community during an emergency.

Good PR improves sales by creating an environment in which people choose to spend their time and money. As said before, PR is getting credit for being an upstanding member of your community. If you are not, PR cannot make you look like you are. PR accentuates the positive and creates lasting value by highlighting what makes your establishment special. PR cannot create lasting value if none is there to begin with. What it can do is communicate existing value effectively, so it lives in your customers' minds.

Good PR can make a good story great and a bad story less bad. But PR is not just the public's opinion of your business; it is also the physical state of your establishment. People are not just interacting with your staff; they are interacting with your facility. If the media are reporting on something wonderful that happened at your restaurant, but the place is in a state of disrepair, what are you communicating about your establishment?

The key to implementing an effective PR campaign is determining what your business's image is, what you want it to be and how best you can create that image in the eyes of the public. You need to clearly define your objectives and create a plan that will implement them. PR is not a way to gloss over a tarnished image or to keep the press at a safe distance; it is an organized and ongoing campaign to accentuate the positives of who you truly are.

The Marriage of PR and Marketing

Public relations is one of marketing's tools. As a result, most businesses keep these two functions close together. This is because PR is one of the crucial aspects of a successful marketing plan. In fact, in many instances the two have been combined and are referred to as marketing public relations or mega-marketing. Both these terms reflect the symbiotic relationship between PR and marketing.

On a practical level, this close relationship obtains and retains customers, which is the obvious goal of any marketing plan. When management is communicating effectively with guests, employees, and community leaders, it is implementing an effective marketing plan.

Fundamentally, all marketing is integrated. Consumers do not distinguish between one message from your business and another; all the messages are yours. In that light, since it is your job to communicate as well as possible, understanding that all your marketing is integrated allows you to focus on an overall approach to building good PR.

How to Apply Your PR Plan

Once you have established the objectives of your PR campaign and integrated them into your marketing plan, it is time to execute. These questions can help you do just that:

- What's the right medium for this strategy?
- Who are the key contacts?
- How strong are the necessary personal relationships required for this plan? Do any need to be established or reestablished?
- Is this plan thorough? Have we considered all the downside risks?
- Are we prepared to deliver a package to the media?

This delivery package is an essential part of your plan. It contains descriptions, plots, contacts, phone numbers — all the pertinent information that will inform the media and direct them to you. The press may not use one word of your materials, but a much greater likelihood is that they will describe you the way you want them to if you have given them the resources to do just that. Following is a list of practical factors that will help you gain recognition:

- **Be honest.** The media want credible, honest material and relationships. Your message should be genuine and factual. This does not mean you have to reveal confidential data; it just means that your materials should be thorough and truthful.

- **Respond.** Do not lie, dodge, or cover up. If you do not have an answer to a question — and you might not — do not say "no comment," or "that information is unavailable." Simply respond that you do not have that information, but will provide it as soon as humanly possible. Then provide it as soon as humanly possible.

- **Give the facts, and follow up.** If you supply the media with a printed handout of key facts, it greatly lessens the chances of your getting misquoted. Make a concentrated effort to follow up and go over information with the media. Again, if you do not have a requested piece of information, get it and follow up with a note and/or call to make sure the correct data reaches the media.

- **Be concise.** Usually, the media will burn you for what you do say, not what you do not. Be deliberate about providing the facts without editorializing, exaggerating, or pulling things out of thin air.

- **Nurture relationships.** If you follow the above steps, you are on your way to building a strong and lasting relationship with the press. These relationships can sour instantly if you are reactionary, hostile, aloof, hypersensitive, or argumentative in any way. No matter what you think of an interviewer, treat him or her with respect, courtesy, and professionalism. Causing negative reactions from the press will deny you print space and airtime.

How you interact with the press is crucial, but it is only half the process. The content of what you communicate to them — having a clear and deliberate focus about how you are going to tell your story — is the other side of press relations. The following list will help you identify your purpose and communicate it effectively to the press:

- **Identify your purpose.** Why do you want public exposure? To what are you specifically trying to draw attention? Be sure you are conveying your purpose.

- **Identify your target.** Who are you targeting? Prospective customers? Your employees? The local business community? Civic leaders? Lay out whom you want to reach, and then determine who in the media will speak to them most effectively.

- **Think as they are thinking.** Why would this be interesting to the media? Figure out how your interests can be packaged in a way that directly matches the press's interests. Make your story one they want to print; i.e., one that will help them sell papers, gain listeners, etc.

- **Customize your materials.** Once you have identified your purpose, who your target is and the media's angle, tailor your materials to include all three. Give the press everything they need to tell the story — photos, copy, etc. — and be sure it is in exactly the style and medium they are using.

- **Know where to send your materials.** Is your story a news story or a feature story? Do you know the difference? A news story goes to a newspaper's city desk. Feature stories go to the appropriate editor: travel, lifestyle, etc. It is a very good idea to cultivate relationships with these editors beforehand so that when the time arises, they are thinking well of you and would like to help.

- **Make their jobs easy.** Do not ask the media the ground rules for getting press and building relationships — learn these on your own, and then meet them. Spending valuable time and resources building a relationship with a reporter, only to then submit materials at the last minute or give them insufficient or inaccurate information, burns bridges quickly. Do as much of their work for them as possible; give them something that is ready to go, answers all their questions, and is interesting. Also, be available immediately to answer questions.

Building and Supporting Strong Media Relations

Media relations is one of the most important aspects of PR because effective media relations generates publicity. Effective media relations opens the channels for your public to receive the messages you want them to receive. Media relations is how you build your relationships with the press, and this determines how they respond when you want them to report on a story.

The first goal in building strong media relations is to determine who your target media are. News media should be classified by the audiences they reach and the means they use to carry their messages. Your target media will change according to the type of message you wish to send and the type of audience you wish to reach. Your advertising agency can supply you with contact information for the newspapers, radio, and television stations in your area.

Marketing Your Coffee, Espresso & Tea Shop

Marketing a specialty beverage business can often prove frustratingly difficult for the simple reason that a large proportion of the potential customer base is likely to consist of commuters and foot traffic. Since these people are all coming from different places and heading in different directions, it is not easy to find a marketing medium, apart from your shop front, that can capture their attention.

It may, therefore, be a good idea to hire a part-time PR consultant, former reporter, or editor who can help you present your business to the press. If this is beyond your budgetary limits, the following is a list of essentials for building a good relationship with the press:

- **Fact sheet.** One of the most helpful items of media information, the fact sheet does most of the reporter's research for them. It also shortens the length of interviews by answering questions in advance. It should describe your shop and what you are trying to get press for. At a glance, it tells where you are located, when you opened, your architectural style, capacity, and number of employees. It also should specify the types of facilities you have and what kind of specialty beverages you serve.

- **Staff biographies.** You will need to write biographies for all of your key employees. These list work experience, professional memberships, honors, and awards. Your senior barista should be given extra coverage.

- **Good photography.** Do not take chances with an amateur photographer. Space is very limited in the print media, and editors go through thousands of photographs to choose just a few. This is true even for local editors. Do not give them any reason to ignore your pictures. Have them taken by a pro. Ask for references and check them thoroughly. When the photos are done, write an explanatory caption for each picture in your collection. This gives editors an easy understanding of what they are looking at. Then, before sending photos to the media, be sure you find out whether they prefer black and white, slides, transparencies, etc., and send them in the desired format.

- **Press kit folder.** Put all of these materials into a single folder with your property's name and logo on the cover. You also might include brochures, rate cards, package flyers, a brief on your involvement with local charities, etc. Do not overstuff it, but give the press a solid idea of what distinguishes you from the competition.

Before you begin your media campaign, you should get to know the media as much as possible. This may mean inviting them, one at a time, to have a brief tour or visit of your establishment and, certainly a free beverage of their choice. This gives them a sense of you and your business and begins to build a relationship. These visits are not the time to sell them on doing a story on you. It is a time for you to get to know each other and to build a relationship. If the reporters trust you, they will help you, and vice versa. They need article ideas as much as you need press, and getting to know them will give you insight into how you can help them do their job.

Once you have built this relationship, and your friends in the media trust you will not be barraging them with endless story ideas, you can begin your media campaign. It is important to remember that having a positive rapport with a reporter does not mean he or she will do a story on you. Your relationship with the reporter will help get a newsworthy story printed, but you will not get a boring story to press just because the reporter likes you. Your story needs to be newsworthy on its own. Also, reporters are always working against the clock. The more you can give them pertinent, accurate, concise information, the better your chances of getting their attention.

If you have built a respectful relationship with the media, a reporter who gets a story from an interview or news conference at your establishment will mention your place in his or her story. These "freebies" come from developing strong relationships with the media and learning to think in their terms.

Many businesses go one step further and give their media contacts news releases that are written in journalistic style. A news release describes the newsworthy development in your specialty beverage business in a ready-to-print article. Editors can then change it or print it as is. These can be immensely valuable for getting your message out there.

If writing journalistic articles is beyond your reach or budget, tip sheets can be very effective in getting your story across. A tip sheet gets the message to the media by simply outlining the who, what, when, where, why, and how of your story. It is an outline of the story the reporter will then write. Tip sheets give the spine of the story and, because they are so concise, often get more attention from busy editors.

Here are a few more tips on how to work effectively with the media:

- Earn a reputation for dealing with the facts and nothing else.
- Never ask to review a reporter's article before publication.
- Never ask after a visit or an interview if an article will appear.
- Follow up by phone to see if your fact sheet or press release has arrived, if the reporter is interested and if he or she needs anything else.
- Provide requested information — photos, plans, etc. — ASAP.

What Is News?

Once you have identified your target media and begun your media relations program, you need to learn what makes news. To do this, pick up the paper and turn on the TV. The media is looking for the strange, volatile, controversial, and unusual. It is not newsworthy that you run a nice coffee, espresso, and tea shop that provides great specialty beverages and snacks at a reasonable price. It is newsworthy when a customer gets food poisoning at your shop, or when something goes drastically wrong with the service you offer. You do not want to make this type of news, but it is news. Obviously, you want to be making great news.

One of the foundations of this is taking steps to avoid negative articles: your staff treat guests courteously, etc.

Once you have taken these steps, you are ready to generate positive stories in the media. How? Well, what do editors find newsworthy? Here is a list of basic newsworthiness criteria:

- Is it local?
- Is it timely?
- Is it unique, unusual, strange?
- Does it involve and affect people?
- Will it evoke human emotion?

Think in terms of what it is that sets your establishment apart from the competition and what is newsworthy about those qualities. When this is done, again, target your media. When you have a story, be smart about who would be interested in writing about it and whose audience would love to read about it. Here is a short list of possibly newsworthy ideas:

- A new manager or barista
- Visits by well-known politicians, entertainers, authors, or local heroes
- A new beverage menu
- Hosting a charitable event
- Reduced prices, specialty beverages, promotions such as free espressos, weekend specials, etc.
- Personal stories about the staff: the employee who returned a doctor's medical bag, helped a patron stop choking, returned a tip that was too big, etc.

PR is Different from Advertising

PR is not advertising; PR uses advertising as one of its tools. A good PR campaign usually is coordinated with advertising, but PR is not paid-for time and space. In advertising, clients pay the media to carry a message, and the client has complete control over this message. With PR, the media receives no money. The success of a PR story often depends on how timely it is or whether a newspaper editor feels it is worth reporting on. Furthermore, only a portion of your intended message may be used. The media may not even use your business's name. Because they are choosing to write about your topic, and you have given them only a potential idea for a story, the story could end up in a very different form compared with your original draft.

With PR you have none of the control that you do with advertising in terms of the message being delivered. But when done well, PR garners positive attention for your establishment, is hugely cost-effective, and is more credible than advertising. This is because the public is getting its information from a third party — not directly from a business. Customers assume advertising is self-serving, but a positive message delivered by a third party is considered authentic and trustworthy. Therefore, third-party messages are infinitely more persuasive than advertising.

Seeing the differences between PR and advertising, one sees differences both in guarantees of space and in the effectiveness of the different types of media. The enormous value of securing unpaid media space through your PR campaign becomes clear.

Launching a Campaign

In a small specialty beverage business, the manager may be solely responsible for public relations. In a larger establishment, the director of marketing or sales often plays this role. Regardless of who gets the job, ultimately the PR-buck stops with the general manager. Whoever it is that takes on your PR function, he or she should be your liaison with the media. Having a single person designated as media liaison makes it simple for the press to get their questions answered and makes it much easier for you to control the flow of information to them. This back-and-forth is a critical element in your PR campaign. Once this liaison is determined, notify your staff. Advise them not to talk with the press, but to refer all media inquiries to the liaison.

In launching your campaign, it is important to remember that you will be competing with professionals for a very limited amount of airtime and/or editorial space. Reading newspapers and trying to determine which pieces were inspired by PR people — and what about them made editors choose them — is a good discipline. Many colleges offer courses in public relations. However, it is important that you gain knowledge, the more expertise you have, the more effective your campaign will be.

If your establishment is part of a chain or franchise, PR assistance may be available from the headquarters. If you manage an independent property, PR help may be available from your local chamber of commerce or convention/visitors' bureau. Chambers of commerce often have PR departments that will offer advice on how to launch your program.

When contacting the media, it is important to determine who will be the most useful to you. What type of customer are you seeking to attract? What is the size of your market area? Are you contacting the media who cater to those demographics? Your advertising agency can be helpful with statistical data and the interpretation of it.

Once you know who your target is, begin building media lists. These include names of appropriate editors, reporters, news directors, assignment editors, media outlets, addresses, and contact numbers. From this list you call, visit, or otherwise contact the media who are crucial to your campaign. If you want to mail fact sheets, press releases, press kits, etc., you can hire a company that sells media mailing lists; you can pay them or another firm to do your mailing for you. If that is beyond your budget, calling the editorial department of a newspaper or a newsroom will get you the contact numbers or email addresses of the people you seek to reach, and you can put your mailing together yourself.

During your campaign, it is also important that you search for allies. Allies are businesses and organizations that have similar goals to yours. Your state's tourism/travel promotion office can be a great resource for this. This office is working year-round to bring business and leisure guests to your state. These, of course, are your prospective customers. Your state's travel promotion officials will be happy to give you advice on how to tie in with their advertising, PR, and other promotional programs.

Most states also have a business/economic development department that will be happy to help you, since their goal is to create new business in your state. Their mailing list will keep you informed of planned promotions. When meeting with state officials, it is a good idea to volunteer to assist their promotional and PR programs. Doing this gets you "in the loop" and, often, ahead of your competition, because you will know about the programs your state is developing.

A number of national travel industry organizations work privately to generate travel in the United States. They are natural allies. Locally, your chamber of commerce may organize familiarization (fam) trips to your area. These are trips for travel writers and travel agents that showcase the attributes of your area. Let the organization arranging the fam trip know that you are willing to offer free, unlimited beverages to the visiting journalists and travel agents. If you are selected, make sure time is allotted for a guided tour of your establishment, led by your most knowledgeable manager or salesperson. Present each guest with a press kit. Also, mail press kits to the agents after the tour, since most of them prefer to travel light but accumulate tons of literature and souvenirs on their trips. Making a good impression with travel agents and writers is great for you because their third-party endorsement is the best kind of advertising.

When these agents and writers do visit, make sure that your establishment is in tip-top shape. Your visitors probably will be visiting numerous similar outlets, and you want to stand out in every (positive) way. Only the most memorable operations will be on their "recommend" list, and you want to be one of them.

Special Events

Special events can be very effective in generating publicity and community interest. Any such occasions are opportunities to plan a special event that will support or improve your PR program. There are usually two kinds of special events: one-time and ongoing. Obviously, you are not going to have a groundbreaking ceremony annually, but you might have a famous Fourth of July party every year.

The key question to ask when designing a special event is "why?" Clearly defining your objectives before you start is crucial. Is your goal to improve community opinion of your business? To present yourself as a good employer? To show off a renovation? Once these objectives have been clearly defined, a timetable and schedule of events can be made. Ample time is necessary, since contractors, inspection agencies, and civil officials may be involved. If you are planning an anniversary celebration, research what events were going on in your community when you opened; once you have this information, send it to the press. They will see your event as part of the historical landscape, as opposed to a commercial endeavor that benefits only you, and they will appreciate your community focus.

Special events require preparation to ensure everything is ready when the spotlight of attention is turned on you. Be certain the day you have chosen does not conflict with another potentially competing event or fall on an inappropriate holiday. With a groundbreaking or opening of a new property, you should invite the developer, architect, interior designer, civic officials, and the media. Refreshments should be served, and whatever your occasion, you should provide press kits to the attending media and mail them to all media that were invited. Souvenirs are a good idea; they can be simple or elaborate, but should always be creative, fun, and useful to your guests.

Create Your Own Special Events

You do not have to wait for a special event. Create your own. The calendar highlights something on each day of August.

August

1	2	3	4	5	6	7
National Raspberry Cream Pie Day Birthday: Jerry Garcia	National Ice Cream Sandwich Day Dinosaurs Day	National Watermelon Day Birthday: Tony Bennett	Chocolate Chip Day Birthday: Jeff Gordon	Sisters Day Work Like a Dog Day Birthday: Neil Armstrong	National Gossip Day Birthdays: Lucille Ball Andy Warhol	Beach Party Day Birthday: Charlize Theron

8	9	10	11	12	13	14
Sneak Some Zucchini Onto Your Neighbor's Porch Night	Book Lovers Day Birthday: Melanie Griffith	National S'mores Day Birthday: Jimmy Dean	Son and Daughter Day Birthday: Alex Haley	Middle Child's Day Birthday: Cecil B. DeMille	Left Hander's Day Birthdays: Annie Oakley Alfred Hitchcock	National Creamsicle Day Birthday: Steve Martin

15	16	17	18	19	20	21
Angel Food Cake Day Birthday: Julia Child	National Tell A Joke Day Birthday: Madonna	National Thriftshop Day Birthday: Davy Crockett	Bad Poetry Day Birthday: Robert Redford	Aviation Day Birthdays: Matthew Perry Gene Roddenberry	Bad Hair Day Birthday: Al Roker Don King	Senior Citizens Day Birthday: Kenny Rogers

22	23	24	25	26	27	28
National Tooth Fairy Day Birthday: Norman Schwarzkopf	National Spongecake Day Birthday: Barbara Eden	Knife Day Birthday: Cal Ripken, Jr.	Kiss-and-Make-Up Day Birthday: Regis Philbin	National Dog Day Birthday: Macaulay Culkin	Banana Lover's Day Birthday: Mother Teresa	World Sauntering Day Birthday: Shania Twain

29	30	31				
More Herbs, Less Salt Day Birthday: Ingrid Bergman	National Toasted Marshmallow Day	National Trail Mix Day Birthday: Richard Gere				

Communicating to Your Guests — The Value of Loyalty

We all know first impressions last. Obviously, how you relate to your guests affects their opinion of you. That opinion then translates into potential loyalty, and loyalty boosts your bottom line. In fact, a 5 percent improvement in customer retention translates into a 15 to 50 percent boost in profits. Those are serious numbers. In common terms, that simply means getting your regular customers to return one more time per month. Furthermore, it costs about five times as much to attract a new customer as it does to retain an existing one. This is another huge benefit of loyalty to your bottom line, and it comes through the overall commitment your establishment makes to its repeat customers. Focusing on your repeat customers — your most profitable clients — allows you to keep them coming back. Two things to focus on for retaining clients:

- Pay attention to your most profitable clients. Listen, keep in touch, and find out what they want and need, and why they have chosen you.

- If they go to the competition, find out why.

Brief, succinct comment cards where guests rate your service, facilities, etc., can be a great way to find out what they think of you. You can offer discounts or promotional items for the return of these cards. If you do use a comment card, the one question that must be there is "Would you return to have coffee with us again?" If you get "nos," take immediate action to determine why, and then fix the situation.

Customer Loyalty Schemes

There are many things that small, specialty beverage operations can do to build loyalty. Here are a few:

- Build a database (or at least a mailing list) of your customers.

- Track purchases and behavior: beverage and food preferences, special needs.

- Constantly update your information based on interactions with your customers.

- Recognize birthdays, anniversaries, and special occasions.

- Show your appreciation through holiday greetings, special discounts, and other forms of recognition.

- Thank your customers for their business.

- Whenever you can, individualize your communications.

- Listen to and act on customer suggestions.

- Inform guests of new or improved services.

- Tell guests of potential inconveniences like renovations, and stress their future benefits.

- Put out a newsletter or brochure on the history of coffee or how to brew a good cup of coffee at home.

- Answer every inquiry, including complaints.

- Accommodate all reasonable requests for ingredient substitutions, etc.

- Empower employees to solve problems.

- Talk to your customers and employees so you can let them know you are listening and find out what is going on.

This last point — the back and forth between guests and employees and you — is enormously important. Just as you need to focus on getting your message to your guests, you also need to focus on getting their messages to you. If they think their opinions are important to you, they will think they are important to you, and they will come back. People have more choices than ever about where to spend their money. If they know their individual needs will be met and that they will be taken care of, their choice will be to spend it with you.

Sustainable Coffee

While typically more expensive, organic, fair trade, and sustainable coffees may be an option to look into. Organically grown coffees are certified by a third party to be grown, processed, transported, and stored without chemicals, pesticides, or herbicides.

Fair trade coffees are those that have been produced by cooperatives that have been guaranteed a fair price for their coffee based on an internationally determined price. To find out more about fair trade coffee, visit the Global Exchange® website at **www.globalexchange.org/campaigns/fairtrade/coffee**.

Sustainable coffee growers are those that meet a variety of environmental criteria, such as nonpolluting practices, and economic practices that benefit the welfare of workers and farmers. To find out more about sustainable coffee, visit Coffee Research Institute's website at **www.coffeeresearch.org/politics/sustainability.htm**.

While these coffees generally carry a higher price tag, you may find your customers will to pay the price for socially responsible coffee, and you should advertise that you use such products.

Employee Relations Is Also Public Relations

You cannot succeed in the hospitality industry if your employees do not deliver excellent service. They have the most daily contact with your customers, and are responsible for the opinion — positive or negative — people have of your establishment. One of the most important "relations" that your public relations program should focus on is your staff.

Customers want to be taken care of, and they judge a business as much on the quality of the service as the product. If a member of your waitstaff is grumpy or tired, that is bad PR. Therefore, employee relations should be a focus of your PR campaign. In order to do this, you must have well-trained staff that understand the technical ins and outs of their jobs and also believe in your organization's mission. Your employees need to know the high level of service your customers expect, and they need to be empowered to deliver it. A staff that does this on an ongoing basis is one that generates repeat business through word-of-mouth referrals. And that is good PR.

Keeping your employees informed is a key way of making them feel involved and building positive feelings between staff and management. The following is a list of things to communicate to your staff:

- How your business is doing, and what you are planning
- How the competition is doing, and what you are planning
- What community issues you are concerned about and taking a role in
- Recent personnel changes
- Available training and job openings
- Staff weddings, birthdays, significant accomplishments, or happenings

Communicating this information gives employees the sense that you care and creates a unified work atmosphere where great service becomes a group responsibility. It also shows that you recognize the difference they make to your bottom line and that you are paying attention.

Opening the lines of communication between management and staff is the next step. No one knows the intimate ins and outs of your business like your staff. If they care about your business and know your ears are open, they can be your biggest resource in suggesting improvements and letting you know what is really going on. One-on-one sessions are a great way to let them know you care and to encourage them to make the biggest difference they can.

Talking to Your Community

All business is local. This is especially true in the specialty beverage business. Establishments that are not accepted by their local communities disappear; it is as simple as that. Also, you will not find a prosperous business in a depressed area. Your community and you are the same, and it is crucial to remember this as you design your PR program.

Retail beverage and food outlets often are considered hubs of their communities. They offer facilities for meetings and other important social get-togethers. Many decisions that affect the future of local economies take place in these facilities, so it is easy to see how and why such establishments cannot be successful unless the local community accepts them.

To succeed, your coffee, espresso, and tea shop needs to be a leader in its community. In practice, this means building bridges between your business and your community to maintain and foster your environment in a way that benefits both you and the community. Your goal is to make your immediate world a better place in which everybody can thrive. The following are a few ideas that can be part of an effective community relations program:

- Fill a community need — create something that was not there before.
- Remove something that causes a community problem.
- Include "have-nots" in something that usually excludes them.
- Share your space, equipment, or expertise.
- Mobilize your workforce as a helping hand.
- Promote your community elsewhere.

Being a good citizen is, of course, crucial, but you also need to convince your community of the value of your business as a business. Most businesses provide jobs and pay taxes in their communities. These are real benefits, and they should be integrated into the message you send by being a good citizen. Designing this message is a straightforward but remarkably effective process:

- List the things your establishment brings to the community: Jobs, taxes, well-maintained architecture, etc.
- List what your business receives from its community: Employees, fire and police protection, trash removal, utilities, etc.
- List your business's complaints about your community: High taxes, air pollution, noise pollution, narrow roads, etc.

Once you have outlined these items, look for ways your business can lead the way in improving what does not work. As you do this, consult with your local chamber of commerce or visitors' bureau. They may be able to integrate you into existing community betterment programs aimed at your objectives. An effective community relations program is a win-win situation because it gives you the opportunity to be a deep and abiding member of your community, improving the quality of life and opportunities around you and, at the same time, contributing significantly to your bottom line.

Planning for the Unforeseen

Emergencies make bad news stories. Bad news stories are bad PR, and they can destroy the image you have worked so hard to build. They can wipe away years of hard-won customer relations. There are numerous kinds of emergencies: earthquakes, fires, floods, political protests, crime, and more. Any of these events, if not managed properly, can destroy your public image. The law insists you have fire-prevention programs and insurance, but no one is forcing you to create a crisis–public relations program in case of emergency.

In order to meet a PR emergency, you must prepare now. If you have a strategy developed in advance, then when something bad does happen, you assure the most accurate, objective media coverage of the event. It is important that all your employees are aware of this plan and that they are reminded of it regularly. Since your employees generate a huge amount of your PR, it is crucial for them to know how to act and what to say (and not to say) during a crisis. This simple detail can make all the difference in the world.

Here are three basic aspects to a crisis-public relations plan:

1. Your manager or owner should be the only spokesperson during the time of the emergency. Make sure your employees know not to talk to the press and to refer all inquiries to the manager or publicity coordinator.

2. Know the facts of the situation before answering questions from the media.

3. Initiate contact. Once the story is out, do not wait for the media to call you.

The media always will ask the same who, what, when, where, and how questions. Knowing this and being prepared to anticipate their questions, you should be able to answer accurately. If you do not know the answer to a question, do not say, "No comment." Explain why you cannot comment: the police are investigating, for example, and you do not have enough information to answer now, but you will try to find the answer and get back to them. Make a point to do as promised.

In times of crisis, it is crucial to put a positive slant on the news. Try to focus press attention on the diligent efforts of management to handle the emergency, or on employees whose compassion and assistance made a difference. If something happens in your establishment that is not your fault and your establishment handles it well, it is an opportunity to showcase your heart and responsiveness.

The importance of a crisis-PR plan cannot be overstated. When an employee is injured or killed in your establishment, or a guest suffers from food poisoning, the public assumes you are responsible. Whether you are even mildly at fault, people assume you are. Therefore, how you handle public relations during this time means the difference between a temporary loss of public support or the permanent loss of a great deal of your business. Ultimately, having built strong media relations pays off during an emergency. Public opinion depends on how effectively you manage information and how well you get your story across.

Etc.

It takes a coffee tree five years to reach full maturity; the trees can live up to 100 years. The average yield from one tree is the equivalent of one roasted pound of coffee. Coffee sacks weigh approximately 132 pounds when they are full of green coffee beans. It takes more than 600,000 beans to fill a coffee sack. —**www.essentialwonders.com**

16

Internal Marketing: How to Keep Customers Coming Back to Your Establishment

Profitability is what is going to keep you in business, obviously. How and where you focus to become and stay profitable is the key. Are you crunching numbers and pushing your servers to raise their check averages, or are you creating an environment that leaves patrons feeling served and eager to come back? Are you holding staff meetings that leave your crew energized or deflated? Are all employees working independently or as a complete whole towards a common goal? This chapter will give you invaluable insights into how and where you can make these changes in your business and how you can boost your sales volume 15 to 50 percent in the process.

Customers for Life

Take care of your guests, and your sales will take care of themselves. "Customers for life" means that once guests come to your coffee, espresso, and tea shop, they will never be satisfied with your competitors. Simple, right? It also means that the real work of building sales does not happen with your advertising schedule or marketing plan, but on the floor with your customers.

The key to building sales is to increase volume from your existing customer base. Think about it: If your customers were to return just one more time per month, that would be an increase in sales volume of between 15 and 50 percent. These people already know about you, live within an acceptable travel distance, and will recommend you to their friends if you make them happy. These are the people you want to target in order to build a regular, loyal customer base that shares the pleasures of your establishment with friends.

So how do you do this? Work on building loyalty, not the check average.

It is true: a bigger check is a bigger sale. However, selling techniques designed to boost check averages can be dangerous to the survival of your business. Your income comes from serving people, not beverages and food. Focusing only on the bottom line puts your customers second at best. If everyone who ever frequented your establishment were so pleased that they could not wait to come back with their friends, what would your sales be like? Conversely, if customers felt pressured to order something more expensive, what difference does it make how big their check was when they will not be coming back?

This is not to say that suggestive selling cannot work. If it is done well, it can be very effective. The problem is it is almost never done well, and you run the risk of your guests thinking they come in a distant second to their money. The safest way to achieve sales growth is to have your guests return more often. Focusing on this is a win-win situation. Your goal is to delight them, win their loyalty, and put them first.

Focus Your Attention on Delighting Your Guests

Satisfaction is not even close to good enough. It is an improvement on dissatisfaction, of course, but in today's market, it will not keep people coming back. There is just too much competition. You need to exceed your guests' expectations, every time. The beverage and food service business is built on personal connections. You serve one person at a time, and the more personal that interaction, the more you will exceed his or her expectations.

Efficient Service

Do you know what your customers expect when they come through the door? Are you out to exceed those expectations and give each guest a memorable and delightful meal every time?

Guest expectations must be met at all times. Inconsistent standards of service can be as bad as the occasional lapse; there is no margin for error. For example, beverages and food should always be served at the correct temperatures and within an acceptable turnaround time from order to presentation. Guests expect their servers to know the menus and how the specialty beverages are prepared. Make sure your staff does not keep people waiting after they have been seated or when they are ready to leave.

Ways to Delight

Customers are delighted when you go above and beyond the call of duty. Doing things that demonstrate how much you care will make a huge difference. Part of the trick here, however, is that there is no trick. You have to be sincere. People know when they are being treated with sincerity or with a mechanical technique. Sincerity works. One of the best ways to demonstrate to your customers that you really care is to have the manager or supervisor check with customers that they are satisfied with the service they received.

Robotic, routine inquiries from disenchanted servers, simply because they are required to do so as part of their job description, actually can do more damage than good. People like to meet the person in charge. They appreciate that someone important is checking in on them.

Other simple touches like providing guests with daily newspapers and reading material will also encourage them to linger over an extra latté or slice of dessert. Also, if you serve a lot of elderly customers, or even a few, have chairs with arms to make it easier for them to get in and out. Let them know you did it just for them. They certainly will appreciate it.

Or, how about offering free wi-fi in your shop. Let customers know it is a service you offer, and it will create another great point of difference between you and the competition.

Word-of-Mouth

Positive word-of-mouth is the best advertising there is, without question. But does it just come by accident or only from serving great specialty beverages? Yes and no. Great word-of-mouth comes from guests having something great to talk about and sharing it effectively. Do you have a deliberate, creative, and authentic plan in place to create great word-of-mouth? You can and should have everything to do with whether your guests have something to say and whether they are saying it.

Guests do not talk about you unless they are thinking about you. You want them thinking about you in the right way, which means you have to educate your guests on why they come to you. To do this, you must create points of difference between you and your competitors. Then people can tell their friends about why they frequent your establishment.

An effective word-of-mouth program has five main goals:

1. Inform and educate your patrons.
2. Make the guest a salesperson for your shop.

3. Give guests reasons to return.
4. Make sure your service is unique and personal.
5. Distinguish your business from the competition.

Educating Guests on the Differences

Having a great idea in place is not enough; you have to inform your customers about it, and give them the words they can then pass on. Details differentiate your product and make yours the place to go for something extraordinary. Say, for instance, you have gone to great lengths to source a particular type of organic coffee or you are particularly proud of your rigorous standards for fresh roasting your coffee beans. Tell your customers — let them know that you have pulled out all the stops to provide them with an unforgettable coffee experience.

So, how do you get this information across? The secret is to arm your staff with words they can comfortably work into a conversation. Over time, your customers will be repeating your carefully chosen words as if they had thought of them in the first place. An effective word-of-mouth program not only creates points of difference between you and the competition, it educates your guests on those distinctions. If you give your customers a great experience and the words to describe it, they will talk about it to their friends.

Incentives

Incentives work because people do what they are rewarded for doing. It is as simple as that. Reward customers for coming back, and they will.

There are three basic ways to offer incentives:

1. Discounts
2. Promotions
3. Customer loyalty programs

Discounts

An effective deal actually gives your guests a discount and generates more profit for you. How? By making a sale, you would not have made otherwise. The bottom line is that if you discount slow-moving lines, the customer is getting a good deal, and you are making more money. Are your business-card drawings giving customers a chance to buy beverages at half price but bringing in more than twice the business, bringing in people during lunch time when they are hungry, or making your coffee, espresso, and tea shop the first place people think of to go for a drink after work?

Internal coupons can be a great way to increase repeat business. Three of the most widely used coupons are:

1. **Courtesy coupons.** Your staff carries these are wallet-sized coupons. They can be issued to guests and used on return visits. They are great if a guest has a complaint or is put out somehow, or they can be used to reward customers for their ongoing patronage.
2. **Cross-marketing coupons.** If you have very fast and very slow periods, why not offer a discount to customers if they return during the slower times?
3. **Companion coupons.** Encourage your regulars to bring a friend.

Promotions

Five great promotional opportunities:

1. Birthdays
2. Anniversaries
3. Holidays
4. Special events
5. Festivals

Special events could include things like poetry readings or live music at your store. You could also host a tasting class, cater a symphony or museum event in town, or set up a charitable donation project (a quarter of every pound of coffee sold goes to a charity).

Customer-Loyalty Programs

These can be a huge benefit to your business. Rewarding your customers for continued loyalty gives them an added incentive to choose you over the competition and will help bring them back that extra time per month.

Customer-loyalty programs usually come in variations on three basic forms:

1. **Punch cards.** An inexpensive card that is typically issued free and is punched every time the guest purchases a product. When they have purchased a certain number of items, they receive something free. The biggest plus of punch cards is their ease to produce. The biggest negative is the ease with which they can be altered. Keeping the guests' cards, or duplicate cards, on premises can help counter this.
2. **Point systems.** These are often dollar-for-point systems, in which a customer accrues points towards free beverages, food, or merchandise. A point system is

considerably more complicated to implement than a punch card system, often including outside vendors.

3. **Percentage-of-purchase programs.** This involves guests paying full price for items while accruing dollar credits for future purchases. This gets people in the habit of thinking of their purchases as having a larger-than-normal value, and keeps them coming to you.

Punch cards, point systems, and percentage-of-purchase programs are all ways to monitor your guests' patronage, reward them for coming back and increase your opportunities to delight them with your specialty beverages, food, and service. Take some time to figure out which is right for you.

Creative Ways to Win Repeat Customers

Depending on your location and available budget, you can adopt a number of simple, low-cost, yet creative, incentive techniques that will pull in the customers and convert casual customers into loyal patrons. Here are a few suggestions:

- **Freebies.** Use your computer to produce flyers that feature a come-on freebie such as "buy one cappuccino, get the second one free." Distribute the flyers in nearby office blocks, parking lots, or anywhere that is densely populated.

- **"Dual-purpose" business cards.** Have "Good for one free specialty beverage of your choice" printed on the reverse of your business cards; seize every opportunity to hand out your cards at local events, etc., even when you are "off-duty."

- **Commuter program.** Appeal to commuters with a "frequent guest" plan, where they can accrue "points" towards free beverages and snacks. Or, establish a commuter program that involves selling a coffee cup or mug with your shop's name or logo on it, and then offer a discount to commuters who bring their mug in for use at your establishment.

- **Happy hour.** Not just for liquor promotion, the concept of happy hour works equally well for the sales of specialty beverages. Offer discounts or two-for-the-price-of-one during slack periods.

- **Prepay deals.** Encourage customers to pay up in advance for a month's worth of a beverage of their choice, in exchange for significant discounts. A simple index card system and a date stamp that tracks customer purchases is all you need. You will improve your cash flow and your customer enjoys great savings — a win-win situation.

- **Make recommendations.** If a customer is having a difficult time deciding, make sure your servers offer recommendations. For example, a server could say, "My favorite is the Mocha espresso." Remember, these should be suggestions; do not let the servers become pushy.

- **Remember guests' likes and dislikes.** Everyone likes to be remembered. If you have regular customers, encourage your servers to remember their specific food likes and dislikes. For example, if a couple comes in and always orders the same type of coffee, have it ready for them next time before they ask for it. It is guaranteed to charm the customer. It is likely that if they were going to order something different that evening, they will take "the usual" because they appreciate the server remembering their preference.

- **Be willing to customize.** If a customer asks for the a latte with skim milk, say "No problem!" Let your employees know ahead of time what they can offer without checking with someone. It will reflect on the server and you more positively if the server does not have to get permission for everything the customer wants.

- **Go beyond the call of duty.** Make the experience of being in your shop unforgettable. Call the customer a cab, and offer them a free beverage if they have a long wait. If it is raining, have someone escort the customer to the cab with an umbrella.

- **Suggest alternatives.** If the kitchen has sold out of a particular dish or if dietary restrictions do not allow a patron to order a particular dish, severs should have alternatives to suggest. If there is dairy in the mashed potatoes and the guest is lactose intolerant, the server could suggest a another option: "Our roasted potatoes are made with olive oil, perhaps you would like to substitute those?"

- **Resolve problems.** Train your servers to quickly resolve any problems your guests might have. You also need to train the kitchen staff that problems need to be resolved immediately. If a customer gets the wrong order or if their food or beverage is not prepared the way they asked, tell your servers to apologize, and offer to fix the problem. If the server is unsure how to resolve a problem, you or a manager needs to be available to come up with a solution.

- **Anticipate needs.** Bringing a customer something before they ask is an excellent way to win the customer over. Some servers seem to have a sixth sense about it. If you know a particular brand of scotch is very strong, for example, bring the guest a glass of water with the drink they requested. If you are serving red beans and rice to a table, drop off the Tabasco® sauce at the same time.

- **Coffee refills.** Make sure your servers provide coffee refills, but also be sure they ask before they pour. The guest might find it annoying to have the cup refilled without being asked. If a half-filled cup has been sitting for a while, replace the cup with a fresh one rather than filling the lukewarm one.

- **Doggie bags.** Take an extra moment with the doggie bags. Rather than dropping a box off with the customer to fill, fill containers in the kitchen. Add a little something extra as well, perhaps a couple of pieces of bread or extra sauce. Some fine dining establishments form their foil wraps into shapes such as a swan. Also, make sure you have appropriately sized and shaped containers for leftovers. When the customer arrives home and finds her flourless chocolate torte sideways in a soup container it will not reflect well on the server or the restaurant. For doggie bag sources, check with you local paper vending company. You also can find doggie bags online at McNairn Packaging at www.mcnairnpackaging.com.

- **Keep an eye on your tables.** Even if a server is waiting on another table, he or she should keep an eye on their other tables. If they see a guest looking around, stop over immediately, and ask if there is anything you can get them.

- **Knowing personal details.** Knowing personal details about a customer can give the guest a value-added experience. Many restaurants have POS systems that capture information such as birthdays, anniversaries, etc. If you do not have such a system, create your own. You can create a simple database on your computer. Capture the information through customer surveys. If the information pertains to regular customers, create a file just for them. Keep this information with the hostess, and train your hostess to inform servers about special occasions or particular likes and dislikes.

- **Access for disabled.** Make sure that your restaurant is accessible for people with disabilities. Consider a ramp at the front door if there are steps. Also, have a table, or several tables, that have enough space to comfortably fit a wheelchair. If someone who is blind comes in for dinner, ask the guest if you can offer his or her service dog some water or something to eat.

- **Older guests.** Another way to give value-added service is to make special arrangements for older guests. Be sure servers are knowledgeable about the menu's nutrition content. Seat them in an area that provides good light for them to read the menu as well. Also, be sure servers respond to elderly customers with patience and respect.

- **Adding festivity.** Is someone at the table having a birthday? Give your servers ways to make the evening festive for the customers. Some coffee stores and restaurants have special desserts for birthdays and other occasions. Other establishments have the entire staff sing to the individual. Even a simple balloon at a table makes the evening seem a bit more festive.

- **Complimentary items.** Is there a long wait for a table on Saturday nights? Consider sending a server through the waiting area with a tray of appetizers for the people in line. You also may want to offer something complimentary at the table. Perhaps you could give complimentary coffee with dessert. Also, consider giving patrons sips of wine or taste of things if you are able to.

- **Special requests.** Patrons will have special requests for various reasons. A customer may hate the taste of goat cheese and request a different type of cheese on the vegetarian sandwich. Some customers also may have special diets they are required to follow or food allergies to contend with. A restaurant that does not make a big fuss over "substitutions" can easily win the more restricted or finicky customer's heart!

- **Hooks for purses and coats.** If you do not have a coat room, add hooks to booths for coats and purses or provide coat trees in the lobby area so guests do not have to throw their belongings over the backs of their chairs.

- **Fax directions.** Do you have a new customer asking for directions to your restaurant? See if you can fax them directions. Include your phone number, a map, and a coupon.

- **Business customers.** Have your servers go the extra length for your business customers. Offer these guests quick service. You also can provide them with some additional services, such as copying, use of the phone, and pads of paper and pens for making notes.

People, People, People

The hospitality service industry is about personal connection. Of course, it is about beverages and food, too, but if you can establish a connection with your customers, you will exist in their minds as a welcoming friend of the family, not just a place to pop in for a cup of coffee. People want to be treated like individuals, and they will do business repeatedly in a place that does so.

So, how do you connect? You have presence. You get physically and mentally "there" with your guests.

We have wrongly accepted the idea that doing many things at once, "multitasking," is effective. The truth is that we can really only focus on one thing at a time. So, when you talk to your staff or your guests, really talk to them. Listen, say what needs to be said, and move on. Drop distractions, handle each task individually, and then move on to the next. Presence is simply a lack of distraction. If you act distracted with your staff, they will keep asking the same questions or coming to you with the same problems. If you are distracted around your guests, they will not come back at all. Pay attention. People will notice, and you will, too. Be a great listener.

Appreciation

What do you do to let your guests know that you appreciate them? If you recognize them and make them feel important, it will draw them closer to your shop and further differentiate you from your competitors in their eyes. The following list touches on a few tried-and-true examples. Many can be done at little or no cost.

- Put them in your newsletter (you can have either a print or email version).
- Put them on a "wall of fame" or "outstanding customer" plaque.
- Give your regulars awards, and/or honor people in your community that make a difference through charitable work.
- Name menu items after guests. Customers love this, and who knows what soon-to-be famous beverages are brewing in their minds?
- Personalize booths or seats.
- Put guests' names up on your bulletin board.

Getting to Know Your Guests

In a business that lives and dies on personal connection, getting to know your guests is crucial. Go beyond the procedures of service, and start thinking of your guests as individuals. Numbers are important, but your relationship to your customers drives your business. Furthermore, the two easiest things to learn about your customers are also the most useful: who they are and what they like.

People love it when you remember who they are. It instantly makes them feel like they are insiders and makes them feel important in the eyes of their friends. Remember "Norm!" in *s*? Norm felt pretty comfortable, and he definitely came back. As a manager, you probably know your regulars by name, but do you have a system in place that teaches your new staff who these important folks are?

You can train your servers to write the guest's name on the back of the check so they can refer to it throughout, or you can have your greeter put guests' names on their checks when they arrive. However you do it, keeping servers using guests' names will help them remember the names in the future. It will continually remind waitstaff that they are serving people, not anonymous mouths. Using guests' names is another win-win situation because the more you use their names, the easier they will be to remember and the easier it will be to treat them as individuals.

Now that you are talking to customers as individuals, the next step is to find out what they want as individuals. How? You must ask, but you also must remember not only what you have been told, but also what you have observed, such as favorite seats or which newspapers guests prefer to browse through over their beverages. Small note cards kept about regular guests can make this possible. The cards hold information about customers' likes and dislikes, patterns and desires — all the information necessary to treat them like royalty. You can even reward your servers for adding to the cards each time a guest frequents your coffee, espresso, and tea shop.

Throughout this process, it is very important never to pry: Respect your customers' privacy. If a customer were reticent to share about his or her life, a savvy server would note on the biography card not to ask too many questions. In this case, you are serving your customer's preferences simply by leaving him or her alone. Either way, you are finding out what your guests want and giving it to them.

Staff

Your shop is made up of two things in the eyes of your customers: the beverages and food, and the staff. The quality of service your customers receive will determine their opinion of your specialty beverage establishment. Your staff are the ones who delight your guests (or do not), who give them things to talk about and who provide the crucial personal connection. Staff will execute most of your sales promotions and programs, educate your customers about what makes your espresso better than the one down the street, and give your guests information they can pass on to their friends.

It is in your waitstaff's best interests to connect with customers, because it is through that connection that their tip averages will go up. But — here is the thing — your staff will treat your guests the same way you treat your staff. If you want your staff to be gracious, to listen, and delight your guests, you have to do the same for them.

If you take the pressure off your staff to get the check averages up and instead encourage them to treat their customers in a way that will bring them in one more time per month, then your waitstaff can increase their incomes significantly; this is just through being nice and committed to serving your patrons' needs. Also, guests who know their waitpersons usually leave higher tips. As your waitstaff get to know their customers, they are not just increasing the possibility of greater revenue through repeat business, they are also increasing the chance that they will get a bigger tip this time — just by making a personal connection.

Servers are internal marketing tools. They are the link between your customers and sales, so you want a server who is going to be successful at marketing your menu and establishment to their guests. Obviously, knowledge and experience make a person a good server, but what character traits should you look for in an individual that will tell you they would shine as a server?

- **Effective communicator.** One of a server's main jobs is to communicate with customers and the rest of your staff. Servers should be able to communicate with a wide range of personalities. This communication extends to facial expressions and body language. If a server is frowning at a guest, they are communicating negative emotions, whereas a smile implies a welcoming emotion.

- **High energy.** Restaurant serving is a tough job that requires many hours of walking and long periods on your feet. Servers need to be able to maintain this energy level throughout a shift.

- **Flexible.** Servers should be flexible and able to deal with sudden, unexpected rushes that require them to stay longer than they thought they had to that shift. They also need to be flexible and tolerant in dealing with the public. There are many restaurant horror stories about irritating customers. Take, for example, the server who waits on a group of 20 square dancers every Saturday, and every Saturday the group only orders French fries, cheese sticks, and water, and they have the server running their legs off all night for them.

- **Can handle stress.** The restaurant world is a stressful one, and servers will have to deal with physical and mental stress on a daily basis. This stress can take the form of annoying customers, a surly kitchen crew, another server that will not pull his or her own weight, or simply getting all your tables seated at once.

- **Cooperative.** Restaurants require a good deal of teamwork and cooperation. Therefore, servers should be willing to pitch in and help. For example, a good server would help the salad person when he or she was backed up; a less-than-ideal server would stand and wait for his or her salads with hands on hips.

- **Courteous.** Servers should be polite and courteous with their managers, fellow employees, and guests.

- **Desire to please others.** The job of server is aptly named. A person who is working in such a position should get satisfaction from pleasing other people. A server must be able to put his or her ego in check for the good of the customer, as well as for the good of the tip.

- **Empathic.** Good servers can read a customer quickly and see if they want to be alone or are interested in chatting. This ability to feel and reflect another person's mood is helpful for setting the right tone for a guest. If a solitary diner is reading, the server should not loiter, automatically assuming the person is lonely. If the guest encourages conversation, that is fine, otherwise he or she may simply be interested in the book they have brought along.

- **Neat appearance.** Servers need to be neat and clean. Your server indicates to your guest how clean and organized your facility is. It the server runs up to the table frantically searching for a pen with a dirty apron and shirt, the customer is going to feel that this reflects how much you care about the rest of your operation.

Great service does not just happen by accident. Your servers and you can do many things to give your customers exceptional service.

- **Servers stay with diners.** In many restaurants today, managers use multiple employees to wait on a table. While this results in speedy deliver, it also can confuse the customer. Have you ever been to one of these restaurants and you have wanted another drink? You have had so many people stop at your table that you have no idea who your server is and whom you need to flag down for a second cocktail. Give your servers the opportunity to connect to the guest; let them be the sole liaison between restaurant and guest. Of course, this does not mean that no one should help the server if he or she is behind.

- **Maintain a database.** Keep a record of your regular customers' likes, dislikes, birthdays, anniversaries, etc. Nothing makes a customer feel more special than having his or her birthday remembered without even prompting. Use your computer system to develop such a database, or you can simply keep a notebook. If you keep this information with the host/hostess, they can let the server know when there is a special occasion or what a particular person likes to drink.

- **Recognition.** Recognition is very important, but it does not necessarily need to be elaborate. It can be as simple as addressing the customer by name.

- **Listen carefully for information from the customer.** Better to over-communicate than to drop the ball. Servers may want to repeat information back to customers, especially if the order is detailed. This will let the guest know the server wrote it down correctly. If your restaurant does not use guest checks when taking the customer's order at the table, this device can be particularly important for reassuring the customer.

- **Smile.** This is one of the simplest, yet one of the most important things your servers (and management) can do. Smiling sets the tone and sets everyone at ease; it makes the server approachable for the customer. We have all had the experience of going for a quick bite or to the grocery store and have the clerk hand you your change as they continue to talk to their coworker. They never smile at you and never acknowledge you. If you do not care about the customer, why should they care about you? You probably will not go back to the store with the unsmiling, surly clerk if you can find those goods just as easily somewhere else.

- **Rules of the road.** Have set traffic rules in your establishment so aisles do not become clogged. For example, if two servers are heading for the same table, the first one should go to farthest side of the table. Always let the guest go first, then a server with food, and finally the busser.

- **Rules of recovery.** Accidents are bound to happen. How you handle the accident is the important thing. First, promptly offer an honest, sincere apology. Second, take steps to resolve the problem. Let's say one of your servers spills tomato bisque on the white shirt of one of your lunch customers. The server should immediately help clean up the customer, and then the server or a manager should offer to pay for the dry cleaning. Suggest that the customer send you the bill, and you will take care of it for them. If a customer's food is wrong or prepared wrong, get the food to the guest who has had to wait right away. It is extremely uncomfortable for one guest to be waiting for their entrée while the other three people at the table have their food. These three people will either have to let their food get cold while they politely wait for the fourth entrée, or they will have to be impolite and eat in front of the unfortunate customer. This type of situation can throw the pace of the kitchen and dining room off on busy nights, so it might be a good idea to consider having a floater position. This person could work during the rush hours and wander through the restaurant, ready to fix and forestall any problems.

- **Customer-satisfaction survey.** Some people are shy about telling you they have had a bad experience in your restaurant. You can still get feedback from these more reticent customers by using customer-satisfaction surveys. Have the server offer these with the check. They can be self-addressed and stamped for the customer to drop in the mail later, or they can fill them out and leave them at their table. You can share this feedback, good and bad, with your staff later. Use the negative feedback to improve your restaurant. Use positive feedback to give specific employees accolades for their good work.

- **Be courteous.** Seems like common sense, but it is amazing how many servers do not treat guests with common courtesy. Make sure your servers say "thank you" and "you're welcome." The terms "ma'am" and "sir" are appropriate as well.

- **Be knowledgeable.** One of the best resources your servers have for increasing their tips and your customer base is to be knowledgeable about the menu. Most specialty shop customers will expect you and your staff to be knowledgeable about your product — that is why they are drinking specialty coffee. Your customer base will be very sophisticated about the products you are selling, and most likely, they will be quite knowledgeable about it themselves. Make sure you and your staff have been thoroughly trained on the history of coffee and the process of making it as well as the types of product available.

- **Acknowledge the customer quickly.** Customers need to be acknowledged within 60 seconds of being seated. If a server is swamped, train your host staff and bussers to help. Even stopping for a second and saying, "I'll be right with you," will make the customer comfortable in the knowledge that they will receive prompt, good service.

- **Make eye contact.** Do not stare at the table, the floor, or the artwork on the wall. Clear your head, smile, and pay attention. Make sure you are at the table when you are talking. Do not talk to your guests as you are flying by. It makes people feel unimportant, and no one likes that feeling.

- **Do not think about the tip.** Focus your energy on taking care of your guests, making them happy, doing little things that exceed their expectations, and generally making their meals as enjoyable as possible. That is how you will get great tips consistently.

- **Encourage your guests' beverage and food choices.** People can be strange about making decisions. The simple act on your part of telling them that you have had what they are ordering, and it is great, can take away any anxiety they have about making a bad choice.

- **Ask before refilling coffee.** Coffee drinkers can be very particular about the amount of cream and sugar they have in their coffee. Temperature also matters. Do not top off a cup they may have spent considerable time getting just right.

- **Tell the good news to fellow employees.** Just like you need to be sensitive to the mood of your guests, be sensitive to the mood of the beverage and food preparation crew. They do not want to hear about things just when they are wrong. Pass along good news to them, and they will probably make it easier for you to take great care of your guests.

- **Notice lefties.** It is a small thing, but if your guest has moved his or her water glass and silverware to the other side of the plate, serve drinks from there. It will be appreciated.

- **Make your movements invisible.** That means move with the speed of the room. Good service is invisible: beverages and food simply arrive without a thought on the customer's part. If the room is quiet, do not buzz around in it. If it is more upbeat, move a little quicker. You will find fitting in seamlessly with the atmosphere will increase your guests' enjoyment, and it is a great way to stay focused.

- **Tell guests about specific events at your shop, and invite them.** This is a more effective way to let them know you would love them to come back and to build a personal connection. It can be much more effective to invite guests to return for your cappuccino special on Tuesdays than just to say "Thanks. Come again." While you are at it, invite them to sit at your station. You will be more likely to remember their names and what they like.

- **Show gratitude.** People are dealing with a lot in their lives, and you have a chance to "make their day." Express gratitude in the tone of your voice when you thank them for their patronage or invite them to come back. Making them feel appreciated will make them remember you as they fill out the tip.

- **Make personal recommendations.** Tell your guests what you like. This is not suggestive selling, because it is sincere and, therefore, will not alienate your guests. Your enthusiasm will be infectious, even if guests do not order what you recommend. It will not bother them that you are excited about what is on the menu.

Just as there is a list of items that make great service, there is a list of things that lead to poor service. Make sure your servers are not engaging in any of the following practices.

- **All thumbs.** Clumsy servers not only look bad, but they can lead to accidents. You cannot enroll your servers in charm school, but you can give them tips on how to handle trays and plates. To avoid hiring someone who may not have the grace required, have applicants give a demonstration of their serving skills.

- **Unkempt appearance.** Be sure your servers' physical appearance makes a good impression on your guest. Servers' uniforms should be neat, they should be well groomed, and they should not smell offensive.

- **Attitude smattitude.** Do not let your servers get away with ignoring your guests. Even though some waitstaff do the job appropriately, their attitude leaves a lot to be desired. Surly servers who seem to be in a hurry or do not make eye contact do nothing for your guests' appetites.

- **Do not be intrusive.** Customers want attention and service, not another person at the table. Train your waitstaff to be attentive without being overbearing or intrusive. Servers should never get too personal with guests, and they should not engage in lengthy conversations.

Remember, guests leave good tips because they want to leave good tips.

How, as a manager, can you make it easiest for your servers to do these things? For one, waitstaff need to have sampled everything on the menu. Ideally, they should know how every item is made so they can speak knowledgeably about it. Even better, as part of their training, they could work in the preparation area for a day or two. Nothing is more persuasive than a waitperson who knows what he or she is talking about.

Also, let them use their own words to convey their enthusiasm. It is hard to make a personal recommendation using someone else's words. You want them sharing their enthusiasm, not a canned version of yours. Your crew will find their own way of expressing their enthusiasm. Letting them in on what you sell is the best way to give them something to be enthusiastic about.

A Truly Effective Staff Meeting

How are you going to impart all this newfound wisdom and good spirit to your staff, and how are you going to get them excited about delighting your customers? You need a great, truly effective staff meeting.

Most staff meetings are far from invigorating. In fact, they usually result in a drop in energy and a staff that feels like they are on management's bad side. An effective staff meeting is not just a gathering of bodies with one person giving out information; it is primarily a meeting that generates positive feeling in the entire group. An effective staff meeting has three main goals:

1. Generating positive group feeling
2. Starting a dialogue
3. Training

Positive Group Feeling

This will help your staff discover what it has in common and think in terms of working together, as opposed to strictly as individuals. Share good news in order to build good feeling. Staff meetings are not a good time to address individual or group shortcomings. Find the positive, even if you need to hunt for it, and talk about it. This is how you will build a supportive feeling and get people talking.

Dialogue

A good dialogue is a comfortable back-and-forth of ideas that gets people connected and leaves your staff feeling that they are a truly creative part of your establishment. You learn from the staff, and they learn from you. Allowing this flow of ideas reduces or eliminates the "Us vs. Them" mentality in your staff and puts everybody on the same team. If everybody is on the same team, service improves and productivity and profits go up.

Training

Good staff meetings are places to pass on ideas for better performance. If you do not do this, you are passing on the message that things are as good as they could possibly be or that any fool can serve customers. Of course, neither is true, and this is your chance not only to pass along tips to your staff, but also to have them learn from each other. Your staff are intelligent people, and they instinctively know what works. Encourage them to share thoughts about work will turn staff meetings into a forum for discussing ideas. This atmosphere will increase their learning curve dramatically.

Ideally, you should hold a staff meeting before every shift every day. If you frequently cancel staff meetings, it sends the message that they are not important and that the staff's opinions are equally unimportant. An effective preshift meeting should last no longer than 15 minutes. If it is longer, you may lose people's attention; shorter, you will not get enough said. Pick a length, and start and finish on time. Include the prep staff, as well. This may be a good time to let servers sample today's specials and invite them to offer feedback. Have in mind that waitstaff are getting paid for this time, but not tipped, so be sure to not to take advantage of their time.

Possible Format for a 10 to 15 Minute Preshift Meeting

Before you start, remember that the thing that most determines how your meeting will go is your own state of mind. Are you looking at your staff as a group of dedicated people committed to doing a great job or a bunch of layabouts looking to milk the system? Are you a coach on the playing field seeking to facilitate and encourage people's best performances or a judge looking to identify and punish people's mistakes? Rest assured that whichever it is, your staff feel it, and it will affect the work they do. Get committed to building on people's strengths and holding energizing staff meetings:

- **Good news (1 – 2 minutes).** Acknowledge what works and create a good mood. Find something about the business that shows people doing a good job and making guests happy. Acknowledge the doer or bearer of the news with sincerity.

- **Daily news (2 – 3 minutes).** Outline today's specials and upcoming events.

- **Ask your staff (5 minutes).** This is the most important part of the meeting. This is your opportunity to find out what is really going on in your shop and what people are thinking about. Listen. Do not interrupt with your own thoughts, and do not judge people's comments. Create a safe space. How well you listen directly affects how much they are willing to say. If they are shy, ask them questions: What is working for you guys? What is making things tough? Where have things broken down? What questions from customers have you been unable to answer? Once you get the ball rolling, you may find it hard to stop. Good. That means people have things to say, and you will benefit.

- **Training (3–5 minutes).** If staff comments run over, let it cut into this time. It is important that your staff learns from you, but it is more important for you to learn from them. Plus, they will be open to learning from you if they know you are listening to them. Use this time to talk about a single point you want your staff to focus on during this shift, to give out specific knowledge about a product or to train in another targeted way. Focus is important. If you tell people how long the meeting will last and hold to that, they will give you their attention. If you go over, you will lose their attention and their trust. Get to the point, and trust that they got it.

Becoming good at running staff meetings will translate into a feeling of camaraderie among your staff. They will not just be giving you the true insights into how your business is being run; they will be caring about how to improve it, because they know their suggestions count. You will be more effective, because your staff will take weight off your shoulders, helping your coffee, espresso, and tea shop run better and making your job a lot more fun.

Conclusion: Focus on Making Your Guests Happy

Bringing guests back just one time per month will give you a 15 to 50 percent increase in sales volume. If you dedicate your energies towards building an establishment where your servers are treated with respect and gratitude, they will treat you and your customers in the same way. Focus on building an environment that is friendly, helpful, informed, and welcoming, and people will come back again and again. This can happen by taking the weight of sales off your staff's shoulders. Everybody — especially customers — should feel they are on the same page. Again:

- Build loyalty, not a higher check average.

- Dedicate your business to delighting your guests.

- Give your guests something to tell their friends about.

- Give customers incentives to return.

- Get connected. Your staff is your coffee, espresso, and tea shop. Get connected with your staff, and get them connecting with your guests.

17

Internal Bookkeeping: Accounting for Sales and Costs

Internal bookkeeping ties all departments of your business together into one efficient, airtight operation. Internal bookkeeping is the keystone from which all financial transactions are monitored, analyzed, and reconciled. Management involvement in this department is never too much.

This chapter will cover:

- The owner/manager's role in these controls systems
- Basic principles of accounting
- A system of checks and balances to ensure maximum efficiency and profit

The Role of the Bookkeeper

The internal bookkeeping procedures described in this chapter are simplistic. However, to ensure complete accuracy, a couple of hours of every day must be devoted to them. Sometimes, it's best to hire a part-time bookkeeper. The bookkeeper doesn't need to be highly trained or experienced but must be very accurate and thorough. A bookkeeper must be willing to follow his or her work through and dig into the facts and figures that are submitted. Since your bookkeeper will only be required for a few hours each morning, he or she must be well compensated for his or her efforts. The ideal candidate for this position might be a stay-at-home parent wishing to work a few hours each morning while children are at school or day care.

A distinction must be made between the bookkeeper and an outside public accountant. The bookkeeper's primary responsibility is to ensure that all sales and products are accurately recorded and balanced. An outside public accountant should be used from time to time to audit the records, prepare financial and tax statements, and lend management advisory services.

It is not recommended that the bookkeeper be used in any other capacity in the shop, as he or she will be auditing the money and work of the other employees. The bookkeeper must understand and appreciate the confidential nature and importance of the work he or she is doing.

It may be difficult to find a person suitable for this job. Do not settle for just anyone in this crucial position. Once a competent person is located, make every effort to compensate because he or she will be one of your most valuable employees.

This chapter on internal bookkeeping is divided into three separate sections: The first section, Accounts Payable, outlines a unique system for paying and accounting for purchases. The second section, Revenue Accounts and Reconciliation, explains in detail how to account for and reconcile the sales and products from the previous day. The third section, Payroll, describes the steps and procedures used in preparing the payroll.

Accounting Software

We highly recommend the use of a basic accounting program, such as QuickBooks® (**www.quickbooks.com**) or Sage 50 (formerly Sage Peachtree) (**http://na.sage.com**). These programs are inexpensive, easy to use and will save time, money, and countless errors. The procedures detailed below are for a manual system, but they can be easily (and wisely) brought into a computerized environment. Please note that the use of a POS system may also make some of these activities obsolete.

Section 1: Accounts Payable

Accounts payable represents the money your coffee, espresso, and tea shop owes the purveyors from which it has purchased goods, material, or services. Although there are various ways to record the shop's transactions, the procedures and systems described here will become an integral part of your budgeting, controls, and financial management. Therefore, the adoption and use of these procedures is highly recommended.

Invoices

The start of the accounts payable process begins when the invoices are brought to the manager's office at the end of each day. The employees handling the invoices must do so with the utmost of care and concern. Should an invoice become lost or mutilated, it will throw a "monkey wrench" into the bookkeeping records. Ideally, all invoices should be processed on a daily basis so that the transactions are still fresh in everyone's mind and can be easily referred back to. The following are suggested steps for invoice processing:

- Make certain the invoice is actually addressed to your shop. Although this may sound like an improbable mistake, an invoice may be addressed to the business next door or inadvertently left in the wrong invoice box by the delivery person or in the wrong mailbox by the mail carrier.

- Make certain the invoice is signed by one of your employees. This will ensure that the items were, in fact, received intact and accounted for.

- Verify the delivery date.

- Check the price and quantity to make certain the amount delivered was the amount ordered and at the price quoted.

- Check the extensions on the invoice total for accuracy.

- If everything appears to be in order, stamp the invoice "Approved." This will signify that the invoice should be paid. Should any part of the invoice be in question, take the time to call the company, talk to the employee who received the order, and go to the storeroom to check the delivery yourself. A little effort now will save time, money, and many headaches later.

Coding Invoices

Every cost the business incurs is assigned a code number. Coding each invoice is an integral part in setting up and establishing bookkeeping and budgeting procedures. Breaking down each invoice and cost into separate categories helps analyze cost problems later and aids in preparing tax and financial statements.

After approving each invoice, code the invoice to its appropriate category. A rubber stamp for processing invoices may be obtained at most office supply stores. It should contain a space for the following information:

- Date
- Code
- Amount due
- Preparer's initials

After stamping the invoice, simply fill in the appropriate blank with the required data. Some invoices may list purchases or costs that must be entered into the expenditure ledger under different codes. Most purveyors that deliver products for more than one code will be glad to make out a separate invoice for each code if you ask them to.

Every invoice must be copied and filed according to its respective code number and purveyor's company name. Invoices containing two or more codes should have two or more copies prepared, one for each appropriate file. The original invoices also should be filed by code numbers and by the month in which the transaction occurred. Store the originals in a fireproof cabinet.

Most purveyors will issue a monthly statement itemizing all the invoices and the total amount due. Payment may then be made once a month on the total amount rather with a separate check for each invoice received. Paying purveyors on a monthly-statement basis is advantageous. The shop's cash flow will be used more effectively, and there will be less administrative work. Before issuing the check, be certain that the monthly statement is accurate by cross-checking the statement against the invoices in the file. Staple the received invoices to the monthly statement for future reference.

Accounts must be closed out on the last day of each month in order to compute the monthly profits and costs accurately. Most monthly statements will not arrive until the fourth or fifth day of the following month. Thus, the bookkeeper must realize that, even though some bills may be paid in the following month, the cost of the goods and services will be applied to the month they were delivered to the shop. This will be crucial point for computing profits and costs.

In order to record purchases delivered to your premises accurately, you must record these expenditures in a separate ledger, called a purchase ledger. Use a loose-leaf binder to store all the purchase ledger pages. Separate purchase ledger pages are required for each of the following categories:

- Beverage costs
- Food costs
- Liquor costs

- Each operational category: services, utilities, etc.
- Other expenses

All invoices must be recorded in the purchase ledger under the date the items were delivered to the shop (this is a hard-and-fast rule, regardless of whether goods and services are paid for in cash or by credit or other terms). This pertains to all expenses, regardless of whether you intend to use the items during that particular month. For example: Expenses, such as the telephone bill, that may not arrive until the following month must be recorded under the month during which they were incurred.

The purchase ledgers will record all invoices when they are received. The ending inventories will make the necessary adjustments to determine the actual amount used over the month. This is necessary so that actual costs may be projected accurately. The crucial consideration now is to record every invoice in the purchase ledger under the correct expense category. This must be done on the date the material was received to ensure the cost projections calculated at the end of the month are accurate.

Total Monthly Purchases

To compute the total expenditure for each code over the month, simply add each expenditure column, then each page total on the purchase ledger. Credits are subtracted out of the shop's total purchases on the monthly statement.

The cut-off time for each month is the close of business on the last day of the month. Transactions after midnight on the last day of the month are still to be included in the month's totals, as they are a part of the business for that previous month (the measure of one day, for our purposes, is one complete business day or cycle). It is important to make sure that all costs are to be applied to the month the products were received at the shop, regardless of when they were paid for or used.

Some hints on preparing the purchase ledger:

- Enter all figures in pencil.
- Enter all credits in red with parentheses.
- Have purveyors that deliver products for more than one code make out a separate invoice for each code.

Managing the Shop's Cash Flow

Daily involvement and analyses of your financial records are necessary if the shop is to take full advantage of the credit terms and discounts offered by suppliers. Simply managing the operation's cash flow and using its enormous purchasing power can result in substantial savings.

After you have been operating for a few months, most purveyors will extend 30-day net terms if you request them. This is an advantageous situation; through proper management, your inventory may be turned over as many as five or six times in a 30-day period. In effect, the purveyors will be financing your operations. Few businesses can turn their inventories over this quickly, so they are forced to pay interest or finance charges. Quick turnover is one of the blessings of the retail beverage and food industry. Careful planning and synchronization between the purchasing and bookkeeping departments are needed to obtain maximum utilization of the cash flow. The savings are well worth the additional effort.

Section 2: Revenue Accounts and Reconciliation

Revenue is the sales received for the shop's products; primarily beverages and food. The procedures in this section for setting up revenue accounts are the basis of the shop's controls. Every transaction will be checked and balanced. When the procedures are completed, there will be no margin for error and no loss of revenue.

Preparing and Auditing Sales Reports

The procedures for preparing and auditing sales reports are listed below in numerical order. This is the order in which the bookkeeper should begin to record and reconcile the previous day's transactions:

- Remove the cash drawer, tickets, charge forms, prep forms, and reports from the safe where the manager placed at the close of the previous business day.

- Separate the cashier drawer, tickets, and forms into their respective piles. Work in a closed, locked office while the cash is out of the safe.

- Begin by verifying the Cashier's Reports. Count out and separate the cash by denomination. The total amount taken in must equal the difference between the new and old cash register readings. These figures should all be in order, as the manager checked and verified the sales of the previous day with the cashier. Any discrepancies should be immediately brought to the manager's attention.

- Using new Cashier's Report Forms, enter the new register readings in the space provided on the reports.

- Make up new cash drawers for each register. Enter the total and itemized amounts on the reports in the "Cash In" sections. Sign the reports and place them in the cash drawers. Place the drawers back into the safe. Return to the safe the remaining cash, charges, and checks. Later on, you will need all these items to make up the daily deposit.

- Using the Waiter/Waitress Ticket Record Form, verify that all tickets have been turned in. The total number issued must equal the amount used and returned. Should there be any tickets missing, determine which ticket number is missing, and which employee was issued the missing ticket. Notify the manager immediately. The manager should have verified that all tickets were turned in the previous day. This, again, is a double-check.

- From the unused tickets, issue new tickets. Issue the same number of tickets to each employee. Using the employee schedule, write on the appropriate forms the name of each waitperson. Write in the total number of tickets issued and the number sequences of each employee's tickets. Place a rubber band around each pile of tickets. On the top ticket write in the employee's name so that the manager knows to whom they should be issued. When this is completed, place everything in the safe.

- Take the used waitstaff tickets from the previous business day, check each for accuracy. Make certain that: the correct price was charged (this is a double-check on the cashier), the ticket was added correctly, and sales tax was computed and entered correctly. Waitstaff and cashiers may be charged for these mistakes in some states. Regardless of the legality, they must be notified of their errors and correct them in the future. Write up all mistakes and post the sheet on the bulletin board at the completion of each day. Mistakes in writing tickets are caused by careless employees and can be a great expense to your business. Management should use whatever action is necessary to resolve and limit the problem.

- Take the credit card sales drafts and separate them into piles by company. Each employee is responsible for his or her own credit card charges, but they should be double-checked by the cashier. Verify the accuracy of each charge and make sure the charge slip is signed and dated.

- Separate and examine for accuracy any checks received. The manager should have approved personal checks. The customer's driver's license number and telephone number should be listed on the back. Only the manager should approve traveler's checks. The manager must witness the second signature and compare it to the first. Total and verify all the charge and check amounts.

- The total sales multiplied by the percentage of sales tax must equal the total sales tax taken in. After this step, all sales will be completely checked and balanced by three different individuals and against every other transaction that occurred in the shop. There is no possible way items or money could be stolen undetected, unless every single employee — including the manager — were in collusion.

- Make up the daily deposit. Use indelible ink, and prepare two copies of the deposit form. Stamp all checks with the establishment's account number and "For Deposit Only." Put the appropriate employee's name on the back of each check so that, if it is returned, the manager can go back to the employee who accepted it.

- Sort the bills and wrap as much of the coins as possible. Credit card sales receipts can usually be deposited along with your cash deposit or electronically direct from the terminal. If your bank does not offer this service, you will have to mail the receipts directly to the credit card company. The manager should bring the deposit over to the bank every day personally. Change or small bills needed for the following day should be picked up at this time.

- Never let two days' worth of receipts sit in the safe. Make certain the deposit receipt is returned and filed in a fireproof box. Check the duplicate deposit stub against the deposit receipt to make sure the correct amount was deposited. Enter the deposit amount, date, and source onto the check register. Enter the verified figures for the day on the your Daily Sales Report Form.

- To compute individual category percentages, divide the category sales by the total daily sales. "Actual Month-to-Date Sales" is a tally of the daily sales. "Cash, Over/Short" refers to any mistakes made at the register.

This concludes the reconciliation part of the revenue accounts. Every item and sale is accounted for and reconciled against every other transaction in the shop. Keep all of these forms for at least five years in a fireproof storage file. All forms used during the month may be kept in loose-leaf binders in the bookkeeper's office. The daily sales ledger should be left at the manager's desk at the end of the day. Remember that all this information is strictly confidential and should never be the subject of idle conversation.

Preparing the payroll is best left to a computerized payroll program, such as in QuickBooks or Sage North America, or using a computer service.

Tipped Employees

One of the biggest challenges that owners and managers face in retail beverage and food operations, in regard to payroll, is getting employees to report and pay taxes on their tips, as required by the IRS. Complying with the intricacies of the tip-reporting and allocation rules can be difficult and confusing. Tip tax laws are constantly changing. You must use extreme caution in this area; get assistance from your accountant or attorney.

Tip Rate Determination and Education Program

The Tip Rate Determination and Education Program was developed by the Internal Revenue Service in 1993 to address the concern of widespread underreporting of tip income in the food and beverage industry. The goal was to involve employers in monitoring their employees' tip-reporting practices.

There are two different IRS programs available: the Tip Rate Determination Agreement (TRDA) and the Tip Reporting Alternative Commitment (TRAC). Participation in one of these programs is voluntary, but you may only enter into one of the agreements at a time. Please note that 1998 tax legislation specifies that IRS agents cannot threaten to audit you in order to convince you to sign a TRDA or TRAC agreement.

The big benefit for you as an employer is that you will not be subject to unplanned tax liabilities. Those who sign a TRAC or a TRDA agreement receive a commitment from the IRS that the agency will not examine the owner's books to search for under-withheld or underpaid payroll taxes on tip income. There are benefits to employees, also, including increases in their Social Security, unemployment compensation, retirement plan, and workers' compensation benefits.

Under TRDA, the IRS works with you to arrive at a tip rate for your employees. Then, at least 75 percent of your tipped workers must agree in writing to report tips at the agreed-upon rate. If they fail to do so, you are required to turn them in to the IRS. If you do not comply, the agreement is terminated, and your business becomes subject to IRS auditing.

The TRAC is less strict but requires more work on your part. There is no established tip rate, but you are required to work with employees to make sure they understand their tip-reporting obligations. You must set up a process to receive employees' cash tip reports, and they must be informed of the tips you are recording from credit card receipts.

Tip Credits for Employers Are Possible

As an employer, you also may be eligible for credit for taxes paid on certain employee tips (IRS Form 8846). You will not, however, get credit for your part of Social Security and Medicare taxes on those tips that are used to meet the federal minimum wage rate applicable to the employee under the Fair Labor Standards Act. This is also subject to state laws. You must increase the amount of your taxable income by the amount of the tip credit. Note the following changes to this credit:

- The credit is effective for your part of Social Security and Medicare taxes paid after 1993, regardless of whether your employees reported the tips to you or when your employees performed the services.
- Effective for services performed after 1996, the credit applies to the taxes on tips your employees receive from customers in connection with providing, delivering, or serving food or beverages, regardless of whether the customers consume the food or beverages on your business premises.

Additional Information on Tip Reporting

The following IRS forms and publications relating to tip income reporting can be downloaded directly from the IRS's Web site: **www.irs.gov**. Look under the heading Forms and Publications by Number.

- Pub 505 — Tax Withholding and Estimated Tax
- Pub 531 — Reporting Tip Income
- Form 941 — Employer's Quarterly Federal Tax Return
- Form 4137 — Social Security and Medicare Tax on Unreported Tip Income
- Form 8027 — Employer's Annual Information on Tip Income and Allocated Tips

Employee Tip Reporting "Frequently Asked Questions"

As an employee, the tip income received, whether it is cash or included in a charge, is taxable income. As income, these tips are subject to federal income tax and Social Security and Medicare taxes, and may be subject to state income tax as well.

Q: *What tips do I have to report?*

A: If you received $20 or more in tips in any one month, you should report all your tips to your employer so that federal income tax, Social Security and Medicare taxes — maybe state income tax, too — can be withheld.

Q: *Do I have to report all my tips on my tax return?*

A: Yes. All tips are income and should be reported on your tax return.

Q: *Is it true that only 8 percent of my total sales must be reported as tips?*

A: No. You must report to your employer all (100 percent) of your tips except for the tips totaling less than $20 in any month. The 8-percent rule applies to employers.

Q: *Do I need to report tips from other employees?*

A: Yes. Employees who are indirectly tipped by other employees are required to report "tip-outs." This could apply to bus persons, for instance.

Q: *Do I have to report tip-outs that I pay to indirectly tipped employees?*

A: If you are a directly tipped employee, you should report to your employer only the amount of tips you retain. Maintain records of tip-outs with your other tip income (cash tips, charged tips, split tips, tip pool).

Q: *What records do I need to keep?*

A: You must keep a running daily log of all your tip income.

Q: *What can happen if I do not keep a record of my tips?*

A: Under-reporting could result in your owing substantial taxes, penalties, and interest to the IRS and possibly other agencies.

Q: *If I report all my tips to my employer, do I still have to keep records?*

A: Yes. You should keep a daily log of your tips so that, in case of an examination, you can substantiate the actual amount of tips received.

Q: *Why should I report my tips to my employer?*

A: When you report your tip income to your employer, the employer is required to withhold federal income tax, Social Security and Medicare taxes and, maybe, state income tax. Tip reporting may increase your Social Security credits, resulting in greater Social Security benefits when you retire. Tip reporting also may increase other benefits to which you may become entitled, such as unemployment benefits or retirement benefits. Additionally, a greater income may improve financing approval for mortgages, car loans, and other loans.

Q *I forgot to report my tip income to my employer, but I remembered to record it on my federal income tax return. Will that present a problem?*

A: If you do not report your tip income to your employer, but you do report the tip income on your federal income tax return, you may owe a 50-percent Social Security and Medicare tax penalty, be subject to a negligence penalty, and possibly an estimated tax penalty.

Q: *If I report all my tips, but my taxes on the tips are greater than my pay from my employer, how do I pay the remaining taxes?*

A: You can either pay the tax when you file your federal income tax return or you can reach into your tip money and give some to your employer to be applied to those owed taxes.

Q: *What can happen if I do not report my tips to the IRS?*

A: If the IRS determines through an examination that you under-reported your tips, you could be subject to additional federal income tax, Social Security and Medicare taxes, and possibly state income tax. You also will be accessed a penalty of 50 percent of the additional Social Security and Medicare taxes and a negligence penalty of 20 percent of the additional income tax, plus any interest that may apply.

Q: *What is my responsibility as an employee under the Tip Rate Determination Agreement (TRDA)?*

A: You are required to file your federal tax returns. You must sign a Tipped Employee Participation Agreement, proclaiming that you are participating in the program. To stay a participating employee, you must report tips at or above the tip rate determined by the agreement.

Q: *What is my responsibility as an employee under the Tip Reporting Alternative Commitment (TRAC)?*

A: Directly tipped employee: Your employer will furnish you a written statement (at least monthly) reflecting your charged tips:

- You are to verify or correct this statement.
- You are to indicate the amount of cash tips received.
- When reporting your cash tips, keep in mind that there is a correlation between charged tips and cash tips.
- You may be asked to provide the name and amount of any tip-outs you have given to indirectly tipped employees.

A: Indirectly tipped employee: You are required to report all your tips to your employer.

What an Employer Must Record for Tip Records

It is in your company's best interest to insist that all employees accurately report their income from tips. The IRS will hold you responsible. Establishments that do not comply are subject to IRS audit and possible tax liabilities, penalties, and interest payments. As a precaution, if you have any employees who customarily receive tips from customers, patrons, or other third parties, we recommend you keep the following additional information about tipped employees:

- Indicate on the pay records — by a symbol, letter, or other notation placed next to his or her name — each tipped employee.
- Weekly or monthly amount of tips reported by each employee
- The amount by which the wages of each tipped employee have been increased by tips
- The hours worked each workday in any occupation in which the employee does not receive tips, and the total daily or weekly earnings for those times

- The hours worked each workday in any occupation in which the employee receives tips, and the total daily or weekly straight-time earnings for those times.

Large Food or Beverage Establishments Need to File Form 8027 with the IRS

You may meet the definition of a "large food or beverage establishment" if you employ more than 10 employees. If you do, the law requires that you file Form 8027, Employer's Annual Information Return of Tip Income and Allocated Tips, with the IRS.

If you meet the definition, the law requires that you report certain tip information to the IRS on an annual basis. You should use Form 8027 to report information such as total charged tips, charged receipts, total reported tips by employees, and gross receipts from food and beverage operations. Also, employers must allocate tips to certain directly tipped employees and include the allocation on their employees' W-2 forms when the total of reported tips is less than 8 percent.

To find out more about tip-reporting programs and whether you should be filing Form 8027, contact the tip coordinator of your local IRS office. Check your telephone directory for the IRS office in your area. They can provide the mailing address and phone number for the tip coordinator.

You can get a copy of Form 8027 and its instructions by calling 800-TAX-FORM (800-829-3676) or visit **www.irs.gov/Forms-&-Pubs**.

Section 3: Payroll

Payroll Accounting

Although you may decide to use an outside payroll service or a software program, your bookkeeper must still be involved in the computation of the daily labor costs. After each pay period, the bookkeeper will need to compute each employee's time card and call the information to the payroll service company or key the information into the accounting software. There are time clocks now available that can link employee scheduling, time clock administration, and accounting all into one fool-proof system. Described in this section are the procedures used to compute and analyze by manual system daily and monthly labor costs.

On a daily basis the bookkeeper should:

- Gather all of the employees' time cards.

- Using the posted schedule, ensure that each employee punched in at the scheduled time.

- Compute the number and fraction of hours worked.

- Enter hours worked on the time card and on the Daily Payroll Form. Any overtime should be written in red on a separate line. Notify the manager of any overtime or of any employee who is approaching overtime status. The manager may be able to rearrange the schedule to avoid paying overtime.

- Fill in the hourly rate of pay. If the employee performs more than one job, make sure the rate of pay corresponds to the job performed.

- Extend the gross amount to be paid.

- Divide each salaried employee's total monthly salary by the number of days in the month. Enter this figure in the "Gross Paid" column for each day. Although the employee will be paid the same each week, the salary is broken down this way so that labor may be analyzed and budgeted accurately.

- The manager's and owner's salaries should be listed separately at the bottom of the Daily Payroll Form. These costs are separated, as they will be budgeted differently. Also, by separating them out, you may get some additional tax advantages.

- Total the gross amount payable for each day at the bottom of the form. When the week is completed (seven days), total each employee's hours worked and total gross pay. Check your calculations by cross-checking all of the figures against each other.

- Enter the daily sales and labor costs on the Labor Analysis Form. An example of this form can be found at the end of this chapter. Remember that manager's and owner's salaries are computed separately and are not in the total labor cost computations. The Labor Analysis Form is divided into two sections: the daily payroll and the month-to-date payroll. These are computed by adding each day's transactions to the previous day's balance. Budget figures will be explained in the next chapter.

The month-to-date payroll percentage is computed by dividing month-to-date sales by the month-to-date actual payroll costs. The budget figures are the budgeted total labor costs divided by the number of days in the month. The month-to-date payroll column is the prorated budgeted amount.

Use caution: Regulations and laws on tips and tip reporting are constantly changing.

Employer Tax Calendar

This calendar covers various due dates of interest to employers. Principally, it covers the following three federal taxes:

- Income tax you withhold from your employees' wages or from non-payroll amounts you pay out.

- Social Security and Medicare taxes (FICA taxes) you withhold from your employees' wages and the Social Security and Medicare taxes you must pay as an employer.

- Federal unemployment (FUTA) tax you must pay as an employer.

The calendar lists due dates for filing returns and for making deposits of these three taxes throughout the year. Use this calendar with Publication 15, which lists the deposit rules.

Forms You May Need

The following is a list and description of the primary employment tax forms you may need:

- **Form 940 (or 940-EZ), Employer's Annual Federal Unemployment (FUTA) Tax Return.** This form is due one month after the calendar year ends. Use it to report the FUTA tax you paid. Most employers can use Form 940-EZ, which is a simplified version of Form 940.

- **Form 941, Employer's Quarterly Federal Tax Return.** This form is due one month after the calendar quarter ends. Use it to report Social Security and Medicare taxes and withheld income taxes on wages if your employees are not farm workers.

- **Form 943, Employer's Annual Tax Return for Agricultural Employees.** This form is due one month after the calendar year ends. Use it to report Social Security and Medicare taxes and withheld income taxes on wages if your employees are farm workers.

- **Form 945, Annual Return of Withheld Federal Income Tax.** This form is due one month after the calendar year ends. Use it to report income tax withheld on all non-payroll items. Non-payroll items include the following:

- Backup withholding
- Withholding on pensions, annuities, IRAs, and gambling winnings
- Payments of American Indian gaming profits to tribal members

- **Fiscal-year taxpayers.** The dates in this calendar apply whether you use a fiscal year or a calendar year as your tax year. The only exception is the date for filing Form 5500 and 5500-EZ. These employee benefit plan forms are due by the last day of the seventh month after the plan year ends. See July 31, later.

- **Extended due dates.** If you deposit, in full and on time, the tax you are required to report on Form 940, 941, 943, or 945, you have an additional 10 days to file that form.

FIRST QUARTER

The first quarter of a calendar year is made up of January, February, and March.

- All employers. Give your employees their copies of Form W-2 for 2014 by January 31, 2015.

January 2

Earned income credit. Stop advance payments of the earned income credit for any employee who did not give you a new Form W-5 for 2014.

January 15

Social Security, Medicare, and withheld income tax. If the monthly deposit rule applies, deposit the tax for payments in December 2014.

Non-payroll withholding. If the monthly deposit rule applies, deposit the tax for payments in December 2014.

January 31

All employers. Give your employees their copies of Form W-2 for 2014.

- **Payers of gambling winnings.** If you either paid reportable gambling winnings or withheld income tax from gambling winnings, give the winners their copies of Form W-2G.

- **Non-payroll taxes.** File Form 945 to report income tax withheld for 2014 on all non-payroll items, including backup withholding and withholding on pensions, annuities, IRAs, gambling winnings, and payments of American Indian gaming profits to tribal members. Deposit any undeposited tax. (If your tax liability is less than $2,500, you can pay it in full with a timely filed return.) If you deposited the tax for the year in full and on time, you have until February 11 to file the return.

- **Social Security,** Medicare, and withheld income tax. File Form 941 for the fourth quarter of 2014. Deposit any undeposited tax. (If your tax liability is less than $2,500, you can pay it in full with a timely filed return.) If you deposited the tax for the quarter in full and on time, you have until February 11 to file the return.

- **Farm employers.** File Form 943 to report Social Security and Medicare taxes and withheld income tax for 2014. Deposit any undeposited tax. (If your tax liability is less than $2,500, you can pay it in full with a timely filed return.) If you deposited the tax for the year in full and on time, you have until February 11 to file the return.

- **Federal unemployment tax.** File Form 940 (or 940-EZ) for 2014. If your undeposited tax is $100 or less, you can either pay it with your return or deposit it. If it is more than $100, you must deposit it. However, if you already deposited the tax for the year in full and on time, you have until February 11 to file the return.

February 11

Non-payroll taxes. File Form 945 to report income tax withheld for 2014 on all non-payroll items. This due date applies only if you deposited the tax for the year in full and on time.

Social Security, Medicare, and withheld income tax. File Form 941 for the fourth quarter of 2014. This due date applies only if you deposited the tax for the quarter in full and on time.

Farm employers. File Form 943 to report Social Security, Medicare, and withheld income tax for 2014. This due date applies only if you deposited the tax for the year in full and on time.

Federal unemployment tax. File Form 940 (or 940-EZ) for 2014. This due date applies only if you deposited the tax for the year in full and on time.

February 15

Social Security, Medicare, and withheld income tax. If the monthly deposit rule applies, deposit the tax for payments in January.

Non-payroll withholding. If the monthly deposit rule applies, deposit the tax for payments in January.

February 19

All employers. Begin withholding income tax from the pay of any employee who claimed exemption from withholding in 2014, but did not give you a new Form W-4 to continue the exemption this year.

February 28

Payers of gambling winnings. File Form 1096, Annual Summary and Transmittal of U.S. Information Returns, along with Copy A of all the Forms W-2G you issued for 2014.

If you file Forms W-2G electronically (not by magnetic media), your due date for filing them with the IRS will be extended to April 1. The due date for giving the recipient these forms will still be January 31.

All employers. File Form W-3, Transmittal of Wage and Tax Statements, along with Copy A of all the Forms W-2 you issued for 2014.

If you file Forms W-2 electronically (not by magnetic media), your due date for filing them with the Social Security Administration (SSA) will be extended to April 1. The due date for giving the recipient these forms will still be January 31.

Large food and beverage establishment employers. File Form 8027, Employer's Annual Information Return of Tip Income and Allocated Tips. Use Form 8027-T, Transmittal of Employer's Annual Information Return of Tip Income and Allocated Tips, to summarize and transmit Forms 8027 if you have more than one establishment.

March 15

Social Security, Medicare, and withheld income tax. If the monthly deposit rule applies, deposit the tax for payments in February.

Non-payroll withholding. If the monthly deposit rule applies, deposit the tax for payments in February.

SECOND QUARTER

The second quarter of a calendar year is made up of April, May, and June.

April 1

Electronic filing of Forms W-2. File Copy A of all the Forms W-2 you issued for 2014. This due date applies only if you file electronically (not by magnetic media). Otherwise, see February 28.

The due date for giving the recipient these forms will still be January 31.

Electronic filing of Forms W-2G. File copies of all the Forms W-2G you issued for 2014. This due date applies only if you file electronically (not by magnetic media). Otherwise, see February 28.

The due date for giving the recipient these forms will still be January 31.

For information about filing Forms W-2G electronically, see Publication 1220, Specifications for Filing Forms 1098, 1099, 5498, and W-2G Magnetically or Electronically.

April 15

Social Security, Medicare, and withheld income tax. If the monthly deposit rule applies, deposit the tax for payments in March.

Non-payroll withholding. If the monthly deposit rule applies, deposit the tax for payments in March.

Household employers. If you paid cash wages of $1,300 or more in 2014 to a household employee, file Schedule H (Form 1040) with your income tax return and report any employment taxes. Report any federal unemployment (FUTA) tax on Schedule H if you paid total cash wages of $1,000 or more in any calendar quarter of 2014 to household employees. Also, report any income tax you withheld for your household employees. For more information, see Publication 926.

April 30

Social Security, Medicare, and withheld income tax. File Form 941 for the first quarter of 2015. Deposit any undeposited tax. (If your tax liability is less than $2,500, you can pay it in full with a timely filed return.) If you deposited the tax for the quarter in full and on time, you have until May 10 to file the return.

Federal unemployment tax. Deposit the tax owed through March if more than $100.

May 10

Social Security, Medicare, and withheld income tax. File Form 941 for the first quarter of 2015. This due date applies only if you deposited the tax for the quarter in full and on time.

May 15

Social Security, Medicare, and withheld income tax. If the monthly deposit rule applies, deposit the tax for payments in April.

Non-payroll withholding. If the monthly deposit rule applies, deposit the tax for payments in April.

June 17

Social Security, Medicare, and withheld income tax. If the monthly deposit rule applies, deposit the tax for payments in May.

Non-payroll withholding. If the monthly deposit rule applies, deposit the tax for payments in May.

THIRD QUARTER

The third quarter of a calendar year is made up of July, August, and September.

July 15

Social Security, Medicare, and withheld income tax. If the monthly deposit rule applies, deposit the tax for payments in June.

Non-payroll withholding. If the monthly deposit rule applies, deposit the tax for payments in June.

July 31

Social Security, Medicare, and withheld income tax. File Form 941 for the second quarter of 2015. Deposit any undeposited tax. (If your tax liability is less than $2,500, you can pay it in full with a timely filed return.) If you deposited the tax for the quarter in full and on time, you have until August 12 to file the return.

Federal unemployment tax. Deposit the tax owed through June if more than $100.

All employers. If you maintain an employee benefit plan, such as a pension, profit-sharing or stock bonus plan, file Form 5500 or 5500-EZ for calendar year 2014. If you use a fiscal year as your plan year, file the form by the last day of the seventh month after the plan year ends.

August 12

Social Security, Medicare, and withheld income tax. File Form 941 for the second quarter of 2013. This due date applies only if you deposited the tax for the quarter in full and on time.

August 15

Social Security, Medicare, and withheld income tax. If the monthly deposit rule applies, deposit the tax for payments in July.

Non-payroll withholding. If the monthly deposit rule applies, deposit the tax for payments in July.

September 16

Social Security, Medicare, and withheld income tax. If the monthly deposit rule applies, deposit the tax for payments in August.

Non-payroll withholding. If the monthly deposit rule applies, deposit the tax for payments in August.

FOURTH QUARTER

The fourth quarter of a calendar year is made up of October, November, and December.

October 15

Social Security, Medicare, and withheld income tax. If the monthly deposit rule applies, deposit the tax for payments in September.

Non-payroll withholding. If the monthly deposit rule applies, deposit the tax for payments in September.

October 31

Social Security, Medicare, and withheld income tax. File Form 941 for the third quarter of 2015. Deposit any undeposited tax. (If your tax liability is less than $2,500, you can pay it in full with a timely filed return.) If you deposited the tax for the quarter in full and on time, you have until November 12 to file the return.

Federal unemployment tax. Deposit the tax owed through September if more than $100.

During November

Income tax withholding. Ask employees whose withholding allowances will be different in 2016 to fill out a new Form W-4.

Earned income credit. Request each eligible employee who wants to receive advance payments of the earned income credit during the year 2016 to fill out a Form W-5. A new Form W-5 must be filled out each year before any payments are made.

November 12

Social Security, Medicare, and withheld income tax. File Form 941 for the third quarter of 2015. This due date applies only if you deposited the tax for the quarter in full and on time.

November 15

Social Security, Medicare, and withheld income tax. If the monthly deposit rule applies, deposit the tax for payments in October.

Non-payroll withholding. If the monthly deposit rule applies, deposit the tax for payments in October.

December 16

Social Security, Medicare, and withheld income tax. If the monthly deposit rule applies, deposit the tax for payments in November.

Non-payroll withholding. If the monthly deposit rule applies, deposit the tax for payments in November.

General Tax Calendar

This tax calendar has the due dates for 2015 that most taxpayers will need. Employers and persons who pay excise taxes should also use the Employer's Tax Calendar and the Excise Tax Calendar.

Fiscal-year taxpayers. If you file your income tax return for a fiscal year rather than the calendar year, you must change some of the dates in this calendar. These changes are described under Fiscal-Year Taxpayers at the end of this calendar.

FIRST QUARTER

The first quarter of a calendar year is made up of January, February, and March.

January 10

Employees who work for tips. If you received $20 or more in tips during December, report them to your employer. You can use Form 4070, Employee's Report of Tips to Employer.

January 15

Individuals. Make a payment of your estimated tax for 2014 if you did not pay your income tax for the year through withholding (or did not pay in enough tax that way). Use Form 1040-ES. This is the final installment date for 2014 estimated tax. However, you do not have to make this payment if you file your 2014 return (Form 1040) and pay any tax due by January 31, 2015.

Farmers and fishermen. Pay your estimated tax for 2015 using Form 1040-ES. You have until April 15 to file your 2014 income tax return (Form 1040). If you do not pay your estimated tax by January 15, you must file your 2014 return and pay any tax due by March 1, 2015, to avoid an estimated tax penalty.

January 31

Individuals. File your income tax return (Form 1040) for 2014 if you did not pay your last installment of estimated tax by January 15. Filing your return and paying any tax due by January 31 prevents any penalty for late payment of the last installment.

All businesses. Give annual information statements to recipients of certain payments you made during 2014. (You can use the appropriate version of Form 1099 or other information return.) Payments that are covered include the following:

- Compensation for workers who are not considered employees (including fishing boat proceeds to crew members)
- Dividends and other corporate distributions
- Interest
- Amounts paid in real estate transactions
- Rent
- Royalties
- Amounts paid in broker and barter exchange transactions
- Payments to attorneys
- Payments of American Indian gaming profits to tribal members
- Profit-sharing distributions
- Retirement plan distributions
- Original issue discount
- Prizes and awards
- Medical and health care payments
- Debt cancellation (treated as payment to debtor)
- Cash payments over $10,000 (See the instructions for Form 8300, Report of Cash Payments Over $10,000 Received in a Trade or Business.)

See the 2014 Instructions for Forms 1099, 1098, 5498, and W-2G for information on what payments are covered, how much the payment must be before a statement is required, which form to use, and extensions of time to provide statements.

February 11

Employees who work for tips. If you received $20 or more in tips during January, report them to your employer. Use Form 4070.

February 15

Individuals. If you claimed exemption from income tax withholding last year on the Form W-4 you gave your employer, you must file a new Form W-4 by this date to continue your exemption for another year.

February 28

All businesses. File information returns (Form 1099) for certain payments you made during 2014. These payments are described under January 31. There are different forms for different types of payments. Use a separate Form 1096 to summarize and transmit the forms for each type of payment. See the 2014 Instructions for Forms 1099, 1098, 5498, and W-2G for information on what payments are covered, how much the payment must be before a return is required, what form to use and extensions of time to file.

If you file Forms 1098, 1099 or W-2G electronically (not by magnetic media), your due date for filing them with the IRS will be extended to April 1. The due date for giving the recipient these forms will still be January 31.

March 1

Farmers and fishermen. File your 2014 income tax return (Form 1040) and pay any tax due. However, you have until April 15 to file if you paid your 2014 estimated tax by January 15, 2015.

March 11

Employees who work for tips. If you received $20 or more in tips during February, report them to your employer. You can use Form 4070.

March 15

Corporations. File a 2014 calendar year income tax return (Form 1120 or 1120-A) and pay any tax due. If you want an automatic six-month extension of time to file the return, file Form 7004, and deposit what you estimate you owe.

S corporations. File a 2014 calendar year income tax return (Form 1120S) and pay any tax due. Provide each shareholder with a copy of Schedule K-1 (Form 1120S), Shareholder's Share of Income, Credits, Deductions, Etc., or a substitute Schedule K-1. If you want an automatic six-month extension of time to file the return, file Form 7004, and deposit what you estimate you owe.

S corporation election. File Form 2553, Election by a Small Business Corporation, to choose to be treated as an S corporation beginning with calendar year 2013. If Form 2553 is filed late, S treatment will begin with calendar year 2016.

Electing large partnerships. Provide each partner with a copy of Schedule K-1 (Form 1065-B), Partner's Share of Income (Loss) From an Electing Large Partnership. This due date is effective for the first March 15 following the close of the partnership's tax year. The due date of March 15 applies even if the partnership requests an extension of time to file the Form 1065-B by filing Form 8736 or Form 8800.

SECOND QUARTER

The second quarter of a calendar year is made up of April, May, and June.

April 1

Electronic filing of Forms 1098, 1099, and W-2G. File Forms 1098, 1099 or W-2G with the IRS. This due date applies only if you file electronically (not by magnetic media). Otherwise, see February 28.

The due date for giving the recipient these forms will still be January 31.

For information about filing Forms 1098, 1099, or W-2G electronically, see Publication 1220, Specifications for Filing Forms 1098, 1099, 5498, and W-2G magnetically or electronically.

April 10

Employees who work for tips. If you received $20 or more in tips during March, report them to your employer. You can use Form 4070.

April 15

Individuals. File an income tax return for 2014 (Form 1040, 1040A or 1040-EZ) and pay any tax due. If you want an automatic four-month extension of time to file the return, file Form 4868, Application for Automatic Extension of Time to File U.S. Individual Income Tax Return, or you can get an extension by phone if you pay part or all of your estimated income tax due with a credit card. Then file Form 1040, 1040A, or 1040-EZ by August 15. If you want an additional two-month extension, file Form 2688, Application for Additional Extension of Time to File U.S. Individual Income Tax Return, as soon as possible so that your application can be acted on before August 15.

Household employers. If you paid cash wages of $1,300 or more in 2014 to a household employee, file Schedule H (Form 1040) with your income tax return and report any employment taxes. Report any federal unemployment (FUTA) tax on Schedule H if you paid total cash wages of $1,000 or more in any calendar quarter of 2014 or 2015 to household employees. Also, report any income tax you withheld for your household employees. For more information, see Publication 926.

Individuals. If you are not paying your 2015 income tax through withholding (or will not pay in enough tax during the year that way), pay the first installment of your 2015 estimated tax. Use Form 1040-ES. For more information, see Publication 505.

Partnerships. File a 2014 calendar year return (Form 1065). Provide each partner with a copy of Schedule K-1 (Form 1065), Partner's Share of Income, Credits, Deductions, Etc., or a substitute Schedule K-1. If you want an automatic three-month extension of time to file the return and provide Schedule K-1, file Form 8736. Then file Form 1065 by July 15. If you need an additional three-month extension, file Form 8800.

Electing large partnerships. File a 2014 calendar year return (Form 1065-B). If you want an automatic three-month extension of time to file the return, file Form 8736. Then file Form 1065-B by July 15. If you need an additional three-month extension, file Form 8800. See March 15 for the due date for furnishing the Schedules K-1 to the partners.

Corporations. Deposit the first installment of estimated income tax for 2015. A worksheet, Form 1120-W, is available to help you estimate your tax for the year.

May 10

Employees who work for tips. If you received $20 or more in tips during April, report them to your employer. You can use Form 4070.

June 10

Employees who work for tips. If you received $20 or more in tips during May, report them to your employer. You can use Form 4070.

June 17

Individuals. If you are a U.S. citizen or resident alien living and working (or on military duty) outside the United States and Puerto Rico, file Form 1040, and pay any tax, interest, and penalties due. Otherwise, see April 15. If you want additional time to file your return, file Form 4868 to obtain two additional months to file. Then file Form 1040 by August 15. If you still need additional time, file Form 2688 to request an additional two months as soon as possible so that your application can be acted on before August 15.

However, if you are a participant in a combat zone, you may be able to further extend the filing deadline. See Publication 3, Armed Forces' Tax Guide.

Individuals. Make a payment of your 2015 estimated tax if you are not paying your income tax for the year through withholding (or will not pay enough in taxes that way). Use

Form 1040-ES. This is the second installment date for estimated tax in 2015. For more information, see Publication 505.

Corporations. Deposit the second installment of estimated income tax for 2015. A worksheet, Form 1120-W, is available to help you estimate your tax for the year.

THIRD QUARTER

The third quarter of a calendar year is made up of July, August, and September.

July 10

Employees who work for tips. If you received $20 or more in tips during June, report them to your employer. You can use Form 4070.

July 15

Partnerships. File a 2014 calendar year return (Form 1065). This due date applies only if you were given an automatic three-month extension. Provide each partner with a copy of Schedule K-1 (Form 1065) or a substitute K-1. If you need an additional three-month extension, file Form 8800.

Electing large partnerships. File a 2014 calendar year return (Form 1065-B). This due date applies only if you were given an automatic three-month extension. If you need an additional three-month extension, file Form 8800. See March 15 for the due date for furnishing the Schedules K-1 to the partners.

August 12

Employees who work for tips. If you received $20 or more in tips during July, report them to your employer. You can use Form 4070.

August 15

Individuals. If you have an automatic four-month extension to file your income tax return for 2014, file Form 1040, 1040A or 1040-EZ, and pay any tax, interest, and penalties due. If you need an additional two-month extension, file Form 2688.

September 10

Employees who work for tips. If you received $20 or more in tips during August, report them to your employer. You can use Form 4070.

September 16

Individuals. Make a payment of your 2015 estimated tax if you are not paying your income tax for the year through withholding (or will not pay in enough tax that way). Use Form

1040-ES. This is the third installment date for estimated tax in 2013. For more information, see Publication 505.

Corporations. File a 2014 calendar year income tax return (Form 1120 or 1120-A) and pay any tax due. This due date applies only if you timely requested an automatic six-month extension. Otherwise, see March 15.

S corporations. File a 2014 calendar year income tax return (Form 1120S) and pay any tax due. This due date applies only if you timely requested an automatic six-month extension. Otherwise, see March 15. Provide each shareholder with a copy of Schedule K-1 (Form 1120S) or a substitute Schedule K-1.

Corporations. Deposit the third installment of estimated income tax for 2015. A worksheet, Form 1120-W, is available to help you make an estimate of your tax for the year.

FOURTH QUARTER

The fourth quarter of a calendar year is made up of October, November, and December.

October 10

Employees who work for tips. If you received $20 or more in tips during September, report them to your employer. You can use Form 4070.

October 15

Individuals. File a 2014 income tax return and pay any tax due if you were given an additional two-month extension.

Partnerships. File a 2014 calendar year return (Form 1065). This due date applies only if you were given an additional three-month extension. Provide each partner with a copy of Schedule K-1 (Form 1065) or a substitute K-1.

Electing large partnerships. File a 2014 calendar year return (Form 1065-B). This due date applies only if you were given an additional three-month extension. See March 15 for the due date for furnishing the Schedules K-1 to the partners.

November 12

Employees who work for tips. If you received $20 or more in tips during October, report them to your employer. You can use Form 4070.

December 10

Employees who work for tips. If you received $20 or more in tips during November, report them to your employer. You can use Form 4070.

December 16

Corporations. Deposit the fourth installment of estimated income tax for 2015. A worksheet, Form 1120-W, is available to help you estimate your tax for the year.

Fiscal Year Taxpayers

If you use a fiscal year (rather than the calendar year) as your tax year, you should change some of the dates in this calendar. Use the following general guidelines to make these changes.

Note: The three months that make up each quarter of a fiscal year may be different from those of each calendar quarter, depending on when the fiscal year begins.

Individuals

Form 1040. This form is due on the 15th day of the fourth month after the end of your tax year.

Estimated tax payments (Form 1040-ES). Payments are due on the 15th day of the fourth, sixth, and ninth months of your tax year and on the 15th day of the first month after your tax year ends.

Partnerships

Form 1065. This form is due on the 15th day of the fourth month after the end of the partnership's tax year. Provide each partner with a copy of Schedule K-1 (Form 1065) or a substitute Schedule K-1.

Form 1065-B (electing large partnerships). This form is due on the 15th day of the fourth month after the end of the partnership's tax year. Each partner must be provided with a copy of the Schedule K-1 (Form 1065-B) or a substitute Schedule K-1 by the first March 15 following the close of the partnership's tax year.

Corporations and S Corporations

Form 1120 and Form 1120S (or Form 7004). These forms are due on the 15th day of the third month after the end of the corporation's tax year. S corporations must provide each shareholder with a copy of Schedule K-1 (Form 1120S) or a substitute Schedule K-1.

Estimated tax payments. Payments are due on the 15th day of the fourth, sixth, ninth, and 12th months of the corporation's tax year.

Form 2553. This form is used to choose S corporation treatment. It is due by the 15th day of the third month of the first tax year to which the choice will apply or at any time during the preceding tax year.

> ### Etc.
>
> Some of the world's most powerful businesses, including Lloyds of London and the New York Stock Exchange, started life as coffee houses. The French and the American Revolutions were planned in coffee houses as well. —**www.justaboutcoffee.com**

18

Successful Budgeting and Profit Planning – For Maximum Results

All beverage and food operations are in business to make a profit. In order to plan financially, you must first set up a long-range plan detailing how much money you want the business to return and when. This financial plan is the shop's budget. This chapter will detail the steps for setting up a budget and the procedures on projecting actual operating costs.

Aside from being the shop's financial plan, the budget also is used to control costs and account for sales and products. Budgeting is an accounting record and a tool used to evaluate how effectively the shop, management, and employees operated during the month. Based on this information, management can then recognize cost problem areas and act accordingly to correct them.

Although many businesses maintain a yearly or quarterly budget, retail beverage, and food outlets, because of their fluctuating operating performances, should use a monthly budget. The annual budget and profit and loss statement then can be computed easily by totaling all 12 monthly budgets. Monthly budgeting is the system described in this book. Once set up and operating, about four hours each month is all that will be required to compute the old budget and project a new one. Although the shop may only be in the pre-opening stage, it is imperative that you start to develop an operating budget now. As soon as the budget is prepared, you will possess the control for guiding the business towards your financial goal.

Initially the proposed budget may be underflated or overinflated. You may have overruns, but at least you will be starting to gain control over the organization, rather than the organization controlling you. After a few months, you will have past operating budgets to guide you in projecting new ones. The budgeting process will become easier and more accurate as time goes by.

There are many other benefits to preparing and adhering to a monthly operational budget. Supervisors and key employees will develop increased awareness and concern about the business and controlling its costs. This involvement will invariably rub off on the other employees. A well-structured, defined budget and orderly financial records will aid you greatly in obtaining loans and will develop an important wealth of information should you decide to expand or sell in the future. Cost problems can be pinpointed easily once the expense categories are broken down. Last, but not least, you will become a better manager. Your financial decisions and forecasts will become increasingly consistent and accurate, as more information will be available to you. Financial problems may be seen approaching down the road rather than suddenly cropping up and forcing you to act quickly when you are uninformed. Management all too often reacts to a problem's symptoms, instead of curing the disease. Budgeting will give you the tool for an accurate diagnosis.

Projecting the Operational Budget

The following information describes in detail all of the operational costs listed on the operational budget, as well as how to accurately project each expenditure and revenue for the following month.

Sales

Projecting total sales is the most crucial and difficult aspect of budgeting. The fact that it is impossible to know how business will be from day to day makes budgeting total sales a perplexing task. Most costs are either variable or semi-variable, which means they will fluctuate directly in relation to the total monthly sales. Thus, projecting these costs depends largely upon using an accurate total sales figure. Projecting total sales, at first, will be difficult (and most likely inaccurate) but after several months of operation, your projections will be right on target. You will be surprised at how consistent sales and customer counts are and how easy it will be to consistently budget accurately.

The initial budgets may show unrealistic expectations. Sales probably will be low, as you will not have been able to build a substantial clientele or reputation. Operating costs will be higher than normal. It will take a couple of months to streamline and build an efficient coffee, espresso, and tea shop, even with the best laid plans. Labor and material costs will be extremely high, as there will be a lot of training, low productivity, and housed food, liquor, and wine. All of these costs are normal and should be anticipated. Profit margins will be small and possibly even nonexistent.

This period (4 to 12 weeks) should be used to ensure that your products are perfected and all the bugs are worked out of the systems. This is no time to cut back on costs. Your intention is to be in business for a long time. Allocate sufficient funds now to make sure the business gets off on the right foot and profits will be guaranteed for many years. Schedule a full staff every day to make certain all details will be covered. Discontinue those items that are passable but not of the quality level desired. Slow, clumsy service and only average coffees, teas, and food will never build sales. Strive for A-1 quality products and service. Constantly reiterate to employees this primary concern, and before long, they will self-monitor the quality. Once you develop a clientele and a solid reputation for serving consistent, quality products, the budget and profits will fall into place.

There are eight basic steps for projecting total sales:

1. If possible, use last year's customer count. This information can be found in last year's Daily Sales Report Form. Projections for the first year can be based upon prior months' reports and educated estimates.

2. Using a Sales Projection Form and a calendar, calculate the number of days in the month. Enter this figure in the first column. From the information in #1, calculate the average number of customers served each day. Enter this figure in the second column. Compute the average number of customers served on any holidays that may be in the month.

3. Multiply the number of days in the month by the average number of customers served for that day; enter the result in the "Subtotal" column. Add the eight "Subtotal" columns to arrive at the grand total.

4. Review and analyze the growth in customer counts during the past year (if applicable), current year, and current month. Based upon past customer counts, determine the percentage of growth or decline in growth anticipated in the coming month. Percentage of growth or decline can be computed by subtracting the most recent period of customer counts by the past period of customer counts. The difference is then divided by the actual number of customers served during the past period. A negative percentage figure shows a drop in customer counts. A positive figure indicates the percentage of increase. When computing and analyzing these computations, keep in mind that each period must have the same number and type of days. In other words, you can only accurately compare months that have the same number of Mondays, Tuesdays, and so forth, since sales are different for each day; the results and analysis would be inaccurate. The most accurate way to

analyze the percentage of growth or loss is to compare the previous month to the same month last year and then compare the percentage to the current month. Remember to examine only actual customer counts as indicators of growth; changes in sales may be the result of a price change.

5. Multiply the percentage of growth or loss by the grand total. Add the result to the grand total to compute the projected volume, or number of customers. Subtract this figure instead if you are multiplying by a negative percentage figure that indicates a loss in customer counts.

6. Multiply the projected volume by the average check of the past month. The average check amount may be located on the Daily Sales Report Form. Adjust this figure if a price increase will be occurring during the month. Separate menu sales all may be projected together unless the percentage of growth or loss is suspected in one area and not in the other two. A separate chart for each menu should then be used to project each sales amount; simply add the figures together from each separate category to compute grand total sales.

7. Compute individual beverages, food, and liquor sales by simply dividing total sales by the average percentage of sales on last month's Daily Sales Report Form. For example, a shop budgeted at $25,000 in sales that has a division of sales at 70 percent beverages, 20 percent food, and 10 percent liquor would have a breakdown of $17,500 beverages, $5,000 food, and $2,500 liquor sales.

8. The final step in budgeting sales is to enter the budgeted amount for each day on the Daily Sales Report Form. To compute the budgeted amount for each day, divide the total projected sales by the number of days in the month. This amount is the budgeted sales for one day. Enter this figure on line 1 of the first day of the month. Add this same amount to itself to compute the budgeted sales for day two, and continue adding this same amount to itself until you have computed the sales for each day. Double-check your calculations by running a tape on the sales. The total must equal the total budgeted sales projections. Breaking down sales this way will enable the manager to see exactly where actual sales are in relation to budgeted sales. On a daily basis, enter the amount over or under budget in sales in the appropriate column (use parentheses or a red pencil to enter sales that are under budget).

Material Costs

Material costs will fluctuate directly with the sales variance. More beverages, food, or liquor sales will result in higher material costs. In budgeting material costs, the important figure to analyze is not the actual cost but the percentage of cost, or the cost-of-sales percentage, as it is more commonly known. Compute the cost-of-sales percentage by dividing the actual cost of the category by the category's total sales. The result will be a percentage figure. This formula will present an accurate indication of the category's costs, as the cost of sales are proportionate to each other.

The cost-of-sales percentages for each category — beverages, food, or liquor — are projected when determining the selling price of each item. The projected percentage figure can be used initially in order to project the first month's budget. After several months of operation, the actual figure can be substituted.

Multiply the individual material costs by each respective budgeted percentage; the results are the budgeted cost amounts. For example: If beverage sales were budgeted at $50,000, and the beverage cost percentage was estimated at 40 percent, the budgeted beverage cost would be $20,000. Increases in product costs will raise the actual cost-of-sales amount; adjust the budgeted amount accordingly. However, be certain that if an increase is anticipated, the increase will affect the following month, which is what is being budgeted. Items purchased at a higher price and then stored in inventory will have no effect upon the following months actual cost of sales, as the product will not have been used. Add all three budgeted costs to compute the total budgeted material costs. Subtract the total gross costs from the total sales to compute the gross profit dollar amount. Divide gross profit by total sales to calculate the gross profit percentage.

Labor

Manager Salary

Manager salaries should be a fixed monthly cost. Total all the manager salaries for one year; divide this figure by the number of days in the year (usually 365), and multiply this cost by the number of days in one month. Salary changes during the year will require adjustments. When owners take an active part in the management of the business, or when the company is incorporated, the owners should have their salary amount included in this category.

Employee Salary

The employee salary expense is a semi-variable cost which will fluctuate directly with total sales. Employee labor costs have a break-even point, the point where the labor cost is covered by the profit from sales. As this point is reached and total sales increase, the labor cost percentage will decrease, increasing net profit. Thus, the cost of labor is determined by its efficiency and by the volume of sales it produces. Multiply the projected total sales by the average labor-cost percentage to arrive at the anticipated labor cost dollar amount. Adjust this figure in relation to the amount of employee training anticipated for the month.

Overtime

Overtime should be nonexistent — or at least kept to an absolute minimum. No amount should be budgeted for overtime. Money spent on overtime usually indicates poor management and inefficiency. Bookkeepers should be on the lookout for employees approaching 40 hours of work near the end of the week. Carefully prepared schedules will eliminate 98 percent of all overtime work and pay. Employees who wish to switch their schedules around should only be allowed to do so after approval from the manager.

Controllable Operational Costs

China and Utensils

Cost of china and utensils bought should be a consistent amount and percentage of sales for each month. Review Chapter 9: Successful Management of Operational Costs and Supplies.

Glassware

Same as china and utensils.

Hardware Supplies

Same as china and utensils. Capital expenditures for equipment with utility for more than one year generally must be depreciated over the item's anticipated life span.

Office Supplies

Cost of office supplies should be a fixed dollar amount each month. Capital expenditures must be depreciated.

Uniforms

The uniform expense will depend upon the state in which the shop is located and individual management policies. Some states allow the company to charge the employees for uniforms; others do not. Many establishments that do charge employees for uniforms do so at cost, which, if done correctly, should cost the business nothing but administrative time.

Laundry and Linen

Laundry and linen buying should be a consistent monthly expenditure, as laundry and linen usually is purchased once or twice a year in bulk. This expenditure column is for the purchase price only; cleaning is computed in a separate column, under "Services."

Services

Laundry Cleaning

Cleaning of laundry is a variable expense directly related to total sales. Multiply last month's percentage of cost by budgeted sales. Adjust the figure for price increases.

Protection

Protection should be a consistent, fixed monthly expenditure. Service-call charges should be coded to "Equipment Repairs" under "General Operating Costs."

Freight

This expense may not be applicable to all retail beverage and food outlets. Freight is the expense incurred shipping material via rail, truck, or other method to the shop for its exclusive use. Freight charges are usually only made to businesses in remote areas, or when the shop purchases a product and then has an independent company deliver it.

Legal

Legal service is a variable expense that can fluctuate greatly. Estimates for most legal work can be obtained, but it is best to budget a little each month to cover periodically large legal fees.

Accounting

A semi-fixed expense depending upon the amount and the type of accounting services used. Once set up and operating, the accounting expense should be a consistent monthly charge except for an annual tax-preparation and year-end audit fee.

Maintenance

Maintenance should be a fixed monthly expenditure if using a maintenance service company with contract service.

Payroll

A semi-fixed expense fluctuating directly with the number of employees on the payroll. Operations not using a computerized payroll service will not have a payroll preparation expense. The wages paid to the bookkeeper are included in the employee labor expenditure.

Utilities

Telephone

Telephone service should be a relatively consistent monthly expense. All long-distance phone calls should be recorded in a notebook (your local office supply store has a specially designed book for this purpose). The itemized phone bill should be compared against the recorded phone calls to justify each one.

Water

Water should be a semi-variable expense.

Gas

Gas may be a variable or semi-variable expense depending upon the type of equipment it operates. Gas used in heating will be a variable expense, because more will be used during the winter months than in the summer.

Electricity

Electricity may be a variable or semi-variable expense depending upon the type of equipment it operates. Electricity bills are normally higher during the summer months when the air-conditioning units are used.

Heat

Heat includes the cost of any heating material used but not listed above, such as coal, wood, oil, etc.

Fixed Operating Costs

Rent

This should be the monthly amount of rent or, if the building is leased, the monthly lease. Certain business-rental and lease agreements also include payment of a percentage of the total sales or per-tax profit amount. Should this be the situation, use the budgeted total sales figure, and project the anticipated amount due. Enter this amount and the total rent amount in the "Budgeted" column.

Insurance

Total all insurance premium amounts (fire, theft, liability, workers' compensation, etc.), and divide by 12. This figure will equal the average monthly insurance expense.

Property Taxes

If applicable, divide the annual property tax amount by 12. This figure will equal the average monthly property tax amount.

Depreciation

Depreciation will be discussed in detail in the following section.

General Operating Costs

Labor Taxes

This is the tax amount the employer is required to contribute to the state and federal government. A separate tax account should be set up with your bank to keep all the tax money separate. Labor taxes include: Social Security, federal unemployment tax, and state unemployment tax.

Other Taxes

This includes all miscellaneous taxes, such as local taxes, sales tax paid on purchases, etc. This column is for any tax the shop pays for goods and services. It is not for sales tax or other taxes the business collects, as they are not expenditures. Federal income tax is not a deductible expenditure and should not be listed here either.

Repairs: Equipment

This includes the cost of scheduled and emergency repairs and maintenance to all equipment. Always budget a base amount for normal service. Adjust this figure if major repairs or overhauls are anticipated.

Repairs: Building

This includes the cost of minor scheduled and emergency repairs and maintenance to the building. Always budget a base amount for normal repairs and maintenance. Large remodeling or rebuilding projects should be budgeted as a separate expenditure and depreciated.

Entertainment

Entertainment expenses are deductible only if the amounts spent are directly related to the active conduct of the business.

Advertising

Advertising includes all the costs of advertising your coffee, espresso, and tea shop, including television, radio, mailing circulars, newspapers, etc.

Promotional Expense

This is the expense of promotional items: key chains, calendars, pens, free coffees, T-shirts, sponsorship of sporting events, etc.

Equipment Rental

This cost is the expense of either short- or long-term renting of pieces of equipment or machinery.

Postage
This is postage paid for business purposes.

Contributions
These are all contributions paid to recognized charitable organizations.

Trade Dues and Subscriptions
This includes dues paid to professional organizations; trade magazine subscriptions should be entered in this category. This expense should be divided by 12 to apportion the cost from the month in which it occurs.

Licenses
This is the expense of all business and government licenses: operating licenses, a health permit, liquor licenses, etc. This expense should also be divided by 12 to apportion the cost from the month in which it occurs.

Credit Card Expenses
Credit card expenses can be computed by multiplying the service charge cost-of-sales percentage by the total projected credit card sales volume.

Travel
Travel includes the expense of ordinary and necessary travel for business purposes for yourself and your employees.

Bad Debt
This expense should be nonexistent if the proper procedures for handling credit cards and checks are enforced. Normally, the full amount of a bad debt is a tax-deductible expense. However, you must prove the debt is worthless and uncollectible. In some states, the employee who handled the transaction may be legally held liable for the unpaid amount.

Total Expenditures
Add the total budgeted expenditures from both pages, and enter the figure in this column.

Total Net Profit
Subtract "Total Budgeted Expenditures" from "Total Sales." The result is the total net profit (or loss). Divide the total net projected profit by projected "Total Sales" to compute the projected "Pretax Net Profit Percentage." Total projected sales minus total material costs will equal the gross profit amount.

Depreciation
Depreciation may be defined as the expense derived from the expiration of a capital asset's quantity of usefulness over the life of the property. Capital assets are those assets that have

utility or usefulness of more than one year. Since a capital asset will provide utility over several years, the deductible cost of the asset must be spread out over its useful life, over a specified recovery period. Each year a portion of the asset's cost may be deducted as an expense.

Some examples of depreciable items commonly found in a retail beverage and food outlet include: office equipment, preparation equipment, the building (if owned), machinery, display cases, and any intangible property that has a useful life of more than one year. Items such as light bulbs, china, stationery, and merchandise inventories may not be depreciated. The cost of franchise rights is usually a depreciable expense.

The IRS publishes guidelines for the number of years to be used for computing an asset's useful life.

Conclusion

The specialty beverage business is certainly big business; and it is getting bigger. We hope *How to Open a Financially Successful Coffee, Espresso & Tea Shop* has helped you create a winning strategy that will give you the edge over your competitors. Good luck … and enjoy!

Index

A

accounts payable 96, 242
acidity 107
advertising 18, 210
alcoholic beverages 97
arabica 105
aroma 108
Assam 114

B

bacteria 147
bank account 34
barista 102, 112, 171, 172, 173, 185, 190, 208, 210
black tea 114
body 108
bookkeeping 241
brewing 110, 144
budget/budgeting 20, 273
burns 151
business cards 51
business insurance 14
business plan 14

C

cashier 92

Ceylon 114
China 47, 138, 278
choking 153
city business license 32
Clostridium Botulism 148
Clostridium Perfringens 147
coffee beans 105
communication 191
competition 14, 17, 27, 57
competitive pricing 90
computers 157
conditions 65
cooperative purchasing 133
corporation 22
cost controls 85
cost ratios 88
coupons 225
customers 16-17, 27, 30, 33, 35, 45, 56, 58-60, 62, 71, 89-91, 97, 100-101, 104, 106-107, 110-111, 113, 116-120, 122-125, 127-130, 139, 142, 144-145, 153-154, 158-159, 164-165, 169-172, 174, 177, 181, 191, 195, 198, 203-206, 212, 215-217, 221-234, 237-239, 250, 253, 275-276

D

Darjeeling 114
dark roast 107
desktop publishing 161

E

email 162, 163, 165, 230
employee 167, 217
  handbook 178, 179
  motivation 68, 179, 183-184
  time clock 37, 161
employment interviews 173
equipment 41, 99, 146, 199
espresso 13, 15-20, 23-25, 27, 29,
       37-40, 44, 46-47, 55-56, 61, 75,
       78, 88-89, 97, 99, 101-105, 108,
       110-113, 117-119, 121, 123,
       125, 131, 148, 158-159, 162-
       165, 167, 171-174, 186-187,
       190, 195, 197, 203, 209, 218,
       221, 225, 227, 231, 239, 242,
       275, 281
  recipes 110
extensive menu 122

F

falling 152
financial
  analysis 91
  data 14
  management plan 20
financing 69, 78

fire department permit 33
fires 153
fixtures 50
flatware 47
flavor 108
Formosa 115
franchise 75
Fujan 114
furniture 50

G

glassware 47, 138, 278
goodwill 65
green tea 114
grinders 102
guest tickets 92
Gyokuro 115

H

HACCP 141
cazardous chemicals 153
health department license 32
herbal teas 116
hiring 171

I

iced tea 116
incentives 224
industry trends 26
insects 150
insurance 35

intuitive pricing 90
Inventory 88
  Control 131
invoices 243
issuing 87, 136

K

Keemum 114

L

labor 277
leasing 56
licenses 29
light roast 107
limited liability company 23
limited menu 122
liquor license 33
location 16, 55
  assessment worksheet 28
logo 51

M

management plan 19
marketing 14, 205, 221
  plan 17
medium roast 107
menu 89, 121
  design software 125
milk steamers 103

N

name 23
network 26
nutritional claims 124

O

office supplies 138, 278
Oolong tea 114
operating procedures 14
operational
  budget 274
  costs 137
ordering 94

P

partnership 22
payroll 38, 254, 279
perpetual inventory 132
personnel 14
point-of-sale systems 158
portion size 123
pre-opening promotion 39
prices/pricing 18, 90, 127
products 16
property 28
psychological pricing 90
public relations 18, 203
purchasing 94, 133, 143

R

real estate 63
receiving 87, 135, 143
recruiting 168
restrooms 146
revenue 246
robusta 105, 110
rotation 136

S

safety 151
sales 18, 274
sales tax 32
salmonella infection 148
sanitation 141
SBA Financial Programs 69
scheduling 197
self-service 145
service 16
serving 144
shopping mall 59
sole proprietorship 22
specialty teas 113
staff meeting 237
staphylococci poisoning 148
statement of purpose 14
steeping 116
storage/storing 87, 143
strip mall 59
suppliers 40
supplies 137

T

table service 138
target market 23
terms 65
The 7(a) Loan Guaranty Program 70
tipped employees 249
training 185, 237
trial-and-error pricing 90

U

uniforms 139, 278
utensils 138, 278
utilities 42, 279

W

website 163